VISION FUGITIVE
ezra pound and economics

VISION FUGITIVE

ezra pound and economics

by earle davis

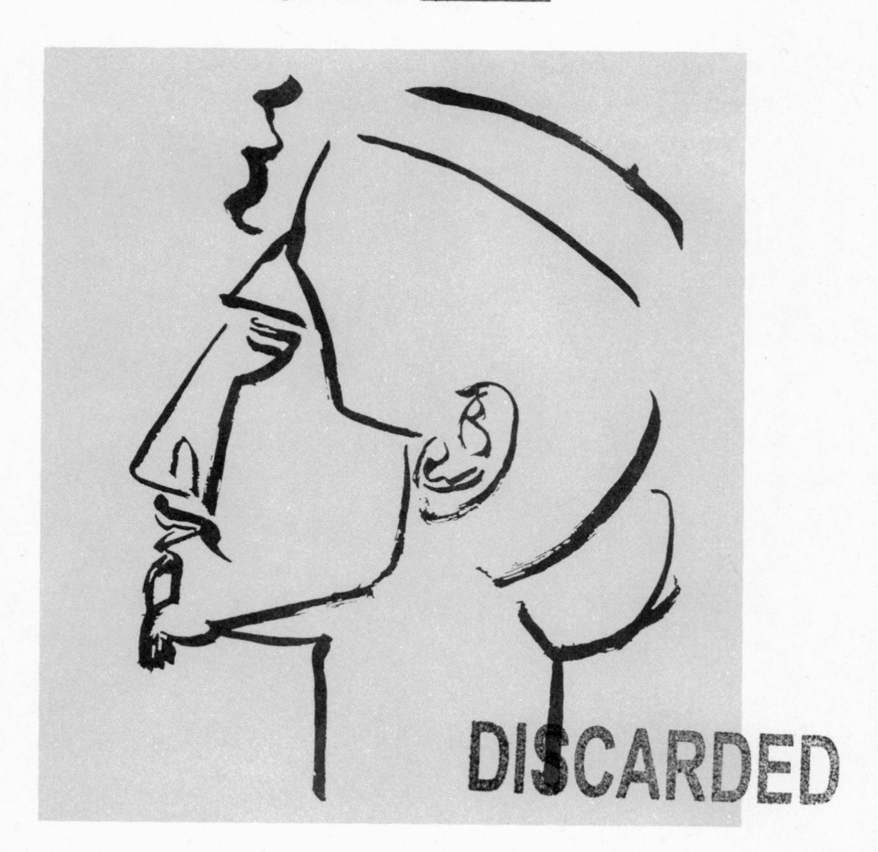

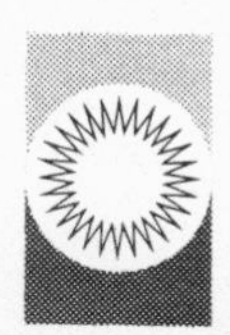

THE UNIVERSITY PRESS OF KANSAS
Lawrence / London

Library of Congress Card Catalog No. 68-25819
Printed in the U.S.A.

For
GEOFF AND NIN DUTTON
and
JOHN AND BETTY YEATMAN
who made a visit to Australia so pleasant . . .

foreword

What or how? That is the question. When dealing with a difficult subject, the critic's dilemma in putting together information and interpretations of importance may be stated simply as a problem in method. What audience does the critic write for? Will it be specialists in the field covered, or some part of the general public, or a combination of readers with varied kinds of interest?

The writings and opinions of a man like Ezra Pound have generally been studied by specialists, their interpretations aimed at the relatively small group which concerns itself with the technical experimentation of modern poetry. Since Pound also emphasized economics, he has been automatically separated from readers who are familiar with arguable theories of national planning by the difficulties inherent in the kind of poetry he wrote. Should the critic's study be aimed at the economics or the poetry? Should one attempt to be all things to all readers? Surely there will be a reasonable audience with special knowledge of one kind willing to investigate knowledge of another kind.

Obviously it would have been possible to construct another book about Pound concentrating on detailed and scrupulous exegesis or description of technique and poetic method. This has been attempted by a number of very able critics like Hugh Kenner. It would also be possible to write about economic theory alone, skimping the poetry. The method assumed in this study mixes the two approaches. If the specialist is interested and the economist amused, Pound may be better understood by the greater audience somewhere between two extremes. The critic must tip his hat in both directions and beg for some allowance in the results attained. Since *The Cantos* are long and complicated, generalizations and capsule summaries must sometimes be attempted. The dangers inherent in compression are that the specialist will find something left out or, in his opinion, misinterpreted. The economist is likely to explode at any moment, especially if he disagrees with Pound's approach. Should Pound be supported or rejected? The critic can wail plaintively that he is not personally to be confused with the opinions of his subject, but many readers will be likely to think that the critic would not have undertaken such a difficult project if he had not begun with some essential sympathy. *Mea culpa.* But the critic deserves a hearing too, and this study is a serious effort to explain and clear up much that is relatively unknown about the writings and opinions of that extraordinary person, Ezra Pound, expatriate, poet, propagandist, and commentator on history.

It is appropriate to note here that all quotations from Pound's writing, poetry or prose, are reproduced as he spelled and arranged them. Part of his idiosyncrasy seems to have been an attempt at some kind of phonetic imitation of the particular language or dialect he was using, perhaps even the pronunciation he imagines. He punctuates oddly or not at all in *The Cantos.* Those familiar with Pound's poetry will recognize his tendencies; others should not be alarmed or feel that the present author has forgotten how to spell.

The reader who wishes to prepare himself for the understanding of Ezra Pound's economic opinions might reasonably investigate several books. Gorham Munson's *Aladdin's Lamp* is the most rewarding exposition of the Social Credit point of view, and Christopher Hollis' *The Two Nations* introduces students to the entire background of the controversy about the banking system, particularly in England. Jerry Voorhis' *Out of Debt, Out of Danger* explores the connection between banking and credit policies controlled or not controlled by the government during the course of American history. I gratefully record my own debt to Mr. Voorhis for his comments and suggestions relating to the section of the book which attempts to explain what Pound recommended.

American economists who contribute to the issues of the Pound thesis are Thorstein Veblen and Irving Fisher. John Galbraith is also very helpful to understanding the theoretical relationship of the government to economic prosperity. Obviously one can read Keynes with profit, and some elementary knowledge of Adam Smith, Malthus, Ricardo, Mill, and Karl Marx is to be taken for granted. The theories of Major C. H. Douglas are scattered through a number of books. Perhaps they can be most easily approached in a selection entitled *The Douglas Manual,* compiled by Philip Mairet. The proposals of Silvio Gesell are all in his major opus, *The Natural Economic Order.*

Pound's application of economic influences to his interpretation of history can be assisted through familiarity with Brooks Adams' *The Law of Civilization and Decay* and Alexander del Mar's *History of Monetary Policy.* Pound refers to many other economists besides those mentioned, including Soddy, McNair Wilson, and Kitson; the ones he likes best are all collected in representative excerpts by Montgomery Butchart in a volume called *Money.* The modern writer most admired by Pound in this field is Odon Por, and the earliest influence on his economic thinking was A. R. Orage. Orage's most helpful book is *Economic Democracy,* and the Por book translated by Pound himself explains why he thinks Italy developed many of his favorite economic nostrums: *Italy's Policy of Social Economics.*

Pound assumes that his readers are familiar with basic issues and principles before they begin to read *The Cantos.* He never explains, but confines himself to illustration, anecdote, quotation, and comment. Some of his theory and argument is on an advanced level of understanding and disagreement. *The ABC of Economics, Jefferson and/or Mussolini,* the six *Money Pamphlets,* and *The Cantos* themselves can best be approached *after* rather than *before* acquiring necessary background, at least if the reader can be expected to assess or comprehend what is being argued. One should be aware from the first that monumental differences of opinion are involved.

Many readers will automatically disagree with some of the conclusions illustrated by Pound's analysis of history. His views of economic right and wrong express so many divergences from the usual perspective of orthodoxy that any critic who attempts an unbiased interpretation or analysis has difficulty in finding a safe station for observation. Nevertheless, understanding of a controversial epic poem demands some attempt at comprehending the author's point of view, whether or not we agree with Pound. Elementary fairness ought to make us look at the unorthodox in order to see whether orthodoxy might occasionally be less than satisfactory. The general public probably misunderstands or condemns Pound for his political and economic opinions without really knowing very much about either. Perhaps rejection is natural because he was accused of treason. Even sophisticated readers have tended to ignore his economic philosophy because of the touchy connection with his wartime activities. This does not stop a number of critics from insisting that Pound is a great poet.

It is my contention that Pound's *Cantos* cannot be absorbed or judged without an excursion into the realm of arguable economic theory. Let us hope that there is profitable stimulus in disagreement as well as praise, whether the subject be poetry or economics. Surely there is light and fascination, for the whole Pound story is extraordinary.

E.D.

acknowledgments

No author is certain that he has sufficiently identified his sources, thanked his friends and colleagues, and acknowledged his debts. I have never met Ezra Pound personally, nor did I attempt to visit him when he was in St. Elizabeths in Washington. He has never seen any of this manuscript, so far as I know. Many of his friends have been helpful, and I mention particularly James Laughlin of NEW DIRECTIONS. Jerry Voorhis, among the economists, read the sections that bear on Pound's economic theories and advised me concerning details of his own activities in Congress. He has been extremely kind. Professor Hugh Kenner criticized an early version of the book with microscopic intensity, and his notation of weaknesses and faulty exegesis was of great assistance. He has generously allowed me to thank him for his criticisms, and he asks that no one be allowed to get the impression that he is responsible for anything said in the book. Obviously I am happy to record my debt and his stricture.

Quotations from Pound's poetry and prose are reproduced by permission of New Directions Publishing Corporation and Ezra Pound. Permission was also granted by Faber and Faber Ltd., since they hold publishing rights outside the United States and Canada. D. D. Paige and Harcourt Brace and World, Inc. granted permission to quote from *Letters of Ezra Pound, 1907-1941*. I note appreciation to John Dos Passos for permission to cite portions of *U.S.A.*, and to Jerry Voorhis and Doubleday and Company for the excerpts from *Confessions of a Congressman.* Marriner Eccles and Alfred A. Knopf have allowed reference to *Beckoning Frontiers.* The Gaudier-Brzeska portrait of Ezra Pound on the title page is reproduced through the services of the Musée National D'Art Moderne in Paris, and to them I register especial thanks for their many courtesies.

EARLE DAVIS

Kansas State University

contents

FOREWORD vii

ACKNOWLEDGMENTS xiii

1 THE MAN AND *The Cantos* 1

2 COUNTERPOINT AND RELATIVITY 17

3 THE PRESENT INFERNO 43

4 MONEY, CREDIT, AND DISTRIBUTION 69

5 THE IDEOGRAMS OF ECONOMIC REFORM 95

6 THE REPEAT IN HISTORY 115

7 MUSSOLINI AND/OR EZRA 147

8 THE TRAGIC FLAW 171

NOTES 203

INDEX 209

1 THE MAN AND THE CANTOS

If we never write anything save what is already understood, the field of understanding will never be extended. One demands the right, now and again, to write for the few people with special interests and whose curiosity reaches into greater detail. (96/11)

Said Yo-Yo:
"What part ob yu is deh poEM??" (104/93)

Everyone who reads a book, everyone who is aware of the course of literature in the twentieth century, everyone who pretends a serious interest in poetry, prose, or criticism eventually comes up hard against the image of Ezra Pound. It may be Pound's own writing or his connection with Yeats, Eliot, Joyce, Frost, Hemingway, Jean Cocteau, Ford Madox Ford, Wyndham Lewis, William Carlos Williams, E. E. Cummings, Gaudier-Brzeska, or even Henry James. Pound in a certain sense has come to epitomize many of the implications of modern literary experimentation, and where the implications are arguable, he has flourished on the ensuing controversies. His poetry reflects the glitter and shine of varying cultures, plus odd and fascinating segments of eternal knowledge. But for the average reader the result *is* odd, even the one who has definable and discernible taste in literature. Some readers have decided to reject him after brave efforts to understand him. He ought by theory to be a supreme example of the artist who is withdrawn from life and usual expression, writing for a limited audience and therefore dismissable. The nature of his appeal constitutes a literary miracle, for he does not dismiss or vanish easily. Erase the poet and the poetry is still there. Or vice-versa.

Look first at Pound as the ordinary reader without special background must occasionally look at him. Pretend for the moment that you have no predilection for the ideogram; in fact you do not know what it is. Imagine that you wish to enjoy great poetry because it has some effect upon you which you expect to be unusual or vital, however it may be defined or explained. Somebody has told you that Pound knows many languages, uses them in his epic, and that he does this to echo the great poetic observations of the ages and recreate them in our time. This means that he may sound like Homer, Ovid, Li Po (call this poet Rihaku, the Japanese form of his name), Dante, Cavalcanti, a host of troubadours like Arnaut Daniel, maybe Catullus, Propertius, Villon, Heine, or any number of nineteenth-century symbolists. Unfortunately for you he has not followed the course of literary study you were exposed to in college, although he does refer to Browning and Whitman. Pound also knows a lot about Confucius, the Greek myths, the Japanese Noh Plays, the legends associated with culture after culture, the Renaissance, the doctrines of Scotus Erigena, the theories of the Neo-Platonists, the explorations and conclusions of the German anthropologist Frobenius, and the whole history of art and music. In one hundred or more *Cantos* you must expect that the man has attempted something more ambitious than anyone else in previous history—if he gets all that in. But wait—you also become aware that he has an interest in recurrent history, the political organization of China, Italy, and the United States, plus a vast and probably unfamiliar field of economic theory—the kind that is rarely emphasized in schools. If you have come across anything written about him by distinguished associates like T. S. Eliot, you may be even more impressed. Hemingway says of Pound, "His own writing, when he would hit it right, was so perfect, and he was so sincere in his mistakes and so enamored of his errors, and so kind to people that I always thought of him as a sort of saint."[1]

Now consider the other portrait. It has little to do, outwardly, with his progress toward writing the great epic of all time. This is the Pound you may have heard about in the newspapers or *Time* or Drew Pearson's column. The impression of creative inspiration does not exactly harmonize with this information. Pound is supposed to be not a saint but a traitor to his country, he is insane—with certificates to prove it, he is violently anti-Semitic, a Fascist (he once referred to Nazi massacres as "fresh meat on the Russian steppes"[2]), a man who apparently encouraged the doubtful extremes of white supremacy in the American Southland, an egotist of supreme and festering potency, a reviler of decent as well as stupid scholarship, an enthusiast for absurd theories of paper money, an unreconstructed rebel—make up your own list. Whatever the case for the poetry, what about the poet himself? If the picture of the man is offensive enough, would you not be forgiven for suspecting that Pound's many literary admirers are in the lunatic fringe of lost literary causes, academic worms who enjoy crawling out of the rhetoric of jargon, quarrelling with each other about the relevance of his theories of imagism, vorticism, non-syllogistic juxtaposition of cumulative entities, or any one of a number of artistic creeds which demand special knowledge to apprehend? Is the real Pound black or white? How can we decide who he really is?

Several points of view can be taken. Perhaps the most usual one ignores the problem of Pound himself by concentrating on the poetry and in effect erasing the man who wrote the poetry. This approach generally harmonizes with the procedures and principles of that perceptive group of writers known in our time as "The New Critics." A parallel position is that the poetry does not mean anything that should be translated into formal ideas or principles. This critical concept seems to argue that poetry is different from ordinary expression. It may be described as "pure," meaning among other things a close reading of the text without reference to the poet who wrote the text, certainly not to his ideas in the realm of patriotism, economics, philosophy, religion, or politics. It is exceedingly tempting to treat Pound this way.

Occasionally one would think that the absolutely pure approach is hard to sustain, particularly when the poet writes about himself. But it can be done. Despite the fact that the *Pisan Cantos* are baldly autobiographical and take their primary appeal from the emotion of Pound's dilemma in a prison camp, he was awarded the first Bollingen Prize for distinguished American poetry, a gesture which had the effect of a national accolade. The judges, many of our finest literary men, had no serious feeling that their lack of sympathy for Pound's ideas or behavior should influence their conclusion that the poetry itself was excellent and worth the award. Bennett Cerf decided to print inoffensive Pound poems in a collected edition of modern poetry, after soliciting opinions from the literary public, saying: "We now have decided to include these poems of Ezra Pound in order to remove any possible hint of suppression, and because we concede that it may be wrong to confuse Pound the poet with Pound the man."[3]

This type of judgment demands logical deductions. Some readers would find justification in concluding Pound did not say anything in his poetry which merited strenuous reaction, or that he writes marvellously when he reflects the poets of other places and times, or perhaps that what he sometimes says should never be considered in terms of arguable theory. There have even been ribald objectors who suggested that modern poetry too often emphasizes the lack of relationship between bare beauty and naked truth. Alternately content and truth may be unlikely associates without damaging the quality of the poetic statement itself: exquisite words in dazzling rhythms; meanings unspecified; comprehension which goes beyond propositions which are better debated in prose; the stimulus to a magical suffusion of emotions.

In any time and place it would be a great temptation to make a purely literary case for a poet like old Ez, to dissociate the man from his explosive and combustible words, put the personal question mark and the literary accomplishment in different compartments. There is much brilliant Pound poetry which concerns itself entirely with aesthetic or literary materials. Surely we may say with sanctification that this is his great work. Then we can exalt his writing as pure poetry, but always hedge properly, as Ray West does (surely speaking for his peers too) when he says, "No one that I know considers Pound correct in his thinking."[4]

The result is that nearly every commentator of importance has so far emphasized the manner rather than the matter. The most reputable of modern critics can be quoted, Eliot himself continually praising the *way* Pound writes but withholding any sympathy for his philosophy, Blackmur suggesting that *The Cantos* are remarkable but still a rag bag of ideas and references, Allen Tate almost completely confusing the issue by saying: "They [the first Cantos] are not about Italy, nor about Greece, nor are they about us. They are not about anything. But they are distinguished verse."[5] Later he added more of the same: "Yet there is no reason to infer . . . that Mr. Pound, outside his craft (or outside his written conversation) knows in the least what he is doing or saying."[6]

The fact remains that Pound himself thought *The Cantos* are about something; they are intended to be didactic, to exploit a point of view, a set of opinions about our world. The reason for this extraordinary conflict between what the poet says and how he says it derives from his unique way of developing his epic. His manner may be the most difficult one ever devised for simple communication, allowing many different kinds of interpretation. Pound has spent much of his life exploring the best way to use language so that it will be intensely effective, effectiveness implying powerful communication. He has published thousands of words about melopoeia, logopoeia, phanopoeia, imagism, vorticism, intaglio, ideograms, and the qualities of superiority attained by his favorite poets. It is paradoxical that most readers do not understand him very well on first reading. No poet in history has been so immediately stimulating to the critical nerve ends of scholars (there are potential doctors' theses for decades in *The Cantos*), and many scholars have already developed opposing interpretations. The greatest critics have read him, described his remarkable experiments with technique in awe, and have supposed that his ideas in the realm of politics, economics, and history are not the point at issue. Obscurity and ambiguity are automatically enshrined and vital objective correlatives are considered for technical immortality. Free association rather than logical thought must be praised.

The most able of the so-called professional critics of Pound, Hugh Kenner, runs a remarkable race between Pound's technique and content. His solution is to praise the poet because he has invented a new way of saying important things. Since Pound never explains anything syllogistically in *The Cantos,* the poetic accomplishment turns out to be "brilliantly realized fusions of multiform experience," or "allotropic components into which the mood, the initial poetic 'idea,' has been fragmented," or a variety of "ineluctible modality," full of "rectificative volition," with "hylomorphic" and "chthonic" entities which somehow turn into "esemplastic power."[7] It may be typical of the trend of modern criticism that a writer of the capacity of Kenner has found it more interesting to describe the technique in such terms rather than concentrate on what Pound is trying to say with each collection of allotropic components. Kenner does not find it important to touch on Pound's economics or his reflections on American history.

In fact, the critics have so far not helped the reader very much in understanding the great long poems, particularly *The Cantos.* Pound himself says that *The Cantos* stand for what he believed, and he even insists that if we do not understand what he is trying to communicate, he will explain later.[8] He calls his poetic goal *concentrated meaning,* implying better writing than prose because the ideas propounded are powerful through implication, indirection, and cumulation of examples rather than through direct and simple exposition. There is a great mass of evidence that Pound thought *The Cantos* coincide with all that he has stood for as a man. One begins to feel that there is more to the poet than the impression that he wrote nothing but literary masterpieces, that he cannot be relegated to another world, or even another country.

Should we then reduce our critical problem to saying that if Pound and his poetry are one, we ought to reject both because Pound is either a traitor, crazy, or full of false ideas? This position has also been taken. The answer is not simple, but extremely complex. The facts of Pound's disloyalty are at the heart of the matter and demand some brief consideration here, since the epic itself depends upon so many of Pound's reasons for being disloyal. The man says, in essence, that he rejected his country on the grounds that he loved it and wanted it to be different. At this point one can take the position that he was not always mentally capable and can be forgiven for a part of his behavior on the grounds of not being responsible. Pound's first full-length biographer, Charles Norman, suggests such a solution: "After Pearl Harbor he took his stand with Italy; and all the apologetic articles about him, and all his own utterances since to the contrary, cannot gainsay what he actually did. But his compulsion to do it is probably a medical, not a political, matter; or so I believe."[9] This is a nice way out if we are talking about Pound the man. But was he sane when he wrote the poems, and not responsible when he did the broadcasts, especially since the poems and broadcasts sometimes say the same things? Does insanity appear only when he got off on economics or Italy, like the interfering vision of Charles the First's head which plagued the harmlessly mad Mr. Dick in *David Copperfield*?

The broadcasts from Italy connect themselves with Pound's reputation for responsibility. Clark Emery, whose study of *The Cantos* called *Ideas into Action* is one of the two or three best books available for any reader of Pound, has the courage to defend the broadcasts. His reasoning is that Pound has always been aggressively American: "The house he wants most to set in order is the American house. . . . had Pound not had the courage of his Americanism, he would not have laid himself open to the ultimate treason charge. . . . And the risks he took, so he thought, were in a very good cause: the rescue of a society which, under the misguidance of evil and of ignorant men, was literally (in Pound's definition of the term) hell-bent."[10]

This may be true. But it is not only offensive to patriotism and good sense to think that Mussolini and Hitler were heaven-bent; one must also understand why Pound thought America was hell-bent. Sometimes in an effort to defend him a Pound partisan will assert that there is nothing treasonable in the broadcasts at all. Eustace Mullins, for example, quotes only reasonable portions of the broadcasts in *This Difficult Individual, Ezra Pound,* insisting that the poet could never have been convicted of treason in a fair trial.[11] According to this view Pound was a kind of political martyr, to be punished because he criticized Franklin D. Roosevelt, not his country.

Several things may be emphasized at this point. It is true that Pound said some things prior to Pearl Harbor which loyal Americans had also expressed vocally and on paper. Mussolini was relatively popular before Ethiopia in the United States, and many businessmen hated the New Deal and Roosevelt with a deep and bitter passion. Their reasons are not exactly the same as Pound's, but in any case they had the luck not to broadcast from Rome. However, Pound did make the broadcasts, even if he was not a simple deserter. Say that he claimed loyalties on a level above patriotism. It follows that we should examine what he thought that level was.

We can assume that Pound is a great poet and an unusual case. It is true that he attempted to leave Italy and come home at the beginning of hostilities. He was lost in the shuffle of arrangements, probably antagonized by the harassed American officials. Since the war he has apparently claimed that he was refused passage to the United States. Citizens caught in a country at war with their own nation are sometimes exposed to the necessity for collaboration to survive. Pound's predicament was complicated by the fact that he had consistently supported Mussolini and Italian economic reform up to that time. In addition he was a supreme egotist, contemptuous of people who let traditional pressures dictate their behavior. We must remember that his son fought in the American army.

The point to be made is that whatever caused Pound to broadcast from Italy, the reasons are all documented in *The Cantos*. An unyielding partisan for his own opinions, he had the habit of quarrelling viciously with other scholars in print. Some of his mildest terms in these quarrels are "sub-human imbeciles," "paid pimps," "simian bastards," "animal excrement," or he simply calls his enemies idiotic or moronic. The poems often incorporate the same kind of vituperation, certainly the broadcasts do. This kind of argument retreats to the world of violent words rather than action. To Pound the United States represented a kind of stupid capitalism disguised as a system of Usury and selfish greed, largely incapable in our time of visible appreciation for living art and eternal literature. In political and economic matters he had faith in Mussolini, practically none in Roosevelt, and he believed that Italian social and economic reforms would be spread round the world when Italy was victorious. The offensive and horrifying side to Fascism and Naziism, the threat to individual freedom which frightened the rest of the world, for some reason never became important to him.[12] An idealist and a dreamer, he wanted to share his dreams and persuade the world to adopt what he recommended for its own good. Does fugitive vision deny partial comprehension of truth?

The problem is that it is hard to judge Pound on a partial or fractional basis. This is the reason why it is simpler to separate the poet from the man, since it is quite a bit easier to judge the poetry as good or bad separated from reality. In a time of survival, treason is the unforgivable sin. Idealistic causes seem unimportant when set next to life or death. There may theoretically be a question of degree in disloyalty, but it is like being partially pregnant. In Canto 74 Pound says:

> and yet petty larceny
> in a regime based on grand larceny
> might rank as conformity nient' altro
> with justice shall be redeemed . . . . (74/12)

In Canto 79 he says: "Neither Eos nor Hesperus has suffered wrong at my hands" (79/66). How much did he hurt the American war effort?

Not much, although this is not relevant to his essential responsibility. The Italians could hardly have viewed the results of his broadcasts with any particular satisfaction, since they must have been mystified by their contents a great deal of the time. No one has suggested that there were hidden code messages to spies in them, although suspicious Italians went through periods wondering whether Pound was actually sending secret information to America. One is reminded of the legendary tale about censors in the first World War studying the manuscripts of *Ulysses* sent by Joyce from Switzerland to France. Since the narrative did not make plain sense, the normal inference was that it might be in code.

Pound's case is, flatly, quite different from that of people like Tokyo Rose or Lord Haw-Haw. The indictment against him charged that he was paid only railroad fares from Rapallo to Rome for his performances. Anyone examining the transcripts can hardly imagine that any American would be influenced or listen very long to one of his programs, except perhaps in wonder mixed with annoyance. Even by the lowest of radio standards the broadcasts are almost completely ineffective.

If there is any importance in these conclusions it derives from the similarities to be found in the epic and the broadcasts. Generally speaking Pound assumes without explanation his interpretation of economic reform in both places. They coincide also in their expression of opinion about Usury, Roosevelt, and the ideal American tradition of Jefferson, Adams, Jackson, and Lincoln. There are several moments when Pound appears to devote his entire time to the explication of a Canto, certainly an extraordinary performance on radio in wartime. The broadcasts include literary criticism, comments on Confucius, and defense of a concept of economic Utopia. Most of this material, and it is a major part, offers little evidence for anything but eccentricity demonstrated by a peculiar medium and a remarkable choice of radio station and time. But there are also extra samples which castigate the United States and praise Italy and Germany in the conflict then raging. The most awful excerpt may be:

> Every hour that you go on with the war is an hour lost to you and your children. And every sane act you commit is committed in homage to Hitler and Mussolini. Every reform, every lurch toward the Just Price, toward the control of the market is an act of homage to Mussolini and Hitler. They are your leaders however much you think you are conducted by Roosevelt or told by Churchill. You follow Mussolini and Hitler in every constructive act of your government.[13]

Let us therefore borrow the vocabulary of the New Critics and say that we reject schizophrenia for syncretism. For those of us who want to consider the impact of his epic on our time and the future there are certain deductions which ought to be faced clearly and honestly. One is that Pound himself thought his *Cantos* were saying much that he was willing to say over the air from an enemy country in time of war. He believed that his poetry ought to convey his political and economic ideas, and that these ideas were of such import that they ought to be explained to people who did not read or understand his poetry. His position is that—war or no war—his interpretation of the issues of history is the best hope for the future of civilization. Considering the circumstances there is need for putting his poetic statements alongside logic and facts, considering them in the classification of all debatable issues—not poetry in a vacuum—with the question of judging *The Cantos* as pure poetry deferrable. Surely there is a good case for saying that we ought not to separate the poetry from the man. Even less possible is the process of putting his words on an altar enshrined to the gods while we quietly dump his ideas in a slop bucket.

One more point needs consideration. For separate reasons it is difficult to examine Pound objectively and without prejudice. This point has to do with the possible influence of his supposed insanity on his ideas. The competence of the psychiatrists who placed Pound in St. Elizabeth's for so many years can hardly be questioned by a layman. Yet most of us are aware of the inexactitude of diagnosis in cases of mental illness. Psychiatrists differ in public trials. The report on Pound had to do specifically with his inability to defend himself properly in a court trial for treason. If the treason charge had not come up, no one would have been in a position to examine him for anything but oddity or peculiarity. We all know that he can tell a hawk from a handsaw.

Years ago, in *The ABC of Reading,* Pound said, "The concept of genius as akin to madness has been carefully fostered by the inferiority complex of the public."[14] There is a like obscurity in the opinion of critics like Charles Norman, who thinks that whatever Pound's essential responsibility, the treatment he received in Italy after he surrendered to the American forces, specifically his confinement in a kind of gorilla cage exposed to glaring light for twenty-four hours a day, drove him over the edge of sanity—perhaps temporarily. But of course this kind of judgment, which may have some vestige of truth, has nothing materially to do with his fixation about Jewish moneylenders, or the ideas he expresses in *The Cantos.* He is merely a "genius" with some extraordinary characteristics which the public may shrug off by saying that they are "akin to madness."

Discussion or judgment of this sort is logically pointless. Ideas are right or wrong, good or bad, without the need for rejecting them on the arguable premise of mental instability. Many critics who do not seem to understand much of what Pound is saying about history or economics have voided their responsibilities by appealing to the psychotic instability argument. Ivor Winters states this attitude beautifully: "I would say that Pound is a talented man who has quite obviously been off his trolley for a great many years; he is a backwash in the development of modern poetry, about 75 years behind the time."[15] This was written to needle the Pound enthusiasts, generally congregated to help explain Pound's many puzzling references in the ten *Newsletters* edited by John Edwards, the critic who later—with William Vasse—published that indispensable guide to understanding Pound: *The Annotated Index to the Cantos.* If you do not like Pound, if you do not understand him, or if you cannot refute him, call him crazy. Since Pound is not a drunkard, a communist, nor a homosexual, one's choice of a ready axe is limited.

Genius akin to madness expresses itself in many ways which in Pound's case appear hyperbolic, even if his genius may be called sane and responsible. He is a brilliant analyst of the literature which has often been unemphasized in our schools and colleges; he is a leader of lost causes, a delver into the depths of unorthodox economics, a discoverer of stray manuscripts, a propagandist for far out movements in art, music, sculpture, and poetry, a writer of eccentric letters to friends, enemies, and politicians, a poet who decorates his great poem with Greek quotations and Chinese characters, or even Arabic squiggles and Egyptian hieroglyphs, the creator of a masterpiece in terms of aesthetic cross-word puzzle acrosticism—for all these qualities he has been praised by somebody at some time or other. He even discussed the virtues of cultivating Brazil nuts in the one interview he had with Mussolini;[16] he explained American history to Franklin D. Roosevelt as if the American President had never examined it; he wore extraordinary clothes before the beatniks—dressing as all long-haired poets are supposed to dress by people who think poets are funny; he petted a hundred cats at Rapallo; he said things like "There's only one thing to do with an Englishman—kick him in the teeth."[17] William Carlos Williams seems to have called Pound "Old Assenpoop." Certainly Pound was different. Should we praise him or blame him for his differences alone?

Let us start by assuming that what he says in his epic represents what he was and is. If it is hard to see him as thinker and artist both, there is no alternative to making the effort. A major break in critical examination of Pound's poems was made by Malcolm Cowley several years ago. Cowley decided to throw his weight against the poet, not on the grounds of technique or incomprehensibility but on the grounds that what Pound says in the realm of ideas is nonsense. Cowley has summed up the extreme argument against the poet's beliefs in an article which attempts to "reweigh Pound," getting him down to ounces instead of tons. As Cowley phrases them, these are the ridiculous ideas, and they need to be examined because they introduce the real argument about the value of *The Cantos:*

> Western civilization is at the mercy of an international conspiracy of bankers, or, as he calls them, usurers.
>
> Wars are caused by this "usurocracy" in order to run nations into debt and create opportunities for manipulating the currency.
>
> The worst of the usurers are Jews, especially a few big Jews conducting a "vendetta on the goyim."
>
> Usury cheapens art, falsifies history, and reduces literature to lying journalism.
>
> The usurocracy could be abolished by a simple reform of currency, namely, the issuance of stamped and dated script based on the goods available for consumption.
>
> Such a reform would have to be instituted by a benevolent despot on the order of Mussolini or the best Chinese emperors.
>
> Confucius laid down the lines of the good society.
>
> American culture, great in the days of John Adams and Jefferson, declined after 1830 and perished in the Civil War, also caused by bankers. "The United States were sold to the Rothschilds in 1863."[18]

Cowley calls these ideas "primer-book notions," and stated more or less out of context they appear somewhat extreme or even "akin to madness," if one may venture euphemism. On these terms alone the poem which exploits them is childishly overpraised. Cowley's service to modern criticism is never more apparent than in his over-stated summary of a challenge not to be answered by explaining Pound's art separated from his subject matter.

One may ask whether Cowley has summed up Pound's ideas clearly or fairly. This is a question which defies a yes or no answer. There are omitted relevant doctrines and propositions which seem to me to alter the entire summary, yet certain parts of Cowley's statements are accurate. The critic's position is that the eventual impact of the epic will depend upon the economic and historical contentions woven into its many strands. Whatever Pound's reflection of Homer, Dante, Ovid, or his literary transfiguration of artistic counterpoint, the epic centers more and more upon the themes which resemble those ridiculed by Cowley. Indeed the economic thesis serves *The Cantos* in the same sense that Catholic theology aided Dante in *The Divine Comedy*.

If we return to the main problem, a critical platform can be formulated. The poet and the important long poems, particularly *The Cantos,* must be considered together and as complements, because the poet intended that his poetry should speak for what he believed. The critical approach which seals literature into a technical compartment will not serve us sufficiently in considering the impact or value of *The Cantos*. We must honestly examine the epic on Pound's essential terms: *concentrated meaning.* While we cannot quit worrying about whether he said it syllogistically, elliptically, or by implication, since it takes study to figure out exactly what he meant, we must nevertheless concentrate on the ideas which he was trying to set down for immortality. Finding out what Pound intends to convey requires a journey as difficult as that of Odysseus; but it is a legitimate quest, even if it is in a different medium. The way leads through the most complex series of references and sources known to literature, although Joyce scholars may wish to argue about that. Above all the attempt to explain Pound and his behavior must direct itself to the realm of economic theory. It is the economic theory which has taken the brunt of the ridicule and opprobrium which have been aimed at Pound the man; it is the economic theory which needs more exegesis and explanation than any other part of the complex Pound story.

In order to pursue our Odyssey in the path of Pound's heroes who visit hell and try to return, we will have to go past what has been called Usury around the unexplored shoals of Social Credit, past paper money cliffs with Gesell's stamps attached, through channels marked with the Just Price for everything sold in the market, into the harbors where banks welcome us by creating money out of nothing. We cannot stop, like the sailors in Homer's epic, to eat the Oxen of the Sun, but we will surely address the gods vainly at appropriate moments. We will also, if one may belabor the figure, sail in an ideogrammic vessel to search out the islands of knowledge, and the islands are not always on plainly marked maps. The decision to make this journey must depend on whether *The Cantos* seem worth discovering. One must say, emphatically, that the whole idea is fascinating because Pound himself is fascinating and his epic may be the great poem of our century. Maybe, since he is such an extraordinary mixture, we have to make the journey to explain the fascination.

2 COUNTERPOINT AND RELATIVITY

Some minds take pleasure in counterpoint
pleasure in counterpoint
and the later Beethoven on the new Bechstein
or in the Piazza S. Marco for example
finds a certain concordance of size
not in the concert hall . . . . (79/63)

No man has dared to write this thing as yet
And yet I know, how that the souls of all men great
At times pass through us,
And we are melted into them . . . . (Histrion)

Pound, like the critics who follow his lead, evidently believes that meaning is more than a perception of sense. The patterns of sound and rhythm supply tones and feelings, a kind of resonance which improves upon plain and simple statements. The problem for the reader, however, is more than a matter of communication. It is not a question of whether or not Pound presents emotions, impressions, or ideas, but it is rather a matter of how much one should read into what he suggests but does not develop or explain. The matter and the manner ought to be one, but both are complicated enough to demand careful description.

The theory of relativity has special bearing upon the composition and the understanding of *The Cantos,* at least in a meticulously special sense. Strangely enough, this is a step in the direction of simplification. It suggests that *The Cantos* can be absorbed on separate but relative levels. All of us must be aware of several dimensions of communication, each successive one being more complex than the last. We begin on the simplest plane, and proceed on later readings to deeper comprehension if we wish. Part of the challenge of *The Cantos* derives from the stimulus to further exploration of the various themes which have been presented. All of us have been driven back to reading some previously unknown example of comparative literature, history, or economics, perhaps because we feel that we have been unaware of something which Pound presents in terms of great beauty or intricate challenge. The attempt to understand Pound can even lead to a complete classical education.

The structure of *The Cantos* is most easily described in terms of several dimensions. A large musical composition achieves a similar effect by playing several main musical themes against each other, bringing them back in different forms, inverted or developed or varied, while contrasting themes play in and out. The burden of Pound's epic does not proceed chronologically or simply. Its manner resembles counterpoint, but not the regular mathematical counterpoint of a Bach fugue, nor the simple statement, recurrence, and combination of parts one hears in a Handel Oratorio. But the basic concept is polyphonic; one theme is presented, another may come in, the first may be restated in other terms, the opposite may be contrasted, several may go on at once—or almost so on the printed page—and the artistic effect depends upon one's interest in the main theme and whether one recognizes its restatement or augmentation in recurrence and repetition. The reader's best course is to attempt perception of the theme in simple dimensions of understanding, then proceed if possible to more complex comprehension. The resemblance of music to poetry is helpful, but not exact; sounds are distinct, but combinations of words may not be recognizable as music separated from sense. Pound's themes, according to this theory, ought to gain effect when they can be stated in terms of "meaning," concepts which directly communicate an emotion, a reaction, or best of all a proposition approximating an idea or opinion.[1]

This analysis is more precise than to describe the method of *The Cantos* entirely in terms of the ideogram. The ideogram derives from the influence of the Chinese written character upon Pound's style, the state of language where the words are pictures of the meaning rather than explanations or definitions in the dictionary sense. A series of impressions joined in related reproduction may eventually supply more satisfactory understanding than an attempt at logical definition. Single ideograms rarely communicate enough, but several reinforcing each other often do. Pound presents his ideogrammic bits in different technical ways, using monologue, climactic highlights from incidents implied rather than narrated, comments or concentrated extracts which also serve as sub-themes. The very first Canto presents a simple illustration of contrast. The short closing quotation from the *Hymni Deorum* is an example of bad translation of a bad poem deliberately set against the appropriate rendering of the *Odyssey* fragment—a sample of how not to do it compared with Pound's idea of effective translation of a great poem.[2]

Examine any typical Canto with the feeling that you are trying to see how the themes expand and play against each other. They are stated, restated, emphasized, developed, and contrasted. Look at one which is concerned with economics. Canto 38 has the main theme in a quotation at the beginning, something Pound rarely provides in simple form:

> *il duol che sopra senna*
> *Induce, falseggiando la moneta.*
> *Paradiso XIX, 118.*

It is in Italian (nothing is ever simple in Pound), but the source is indicated: *The Divine Comedy.* Literally translated it means, "The grief that over the Seine/ Induces, forging the money." Pound would never settle for an interlinear translation, so he might have said, "There is grief in Heaven because man falsifies money and the uses to which money should be put—look at the people who live along the Seine in France!" Simply stated, the unifying theme to be developed in the Canto concerns the false use of money.

The first section, stanza, or paragraph links three short developing motifs: someone named Metevsky, Marconi being presented to the Pope, and a quotation from Dexter Kimball concerning industrial boredom in repetitive piecework in industry. The problem in explication is not so difficult as it looks at first sight. You have to look up or figure out Metevsky; you have to decide why Pound stuck in the reference to the Pope and Marconi (it seems to have little to do with false money and the theme); and you can judge the significance of the Kimball quotation without much outside assistance. Metevsky turns out to be Sir Basil Zaharoff, the international munitions king, whose career is still somewhat difficult to check. We do have some facts about him. Presumably an executive for British munitions firms, he was a master at selling arms to both sides in any war; he secured important or controlling financial contacts with the major munitions companies of many nations, the Harvey United Steel Company, Vickers-Armstrong in England, Schneider-Creusot in France, Skoda, Krupp, Mitsui, Terni-Ansaldo, (du Pont?)—go on down the line. In the first World War he is by legend held responsible for filling orders of the warring countries from whatever plant was best fitted to manufacture the particular weapon of destruction needed, thereby making more profit. After the war it was charged, among other things, that Krupp made the barbed wire used by the French in front of their trenches (shipped to France via Switzerland); that the Turks used guns and bullets at Gallipoli which were supplied by English Vickers; that the German submarines never aimed at a French ship (only the English), and in return the French never bombed the German munitions factories just across the lines in Alsace and Lorraine, a sector of the front where no major campaigns occurred. Metevsky represents in Pound's poem the men of no loyalty but their own interest, the kind of businessman who makes money no matter which country wins, the international cartel manipulator with connections in banks and business that stretch far beyond munitions alone. If you are curious, this reference may send you to further investigation of the rather unbelievable international munitions pirate (did he really do all this?), temporarily stopping the reading of Canto 38 right there. Pound later restates this motif as the climax to the entire group of Cantos, 31 to 41.[3]

It is possible that Pound is suggesting that most of us do not know enough about modern business practices to judge whether money is falsified or acquired dishonestly. We find ignorance in places where one would expect to discover knowledge. Perhaps this is the reason for the contrasting little episode concerning the Pope and Marconi:

> His Holiness expressed a polite curiosity
>   as to how His Excellency had chased those
> electric shakes through the atmosphere.

Funny, one would think the Pope would really be the one most likely to know about the mysteries of the electric atmosphere, considering his connections with divine knowledge or revelation. Unlike his heavenly allies, he is not worrying about the falsifying of money; in fact he is puzzled about natural phenomena. In any case the discovery of electricity bid fair to change the world; it could have been used for the economic benefit of all mankind, not just the power companies. Pound elsewhere says that the discovery of unfalsified money could do as much for mankind.[4]

There follows a restatement of the Metevsky theme, mixing an account of his salesmanship with a reference to the lady he loved (she was married to someone else). His knowledge of business apparently did not carry over into his sex-life, for she had five abortions and died of the last one. Or perhaps Pound is implying that Usury interferes with production.

The Kimball quotation (he turns out to be an economist who wrote a dull book called *Industrial Economics*) points out that modern industry needs to keep its workers happy while they do repetitive and brain-washing work. The restatement of the initial theme must depend upon Pound's desire to add evidence of the callowness of certain business practices where profits grind down the worker instead of stimulating both labor and capital. True money made in business would represent a kind of partnership between owner and worker, would it not? This is what Italy supposedly had in the corporate system under Mussolini. Surely, implies the Kimball quotation, the least the manufacturer could do would be to entertain his workers or educate them while they are performing moronic bits of piecework in the interest of efficient money-making. Perhaps they would work better and make more money for the employer?

The next division piles up a series of short statements commenting on the main theme. Successively you find that

Metevsky-Zaharoff did a fine job of selling munitions to both sides, that Akers (must be Vickers) made large profits in similar trade, importing gold into England through the profits, thus upsetting the international trade balance (one of the causes of wars), that Mr. Whitney (oh yes, the American stockbroker and banker) extolled the practice of selling short on the market (this means that the man on the inside could sometimes make money by special information or privilege, does it not?), that the Afghans tried to buy guns cheap when other nations began to disarm (countries may aim at peace but not at the cost of losing money), that a Secretary (of Cabinet stature?) made money out of oil wells (Harding-Falls-Daugherty scandals?), that an Australian named D'Arcy got a monumental concession from Persia to take oil for fifty years (for the benefit of his company by a "special" deal?—certainly not for the good of any "people" in Persia, Australia, or England?), that Mr. Mellon visited England (on banking business or for the United States as Secretary of the Treasury?), that President Wilson had prostatitis (surely a Messiah would not have anything so embarrassing or common as prostatitis, even one who was responsible for the Versailles Treaty, with all its financial compromises?), that somebody named her Ladyship cut down Jenny's allowance (nobody seems to have figured this bit out, although it had to do with somebody's loss of income because a source of "false" money petered out), and finally the first World War was started by "a louse in Berlin/ and a greasy basturd in Ausstria" (a war which must have had financial or economic causes as well as whatever other reasons explain it?).

This is a relatively long Canto, and the counterpoint becomes complicated, needing sympathetic vision or even second sight. As long as you are intrigued by Pound's remarkable fund of related instances, the impressiveness of the main theme sinks deeper and deeper into your consciousness. You look at each ideogram to see how it comments on the original motif. You are always being prodded to look farther into the suggestion presented briefly—this is Pound's idea of concentrated meaning. For example, there is Gandhi and his attempt to stop wars not only by refusing to buy arms, but also cotton. Do you suppose that there is a connection between international trade (the kind where one nation exploits another) and ensuing wars? There is a fleeting reference to Mussolini's accomplishment in making the Italian marshes cultivatable, something the state did for the benefit of the whole society, business and labor both. This has to be contrast to the main theme. Then there is a reference to the German anthropologist Frobenius:

> The white man who made the tempest in Baluba
> Der im Baluda das Gewitter gemacht hat . . .
> they spell words with a drum beat . . . .

This is a little elliptical in the first dimension of comprehension, but investigation provides possible light. Pound will refer to Frobenius in later Cantos; at the moment we are free to guess that he is celebrating the man who made rain by native rites (he succeeded?), obviously for the good of the agricultural community which needed rain. Public advantage contrasted with selfish or unfair special privilege? There is no grief in heaven over Gandhi, Mussolini, or Frobenius, according to Pound.

The Canto works to a climax in the division where the essential reasoning of the radical economists who urge state management of prices, wages, and profits is summarized:

> "I have of course never said that the cash is constant
> (Douglas) and in fact the population (Britain 1914)
> was left with 800 millions of *"deposits"*
> after all the cash had been drawn, and
> these deposits were satisfied by the
> printing of treasury notes
> A factory
> has also another aspect, which we call the financial aspect
> It gives people the power to buy (wages, dividends
> which are power to buy) but it is also the cause of prices
> or values, financial, I mean financial values
> It pays workers, and pays *for* material.
> What it pays in wages and dividends
> stays fluid, as power to buy, and this power is less,
> per forza, damn blast your intellex, is less
> than the total payments made by the factory
> (as wages, dividends, AND payments for raw material
> bank charges etcetera
> and all, that is the whole, that is the total

of these added into the total of prices
caused by that factory, any damn factory
and there is and must be therefore a clog
and the power to purchase can never
(under the present system) catch up with
prices at large,

and the light became so bright and blindin'
in this layer of paradise
that the mind of man was bewildered.

There is a certain degree of bewilderment on earth too, you will find. If you examine this full statement of counter-theme—the suggestion that intelligence could deal with the falsifying of money—you may eventually look at Social Credit and find that this is Douglas' central contention, usually called "The A plus B proposition." You will also find that most orthodox economists deny its validity, some of them vehemently, which is why Pound blasts their intellects. The proposition has nothing to do with Douglas' proposals for remedy, but merely insists that profits and bank changes on loans for production cost more than the money actually put into circulation in wages and dividends, the latter total being assumed to be the only source from which the manufactured goods can be bought and paid for. The fact that the costs and the money to buy products are never equal (money to buy getting successively less and less equal) causes a clog in distribution. If high enough, the difference produces depression or one of those periodic times when industry grinds to a standstill. All of the Canto up to this point has been preparation for examining the counter-theme, since war profiteers, special interests in defiance of the national interest, and manipulators of value seize part of the money which Pound thinks ought to be used for the prosperity of the whole society. Bank charges take money out of circulation, according to this diagnosis. Further, there are not enough intelligent people who have sufficient information to see what is happening or do anything to remedy it. Thus we have periods of boom and bust; thus we have wars, panics, and suffering; thus heaven is unhappy with the falsifying of money on earth.

The Canto does not stop with this climax; there is anti-climactic contrapuntal repeat and answer. The Krupps and

Schneiders are now exhibited (emphasis for initial Metevsky-Zaharoff material) selling munitions to both sides, but Schneider is nevertheless decorated by a grateful country as a patriot. His manipulations finally happen along the Seine, connecting with the quotation from Dante at the beginning. This man of special privilege has natural alliances with banking interests, the Comité des Forge, the Franco-Japanese Bank, and Schneider purchases most of the main newspapers in France to be sure that his enterprises receive favorable publicity and interpretation. The Canto ends on a description of the Schneider business connections with Japanese munitions and the need for keeping up the Japanese army, not for any real national advantage but for profitable "business" reasons. These private interests

> . . . are destined to have a large future
> "faire passer ces affaires
> avant ceux de la nation."

Literally the quotation reads "to make these matters come before those of the nation," asserting ironically that the business of making money for special interests is more important to the usurer than the health and prosperity of the society which makes up the nation as a whole. This result would have to follow unless labor, for example, profited in some comparable way with the Schneider interests. The quotation is inserted sarcastically. Pound might have said, "What's good for General Motors is good for the country."[5]

The poetic organization of materials in this Canto furnishes a fine illustration of Pound's typical counterpoint. It is not a logical juxtaposition or piling up of examples to illustrate or prove a proposition as Aristotle would recommend. It sets parallel and contrasting ideas and references against a main theme, inserting smaller motifs which are intended to make the main contentions more formidable. From the standpoint of relativity some of the examples are simple, some complex, and the main illustrations demand a great deal of exploration in a dimension which might as well be the fourth one described by Einstein. "It's like a good detective story," said the bright student; "what you don't know about the plot keeps you reading to find out."

Perhaps so. Some of us have difficulties with fourth dimensions, and in detective stories it is frustrating to have the mystery disclosed and still leave the reader perplexed. One wishes wistfully that the direction and scope of Pound's motifs were more easily discernible, even after study. The main theme running through *The Cantos* is his economic interpretation of the meaning of history, but it is not the only theme. Most literary critics have found the other motifs more fun to track down and annotate, depending as they do on so many famous literary models and myths. The literary themes are also presented first, often in Pound's most brilliant verse, and the economic motif presents additional difficulties. It requires knowledge in a confusing field which is highly controversial. Many competent critics and scholars feel hesitancy and lack of experience in barging into another professional area. One even suspects that economists differ more than literary critics about the verities of their subject, which difficulty helps the literary commentator to feel lost. He knows too that if he makes the slightest slip, his entire case may be ridiculed on professional grounds.

The importance of the economic motif in *The Cantos* is subject also to the appropriateness of Pound's poetic method, perhaps the most subtle but eventually the most important question which can be raised in judging the effectiveness of the epic. The contrasting themes which derive from Odysseus' journey to hell and back, Dante's exploration of inferno, purgatory, and paradise, Ovid's examples of metamorphosis and change, all give Pound the opportunity to select, translate, borrow, and rework classical materials in his own inimitable variety of restatement or poetic shorthand. It is even possible to arrange the rhetoric of Confucius, or invoke Usury, Light, or Vanity in the traditional poetic grand manner. But the facts of recurrent history necessary to the development of his economic theme come from sources which have been mainly prose, sometimes undistinguished prose. If Pound quotes Homer, recreating key passages in immortal transformation, he is likely with his capacities to achieve impressiveness and a sense of importance. The documents which illustrate the salient data in the history of China, Italy, or the United States, or even those which concern Jefferson, John Adams, or Sigismondo Malatesta and Ouang-ngan-ché, or Erigena and Pietro Leopoldo, pose problems in translation to impressiveness. When Dante and Cavalcanti are being quoted, Pound started with something; sometimes he has nothing to work with artistically when he quotes Major Douglas or the documents which describe the founding of the Siena Bank. Since Pound is always quoting somebody, even himself, he is to a certain extent bound by his sources. He is a master at recreating the great poetry of other languages in comparable and admirable English; he is much less successful in translating politicians, economists, and historical records, even if his sources are in English. His poetic manner in *The Cantos* varies from the pseudo-traditional to the dialects of many languages to the mere humdrum listing of letters and scholarly references. It is this variance in literary effect which creates much of the impression that the economic theme is less important than the literary ones. The literary motifs sound like the great literature we know; we are likely to ask what the rest of this stuff is doing here.

Because of the ideogrammic arrangement and the multiplication of themes, *The Cantos* appear to present a scattered rather than a unified effect. Let no one mistake Pound's intention—there is a connection between the ideograms in each Canto even if it is difficult to find it. The result may be called unity, but it is a complex kind of unity, apparently obscured by the counterpoint and the multitude of subsidiary themes, each of which has important moments, shedding eventual light and comment on the main theme. Nowhere is this so clear as in the *Pisan Cantos* (74-84) where he recalls briefly some reference to almost everything he has said in the previous Cantos, with much new material added. The counterpoint flashes by, like the symbolic technique of advanced motion pictures, leaping from one motif to another with little transition. Without the early Cantos for assistance in discerning the original themes, much of this material is extremely puzzling. But the structure permits Pound to employ poetic versatility to a degree not always reached in the earlier Cantos, resting as the structure does on so many different poetic masks and poses, urging him on to vivid contrasting manners in verse form and linear exuberance.

It must be emphasized sharply that Pound's art of poetry in *The Cantos* is basically derivative. It is his development, his variation, his selection which constitutes his magic. He is an adapter, an arranger, eventually a commentator. Occasionally the result is extraordinary, achieving effects not present in the original source at all. His epic is intended to be a combination of everything he considers worth borrowing from the storehouse of the past; it might aptly be called an epic writer's epic.

Note the difficulties as well as the accomplishments. Even in terms of the first and second dimensions of comprehension, Pound's themes suffer in some degree because they cannot always be reduced to easy understanding. Every reader hopes for osmosis. If a simple description of basic themes can ever be suggested as a starting point for each Canto, the average intelligent reader will be more easily teased into fruitful exploration. For example, Pound begins in the first Canto with the incident from the *Odyssey* where Odysseus leaves Circe's bower to visit Hades. The hero does this ostensibly to see Tiresias and find out how to get back home to Ithaca. Shortly the reader may realize that this incident has been deliberately not haphazardly selected; it is symbolic. Pound will afterwards describe various times and places where the conditions of hell have operated on earth. Hell is a recurrent condition of man in many ages; the problem faced by Odysseus and a series of selected heroes is how to get out and where to find home or paradise. Pound eventually found himself in this predicament.

Dante's *Divine Comedy* furnishes a related, almost parallel example of theme, since Dante went through hell, purgatory, and eventually saw the light of the thrones of paradise. Pound is interested in how mankind develops and changes under the lash of circumstance and fate, what influences operate in these changes, these "metamorphoses," and the third intersecting motif enters. This one starts with Ovid and his collection of tales about famous changes. The Ovidian theme is not so familiar or so simple as the first two literary ones, but it allows Pound to exploit his admiration for natural human love, to set up for praise Bacchus and a number of famous females who found noble pleasure in the senses. The proper place of sex and/or the Eleusinian mysteries in *The Cantos* is probably in a later dimension of understanding, but the light which beauty sheds on mankind is easily assimilated on first reading. Paradise is a place where body, soul, and intellect find satisfaction.

Pound has always insisted that artists and poets are the antennae of civilization. Another important theme shows literature and art in an exalted state, usually in the past contrasted with the present, and always in conflict with forces which interfere with full appreciation for what Pound feels to be man's noblest capacities. Music joins in this exposition, although not so clearly. Pound continuously refers to the times when the writing was hard and lean, not soft and fat. He quotes troubadours and Cavalcanti, Sordello and Arnaut Daniel. The great artists of the early Italian Renaissance supply a related motif, and in comes Sigismondo Malatesta, the lord who gathered the best artists and thinkers of his day about him. Sigismondo built the Tempio, which Pound thinks gives us the most revealing record of Italian artistic accomplishment. Note that he praises painters like Bellini and Pisano (or Pisanellus or Pisanello, just to confuse things), but never seems to mention Raphael, Michelangelo, or Leonardo da Vinci, who are the best known representatives of Italian art in the minds of the moderns. His references to Rembrandt and Rubens are also contemptuous, so that the reader has to accommodate himself to a shift in estimation of values in order to see why the unstudied Malatesta becomes so important in Pound's evaluation of art history. He does bring in the Medici along with Sigismondo, because they too encouraged great art as well as fair banking policies.

> 1527. Thereafter art thickened, Thereafter design went to hell,
> Thereafter barocco, thereafter stone-cutting desisted.
> 'Hica nefas' (narrator) 'commune sepulchrum.' (46/28)

The art critics can now sympathize with traditional literary scholars, since Pound decries Milton, Spenser, Pope, Dryden, Wordsworth, the Romantics, and Tennyson. He is strangely reluctant to refer to Chaucer or Shakespeare, although he concedes Shakespeare great respect in drama rather than pure poetry.[6]

At this point we can identify another motif, and this one begins to explain where the epic is eventually going. This motif is described by Pound as "the repeat in history." In *Make It New* he partially explained what he meant: "An epic is a poem including history. I don't see that anyone save a sap-head can now think he knows any history until he understands economics."[7] This statement is often quoted by critics without including the second sentence.

Perhaps it is more accurate to call this theme "the economic interpretation of history." The term has reference to but is not precisely what Karl Marx meant by the phrase. The reader who is on the first or second level of dimension may have heard of Vico and his analysis of the resemblances, the turns, the patterns of recurrent history. In the twentieth century Spengler popularized a theory that all known cultures rise and fall according to a set design which fixes their destinies. History really repeated itself for Spengler, and his *Decline of the West* put the events of the past in outlined grooves. It is worth noting that Spengler was a student of Frobenius. Sorokin, Pareto, Toynbee and other historical scholars have continued some part of this analytical game. Pound began to explore the influences of political and economic pressures on art, on human happiness, and upon the health of society in various ages and cultures. He first centered on Renaissance Italy, carrying this study down to the present; then he turned to the United States, and finally to China. Other nations receive passing attention. Similar things have happened in each of these national histories, particularly in the field of economic development, and the epic demonstrates what Pound feels to be the significant patterns of these various cultures.

The main economic theme reinforces the repeat in history motif. Under what conditions do people and art prosper? Pound's historical heroes, distinct from his literary and symbolic ones like Odysseus, are the leaders who helped establish order, prosperity, and culture. Pound finds as a significant factor that unbridled commercialism always interferes with art as well as prosperity in recurrent history. Nor does peace spur the greedy few to power and wealth. The commercial villains form the central evidence for his diagnosis of *Usury,* and Usury implies the love of money beyond all other love, gain at the expense of everything which is admirable in one's fellow men. This concept is broader than the usual idea that usury is merely the practice of charging excessive interest on loaned money. History continually shows mankind going back and forth between economic control by and escape from the bonds of the usurious class, economic good and bad on earth, call this existence boom and bust or hell and paradise. The best times resemble what he finds to be expressed in the "Order" defined or described by Confucius in China, a condition illustrated by economic planning and state-wide tolerance, government encouragement or management of prosperity for the whole society. This view leads to an examination of the conflicts between all the people and predatory private interests as a part of society. In economic matters Pound emphasizes the ideal of social guidance, economic leadership in strong, capable, and somehow unselfish hands, while he castigates the usurers of history. Many usurers are bankers, many money-lenders he discovers to be Jews, and the theme naturally explores the more radical theories of social control of the economic credit of the state for the presumed good of all the people. This latter motif reveals "extreme" economists like Douglas and Gesell, but describes the whole scope of economic contention from Adam Smith to Marx to Keynes. By this time it will be obvious to the reader that he has passed by the second dimension of comprehension of Pound.

Economics is therefore Pound's ultimate theme, a view of society which cannot be stated in simple terms. Yet the economic theme depends upon the other ones. Counterpoint requires several figures of melody played against each other; we cannot ignore any of them. It is mystifying to find so many interpreters of Pound concentrating entirely on the literary materials, ignoring what the poet believed to be the main motif. When critics do mention it they are likely to apologize for it, retreating to what the liberal economist Galbraith calls "the conventional wisdom." Undefined concepts like Socialism enter into this matter. Pound does not imply or urge state ownership, and he declares that what he means by Socialism has no connection with Communism, particularly as it has developed in Russia: "Communism as theory is not only against the best human instincts, it is not even practised by the higher mammals. It suits monkeys more or less, and wild dogs are said to collaborate."[8] He constantly admires the excellent, the unusual, the intelligent, and the artistic; levelling to an average is evil. It is worth noting that he is not opposed to wealth or wealthy classes per se. But he says that it is the stupidity of economic materialism which allowed the Russian Revolution to succeed. Having money or private property is not what he means by Usury, and individualism must be preserved at all costs—except in cheating others to get more money. The rich man should *deserve* his wealth, not have acquired it through manipulation, trickery, or unfair assaults upon the rights and opportunities of others. Capitalism (ordered by rules which keep individuals from cheating the game) is the best economic order if fair practices in production and distribution can be established, money and credit controlled for the prosperity of the deserving many instead of confined to the selfish few.

On selected historical evidence Pound thinks that prosperity and fair dealing are most likely to occur when a strong but benevolent leader either takes charge and dictates social betterment or serves as a director for the needs of economic fortune affecting the whole society. This is why Pound admires John Adams so much, a man he conceives to be wise and benevolent, but who knew that people are hampered when they fight against forces too powerful for them to conquer by themselves. The United States secured a measure of order and prosperity in the days of Jefferson and Adams, one of the few examples of paradise in recurrent history.

Pound believes in democracy which protects the whole society. He presents his own definition of Fascism in this connection, for his idea of the kind of Fascism to be praised is a state where social and economic justice operate, where capital and labor work together, where the man who produces and the man who labors can find equal satisfaction. His emphasis is entirely upon the question of *economic justice,* and at this point one comes into conflict with the much publicized comparison of Italy and America in wartime, to America's disadvantage in his eyes. It is only fair to find out whether what he praised has any exact connection with economic justice in either country. This question demands special and separate examination later.

Considering Pound's motifs and their possible relationship to each other, one must judge whether the main theme has been complemented, augmented, made climactic, or hampered by the subsidiary themes. How much the literary motifs help or interfere with the economic emphasis is arguable, but one must not leap to a quick judgment. The example of the first thirty Cantos presents many alluring glimpses of the literary themes, few relatively effective statements of the economic one. The proportion of effectiveness changes sharply thereafter. The result is a natural process of development. His earliest poetic accomplishment had been entirely devoted to artistic experimentation. He naturally utilized the same techniques in displaying economic and historical materials.

Before we examine his economic and historical opinions in detail, we need to understand how he came to develop his individualistic artistic technique, a technique which is alternately complicated, mystifying, infuriating, exciting, and stimulating. His earliest poems illustrate his experimentation with translation, his assumption of "masks" or "personae" of the poets he admired. Almost every one of these first poems builds upon impersonation or direct translation and imitation. He reproduced selections from his favorite Greek and Latin poets, went on to the unexplored and unexploited collections of troubadour poetry, finally came to the great literary accomplishment of Dante and Cavalcanti. His university education had first directed him to the literature of foreign languages, and he felt that imitating or building upon what had already been done well or ill in our own language would be puerile. He did experiment with transliteration of an Anglo-Saxon poem (almost a foreign language), *The Seafarer,* and he wrote one traditional literary ballad, *The Ballad of the Goodly Fere,* in order to show that he could do that too if he wanted to. Eventually he conceived the poetic ideal of impersonating in his own way whatever had been done well by the great poets of other cultures. Anyone untranslated or relatively unknown became fair game for his borrowing or reproducing anew. We all know that he begins *The Cantos* with a fine version of part of the *Odyssey,* that he sometimes reflects Dante's *Divine Comedy,* that he adds a piece or two from Ovid's *Metamorphoses,* reproduces some troubadour songs, and eventually in Canto 36 inserts a full-length set-piece translation of the poem he might have selected as his favorite, Cavalcanti's masterpiece: "Donna mi priegha."

The penultimate step in Pound's early development of derivative poetic imitation was either to translate freely from the literal text of his source, or to use completely new material in the exact manner of the original (insofar as it could be adapted to English). Particularly interesting are the instances where he "improved" on his inspiration, sometimes in the direction of whimsy or satire. It is generally accurate to call this kind of writing "echo poetry." For example he did not translate directly the ballades of Villon, as Rossetti had done, but composed several new ones as he thinks Villon might have done them in English if he had lived today and had been as good as Pound. He takes a simple middle English lyric, famous but ephemeral, "Sumer is icumen in/ Lhude sing cuccu," and turns it into "Winter is icummen in/ Lhude sing Goddamn." His derivation from the Latin poets, Sextus Propertius mainly, provided him with much opportunity for deft observation or humor, and this kind of verse gained emphasis when he began to utilize Japanese and Chinese models. In *The Cantos* one may not always know what particular poetic mask or manner Pound is assuming, but it is usually safe to say that there is a model somewhere.

Access to the *Fenellosa Papers* (that mass of unpublished studies compiled by Professor Fenellosa and sent to Pound by the widow) gave Pound a tremendous amount of material generally unavailable to other modern poets and scholars, and the short concentrated *haikus* and the suggestive Chinese written characters began to spring into being in Pound's English versions. These models had the added advantage for him of being so different from English types of verse that almost everything he wrote seemed new and artistically exciting. Whatever one thinks of his consistent taste in taking a mask or his accuracy in literal translation, Pound is as good as his source or better on numerous occasions, even in the ungrateful field of parody. The most amazing use of the parodic manner is probably in Canto 80, Browning furnishing the original:

> Oh to be in England now that Winston's out
> Now that there's room for doubt
> And the bank may be the nation's . . . . (80/92)

The point to be noted here is that an epic which shifts contrapuntally from one model to another gives special opportunity for depending upon every poetic mask the poet knows. Pound knew a lot of models. Other epics usually establish a set technical rhythm or rhyme scheme and stick to it.

He has never quite forgotten that he started out to be a traditional scholar. An ancient teaching device is to put something on a blackboard (perhaps in a test), then turn to the class and ask, "Who wrote that and where did it come from?" As he turned into a leader of new artistic creeds, he became aware of the value of establishing a style that not only was unique but gave off the reputation of showing things beyond the casual comprehension of friend or enemy. He always has had a tendency toward saying in effect, "If you don't recognize that quotation, what kind of education did you have?" The next step is to vilify the orthodox teachers who were responsible for your education, and who allowed you to have so many gaps in essential knowledge and understanding.

In all fairness, despite Pound's assumption of more knowledge on the part of his readers than any generation has really needed for literary comprehension in the past, he does attempt to limit himself to the poets and authorities whose work he presents as of genuine importance. He does not quote from the New York telephone directory or sources equally ephemeral. The trouble is merely that he has minutely observed many important and occasionally obscure writers and that he leaps from one to another without much warning. The constant dependence of *The Cantos* on extraordinary sources often gives the impression of an impossible intellectual game with no reasonable purpose beyond the stimulus of detection to be found. This is where knowledge of the central themes and motifs furnishes the really essential clues—that is, as Pound once remarked, *Ariadne's thread* (the thread which in the myth led out of the maze).[9] In single poems he used a single source; in *The Cantos* he arranged many sources and manners about a thread of meaning.

The limitation and selection of his chosen poetic personifications deserves examination. His "impressions," his dramatic monologues, his efforts to imply much in little space were not merely literary exercises in translation but special examples of important poetic accomplishment. "Great literature is simply language charged with meaning to the utmost possible degree," he said in *The ABC of Reading*.[10] In short poems he could take single samples of highly charged moments for his derived style, implying an entire story in the selected instant which resembled the best illustrations of the ideal short short story in verse. The examples of Browning's dramatic monologues and Landor's *Imaginary Conversations* were before him. Concentration became his artistic ideal, and it is always possible to understand without much mental agony single illustrations of his climactic episodes. By the time he came to *The Cantos* he tended to shorten and concentrate even more and more, and the secret of his epic manner lies in the polyphonic combination of brief dramatic moments or observations put together for his larger purpose: the over-all theme of each Canto, or what might be called the illuminating thread of purpose around which it is organized.

Pound's connections with Imagism have been adequately discussed by a great number of critics. *Vorticism* has more to do with *The Cantos*. In his book on Gaudier-Brzeska he said "The image is not an idea. It is a radiant node or cluster; it is what I can, and must perforce, call a VORTEX, from which, and through which, and into which, ideas are constantly rushing."[11] Theoretically each Canto is such a node or cluster of related illustrations of the theme he is exploiting: counterpoint with a reason; emphatic not haphazard or free-associational arrangement. In this manner of composition several illustrations are better than one if they all illuminate the theme. Further, if the reader does not comprehend one illustration or single excerpt, he may eventually see a later one and begin to catch on to the intended central point, even if he has missed part of the so-called "ideogrammic" intention. The vortex reinforces and emphasizes the theme, each successive part of the cluster adding to the final impression. One recalls that a tornado or whirlwind is composed of vast rushing cycles of wind, forming a funnel that has at its tip a "vortex." The tip is the point at which the whirlwind makes contact and gets results. One might say that Pound tries to put only the vortex into his poem, expecting that knowledge of the whirling background will make the intellectual point of contact more effective. Recognition of the unstated residual material aids comprehension if the reason for using the incident is explosive enough, or especially if you do not understand each part of the vortex (the single parts of the "cluster") all by itself.

Pound derived his theory of the vortex from several influences, perhaps coincidentally. As critics like Kenner have said so clearly, he eventually called it the *ideogrammic* manner. However, at one time he used the process of *intaglio* to describe his poetic aims. Intaglio means "to engrave with a sunk pattern or design." This is the opposite of the process which produces a cameo, and it takes special knowledge and training to construct the design which will impress the selected material. The artist works on the *reverse* of what he wishes to create, making a relief impression or die. When the die is then forced upon the gem, metal, or stone, the artist's pattern produces a raised effect. It is obvious that the die itself is not the work of art, but the material struck from it may be. Modern etchings are created in a somewhat similar manner, lines being cut into a plate, inked, and then transferred to paper.

Pound apparently thought of the poetic intaglio process as being like the creation of a die which is then impressed upon the reader:

> the imprint of the intaglio depends
>   in part on what is pressed under it
> the mould must hold what is poured into it
>   in
>   discourse
>   what matters is
> to get it across e poi basta . . . . (79/64)

The engraving agent, or the poet, is then removed from the poem, but the result is unsatisfactory as art unless the reader himself is "impressed." The better the material incised, the more artistic will be the result. Surely the reader has to help, and the more background and atmosphere he can supply, the better will the poet's intention be communicated.

An interesting illustration of this concept is in one of the early dramatic excerpts, Canto 4, where Pound tells a selected part of the tale of the troubadour poet Cabestan:

> And by the curved, carved foot of the couch,
> claw-foot and lion-head, an old man seated
> Speaking in the low drone . . . :
> Ityn!
> Et ter flebiliter, Ityn, Ityn!
> And she went toward the window and cast her down,
> "All the while, the while, swallows crying:
> Ityn!
> "It is Cabestan's heart in the dish."
> "It is Cabestan's heart in the dish?
> "No other taste shall change this."
> And she went toward the window,
> the slim white stone bar
> Making a double arch;
> Firm even fingers held to the firm pale stone;
> Swung for a moment,
> and the wind out of Rhodez
> Caught in the full of her sleeve.
> . . . the swallows crying:
> 'Tis. 'Tis. Ytis! (4/13-14)

Knowledge of the background story of Cabestan and his lady love is necessary to fill in what Pound has poetically incised. You may have to look it up. Almost immediately you will come upon the dramatic story of Cabestan's death, how he loved the young wife of the old lord of the domain and the castle, how the lord sent Cabestan away, how his poetry lived in her spirit, how his murder was arranged, how his heart was cut out and served to the lady for her evening meal, how the old man told her she had eaten the heart of her lover. So she leaped out of the high window to her death.

What else is engraved or incised? Why does the old man say "Ityn!"? Why are the swallows crying? If you do not recognize the reference, you may be directed to the tale of Philomela and Procne, the Ovidian ladies who were metamorphosed into nightingale and swallow after Tereus the king (who raped one of the sisters and cut out her tongue) was also served the flesh of his son in revenge. Tereus pursued the two women, who were miraculously saved by being changed into birds at the last moment. The eaten son's name was Itys, Greek accusative *Ityn*. Simple, says Pound, and why should it have to be explained to the reader? But the reader has to have or get the necessary background or he will not understand the poem.

Pound's combination of the two sources takes on force because of the emotional tension created by their resemblance. This example is only one of a number of selected ideograms in Canto 4. Examination of the many correlated nodes does not help much in finding out exactly what the unifying theme is. One could guess ineffectively, "Passion ends in violence," or "True lovers are willing to die for love," or "Tragedy comes from jealousy and repression." These are obviously inadequate and critics will avoid them. Perhaps Pound is implying that love is a gift of the gods, not the property of privilege attached to religious ceremony. Still, this may or may not be his meaning. It is a difficulty like this which explains why Allen Tate would say that *The Cantos* "are not about anything," or why I. A. Richards would insist that poetry of this kind is there to be responded to, not to be searched for explanation. If we cannot state Pound's themes exactly we are likely to claim that the poet did not intend any particular communication, or that a specific theme does not exist. It would be simpler to suggest that Pound missed part of his intention in this Canto.

Pound is always inviting the reader to react, even to detect. On this level *The Cantos* provide an intellectual puzzle. You may lose the point of the vortex in the background of the wind. There is another explanation offered by Pound which bears upon what he is attempting. In his notes on Fenellosa and the Japanese Noh Plays, he says:

> For 'listening to incense' the company was divided into two parties, and some arbiter burnt many kinds and many blended sorts of perfumes, and the game was not merely to know which was which, but to give each of them a beautiful

> and allusive name, to recall by the title some strange event of history or some passage of romance or legend. It was a refinement in barbarous times, comparable to the art of polyphonic rhyme, developed in feudal Provence four centuries later, and now almost wholly forgotten.[13]

The Noh Plays do not set out, as Shakespeare's *Hamlet* does, a definable situation or problem. Each Japanese play works on an intensification of a single image or emotion, always assuming that the audience knows the story or legend on which the play is built. In a footnote Pound comments: "These plays are also an answer to a question that has several times been put to me: 'Could one do a long Imagiste poem, or even a long poem in vers libre?' "[14] He must have envisaged a poem in which single themes (emotions or perfumes?) were intensified by a number of illustrations or passages from romantic history and legend, examples which connected or illuminated the central image, emotion, or idea. Part of the fun was that it was a guessing game. Presumably Pound transferred a word game from the perfume game, and he certainly demonstrated that the long poem could be written. (Eliot is reputed to have observed, in a whimsical moment, "Can you tell what odor rises from each Canto?")

The exact way in which the ideograms or separate poetic parts are combined in *The Cantos* varies. Some of them seem to be a vortex composed of many nodes which are intended to illuminate a central theme; others, like the Chinese history and John Adams Cantos, proceed chronologically, and the vortex is organized around a central historical or biographical experience. Every Canto is concentrated, suggesting more than it reveals outright. Counterpoint is always present.

In *Guide to Kulchur* Pound says: "I mean to say the purpose of the writing is to reveal the subject. The ideogramic method consists of presenting one facet and then another until at some point one gets off the dead and desensitized surface of the reader's mind, onto a part that will register."[15] In *The ABC of Economics* he explains further: "I am not proceeding according to Aristotelian logic but according to the ideogramic method of first heaping together the necessary components of thought."[16] In *The ABC of Reading* he is even more definite. The Chinaman, when asked to define red, puts together abbreviated pictures of something red.

> That . . . is very much the kind of thing a biologist does (in a very much more complicated way) when he gets together a few hundred or thousand slides, and picks out what is necessary for his general statement. Something that fits the case, that applies in all of the cases.
>
> The Chinese "word" or ideogram for red is based on something that everyone KNOWS.[17]

It is beside the point to say again that there are many references in *The Cantos* to things that everyone does NOT know. But Pound is human; he is occasionally incensed because readers think his ideograms do not communicate their central intent:

> I believe that when finished, *all* foreign words in the Cantos, Gk., etc., will be underlinings, not necessary to the sense, in one way. I mean a complete sense will exist without them; it will be there in the American text, but the Greek, ideograms, etc., will indicate a *duration* from whence or since when. If you can find any *briefer* means of getting this repeat or resonance, tell papa . . . .
>
> There is no *intentional* obscurity. There is condensation to maximum obtainable. It is impossible to make the deep as quickly comprehensible as the shallow . . . .
>
> As to the *form* of *The Cantos:* All I can say or pray is: *wait* till it's there. I mean wait till I get 'em written and then if it don't show, I will start exegesis.[18]

And so we may say, with Kenner, that "things explain themselves by the company they keep," and that "the mode of making complete and properly qualified statements is to present a selection of *examples.*"[19] The contrapuntal resonance communicates on several levels of understanding. Nor can we forget that Pound *intended to communicate* his themes, his poetic emotions, his feelings, even his ideas about life, light, and economics.

Let us, in self-defense, go back to an over-simple observation: when the examples pile up thematic resonance, they indeed accomplish Pound's intention and merit respect. Immortal impression stimulates clear reception of the themes. The effect is blurred when Pound's examples get lost in source hunting or when the reader feels that something important and revealing has been left out. At their best the nodes, the "perfume," the die, the vortex, the counterpoint—whatever you call the techniques—are coherent and cumulative.

T. S. Eliot used many of the same poetic methods in his early poetry, particularly in *The Waste Land*. The "Possum," as Pound eventually calls him, has been much more popular perhaps because he sometimes indicated his unifying themes in headings to his poems. These themes can also be tied in an oblique sense to some variety of religious imagery or feeling. It is easier to applaud outwardly a thesis which says that the modern world is in a wasteland because of spiritual sterility, and that it needs to go back to God, than to try to understand a poet who says that it is not God we need so much as comprehension of economics. Considering the story that *The Waste Land* is printed in the form Pound cut it to, that Eliot originally included more ideograms in additional sections, one legitimately suspects that whatever its poetic effect now, it might have been more revealing in its original state. Kenner says that Pound cut three long parts and all but one of a number of interpolated lyrics. Section Four is the one surviving lyric, made into a division by itself, and not a series of ideograms as are the other parts of the poem.[20] In any case the cumulative effect of Eliot's great poem lives on through the central impression of the ideograms which revolve about the comprehensible themes. One can say that the objective correlatives are objective because they form a pattern.

We must conclude that the central and ultimate accomplishment of Pound's *Cantos* depends upon the effectiveness of the contrapuntal arrangement of concentrated excerpts which develop a "thread of meaning." The reader must not always be mystified by the inadequacy of the first dimension of comprehension. If Pound's largest and most important theme is indeed the economic one, it becomes of vital importance to find out exactly what it was.

3 THE PRESENT INFERNO

I will have another go at it, but up to present I make nothing of it whatever. Nothing so far as I make out, nothing short of divine vision or a new cure for the clapp can possibly be worth all the circumambient peripherization.

Doubtless there are patient souls who will wade through anything for the sake of the possible joke . . . but . . . having no inkling whether the purpose of the author is to amuse or to instruct . . . .

(Letter from Ezra Pound to James Joyce concerning his reading of parts of *Finnegans Wake,* November 26, 1926.)

To communicate and then stop, that is the law of discourse. (80/72)

Many great poems are written in a short space of time. Now and then the work of art covers a life-span, like Whitman's *Leaves of Grass,* being added to as the world and its crises call forth more poetic comment. We cannot forget that Pound's *Cantos* span half a century, and ours has been a violent and eventful century. It has produced many works of protest; Pound is not alone in disgust and rebellion. His compatriot Hemingway found it a bloody era, a time when we would like to say "Farewell to Arms," a time when man fights fate and forces likely to overcome his best defenses, even if he discovers his only solace is stoical but heroic opposition. Dos Passos protested against the century's social and political organization in the vivid complexity of *Three Soldiers, Manhattan Transfer,* and *U.S.A.* Cummings barely succeeded in containing regurgitation as he put down his enormous impressions in prose and poetry. Others objected, despaired, or—like

Yeats—withdrew from an age that displayed the greatest advances in scientific miracles beside man's incapacity to direct discovery toward the best life. The typical historical attitude of many of our greatest writers in the twentieth century is the posture of protest and rejection. Our young men have been angry for a long time. Pound was always angry.

The record of Pound's early poetry shows the development of a creative scholar who began to copy, translate, and assume the masks of the poets of the past, and then was transformed into a commentator on history. For him the first World War climaxed a mounting disgust with modern times, a war which left civilization in the roaring twenties, Europe with the explosive inheritance of the Versailles Treaty, what Americans called "The Jazz Age," or even "The Gin Age." For Americans the war originally possessed the aura of being fought for a noble cause. President Wilson voiced the aims in the resounding rhetoric which was his stock in trade. We hoped that our sacrifices would "make the world safe for democracy," or that the war would somehow be "a war to end all war." The glowing Utopian ideals of the League of Nations broke against the shocking reality of the Treaty of Versailles, and the glamorous League went down the drain in the Lodge-led fight in the United States Senate. It was an unnecessary, useless, disgusting war, said so many people, whoever had started it and whatever its issues.

Today we tend to forget that practically all the important literature which discussed the war after it was over suggested some protest against its uselessness. There was the bitter poetry of Siegfried Sassoon, Wilfrid Owen, Robert Graves, or even the aged Thomas Hardy looking on from afar. Combatants like Remarque wrote the best-selling *All Quiet on the Western Front (Im Westen Nicht Neues),* Robert Sheriff turned out a long-running play called *Journey's End,* and the pseudonymous Mary Lee showed the disillusion of idealistic women in *It's a Great War.* Cummings, Dos Passos, Hemingway, and many others commented from the viewpoint of a generation that eventually was called "lost." Eliot happened to centralize and sum it all up from a literary standpoint by marking these years a "waste land" era.

Pound's reaction to the war consummates general literary disgust, and it is a violent summation. He chose to write it first in *Hugh Selwyn Mauberley,* the collection of poems composed as a mask for the "mythical" poet who had ideals but was unable to realize them in modern times. This poet often seems to speak for Pound, although many critics subtract most of the poems as confessions of an invented, less contrite artist.[1] In any case *Mauberley* prepares the scene for the early *Cantos,* and certainly here and there Pound put down reactions which might easily have been incorporated in his larger epic. He confesses to being "wrong from the start":

> . . . seeing he had been born
> In a half-savage country, out of date . . . .

All that we can expect from our century is that

> . . . a tawdry cheapness
> Shall outlast our days.

We went to war for various reasons:

> Died some, pro patria,
> non "dulce" non "et decor" . . .
> walked eye-deep in hell
> believing in old men's lies, then unbelieving
> came home, home to a lie,
> home to many deceits,
> home to old lies and new infamy;
> usury age-old and age-thick
> and liars in public places.

Those of us who lost loved ones, friends, or fortune had not even the solace that something fine remained because of our sacrifice:

> There died a myriad,
> And of the best, among them,
> For an old bitch gone in the teeth,
> For a botched civilization. . . .[2]

No one has said it any more forcefully, and we should never forget that it represents the testament of an era.

Why was our civilization botched? What caused the war? Many thoughtful analysts began to speculate on political, social, and economic reasons for this destructive holocaust, Pound among them. War is an age-old problem, often written about, but each new outbreak encourages re-examination. It remained for the poet to attempt to document his own conclusions in *The Cantos,* to tell what he thought was wrong with our world, and to suggest whatever remedies he could envisage.

Eight years before the beginning of the first World War, when Pound left America to visit Europe and perhaps to continue scholarly study which could be exhibited by a doctor's degree, he carried with him the seeds of disgust dropping from the state of American culture. To him we had no literature worth mention, the surge of the nineteenth century having faded away in poetry. Art had never progressed very far, and the democratic stimulus envisaged by Whitman seemed to have died out. We had no music except what we imported from abroad, composers like Charles Ives flourishing in oblivion. The average American looked uncultured and prudish beside his European compatriot—see the novels of Henry James, who had found refuge abroad. The bourgeois American was likely to be the kind of fellow later caricatured by Sinclair Lewis, a Babbitt with simple-minded enthusiasms constricted by commercial straight-jackets, or a denizen of a business jungle where one made money or perished. Pound's brief experience as a college teacher left him with the feeling that puritanical intolerance was part of the American intellectual scene. He thought that academic standards in universities were turning into the search for flyspecks on good books; he is supposed to have objected violently to the idea of writing a doctor's thesis on the uses of the verb in Lope de Vega's plays. Today we are likely to suggest that this was a partially distorted view, but little intelligence or liberal imagination was apparent to the departing scholar. A Mark Twain or an Emily Dickinson seems not to have been his type.

The refuge he found abroad was restless. At least there was the record of past greatness, even if it too had deteriorated. Here and there he discovered rebellious talent or genius with which he could sympathize. He saw the remains of great art, and he looked avidly in every direction. In Canto 3 his visit to Venice is recorded:

> I sat on the Dogana's steps
> For the gondolas cost too much, that year,
> And there were not "those girls," there was one face,
> And the Buccentoro twenty yards off, howling "Stretti" .... (3/11)

The beauty of Venice, seen while the advantages of the Venetian prostitutes were advertised—yes, it is a contrast if one has in his mind an image of the "one face" where beauty dwells. If you are in doubt about his meaning here, have an Italian explain to you exactly what "stretti" implies, but do it privately.

Pound studied the living tradition of ideal beauty in art and music, but he found particular appeal in the poetry of Europe's heritage. Culture in all its aspects haunted him. The more he discovered, the more he felt the inadequacies of present appreciation in contrast. Several times in the early Cantos he tells of something which fascinates him from other voices, then says: "And we sit here . . ./there in the arena . . ." (4/16). This was the time when he went "Knocking at empty rooms, seeking for buried beauty" (7/25). Too often he found modern cheap houses, dark brown wallpaper, ugly furniture, slimy and slummy streets, all set against the imagined relics of a more glorious past:

> "Beer-bottle on the statute's pediment!
> "That, Fritz, is the era, to-day against the past,
> "Contemporary." And the passion endures.
> Against their action, aromas. Rooms, against chronicles. (7/25)

In this state of mind he began to celebrate whatever beauty antiquity brought to light wherever he could find it, in old rooms, in old books, in paintings, in architecture, in attitudes. He wanted to bring back to life as much loveliness as he could in the decadent twentieth century. Sigismondo Malatesta attracted him after he looked at the Tempio, and he eventually devoted several Cantos to this early Renaissance Prince, reading everything he could find about him, investigating the artists and philosophers Sigismondo had gathered at Rimini. The story of Sigismondo led him on to other matters, for the Prince had lived a spectacular life, serving as hired general for neighboring states in order to keep his head above financial waters so that he could continue to construct the fantastically costly Tempio.

> And he gone out into Morea,
> Where they sent him to do in the Mo'ammeds,
> With 5,000 against 25,000,
>   and he nearly died out in Sparta,
> Morea, Lakedaemon,
>   and came back with no pep in him
> And we sit here. I have sat here
>   For forty four thousand years . . . .   (11/50)

Other heroes from the past rose in exaggerated glamour in his imagination, and there were lovely women like Helen of Troy, Eleanor of Acquitaine, Cunizza (who loved Sordello), the great passionate heroines of the glorious days of old.

It was little wonder that he complained about modern England. But he found compensations. He believed that the present could equal or surpass the past, if only one could find and encourage men of genius. The ones he found included artists and writers who were in some kind of revolution, who were dissatisfied with the present, or who wanted to construct again some vision of the Golden Age originally located in isolated classical moments of civilization. There were Ford Madox Ford, Wyndham Lewis, and T. E. Hulme. Always there was William Butler Yeats. Young American expatriates gravitated to the revolutionary circle, including Hilda Doolittle (H.D., whom he had known at the University of Pennsylvania). The movement eventually known as the Imagist School began to formulate some principles, principles which were in direct opposition to the "degenerating" tradition of the nineteenth century in poetry. Along came what Pound calls "the telluric mass" of Amy Lowell, and the redoubtable American lady from Boston appropriated Imagism for sale to the public back home. Eventually Frost and T. S. Eliot came over, and finally there was Hemingway. But these recruits came later and the length of their stay varied. Pound settled down as a kind of permanent expatriate.

The American abroad who dabbled or specialized in art, music, or literature had to make a living or get money from home. One supposes that Pound may have drawn on family resources, but he seems to have more or less made his way. He located connections with magazines and took on editorial assignments of varying importance, at the same time that he made some money by contributing articles. He lectured on Provencal poets for pay. He soon became foreign editor for the newly established *Poetry Magazine* and sponsored his revolutionary friends in whatever publications he could wangle. He developed imposing talents as a propagandist for new talent. His own poetry did not succeed enough to support him, although he established himself as a leader of the New Poetry.

One of the most interesting jobs he had turned out to have great importance for the development of his social philosophy. This job was on a magazine called *The New Age,* edited by A. R. Orage, and around 1912 Pound began to do all kinds of hack work for this publication. Eventually he was signing himself B. H. Dias for the art critiques and William Atheling for the music columns. Years later, writing about his memories after Orage died, he refers to a period when the two of them got out the whole magazine between them and Orage supported him financially.[3] This connection had great importance in that it brought Pound into close contact with revolutionary economic policies. Through the magazine he met a number of radical leaders, probably A. J. Penty, certainly S. G. Hobson, and eventually G. D. H. Cole. These men were mainly university idealists, intensely interested in economic and social reform. Orage's purpose was to edit a magazine which would discuss the issues of labor and management relationship. His particular enthusiasm was a movement called *Guild Socialism.*

In Orage's circle Pound became fascinated by the study of economics. All radical protest in this period can be traced in some degree back to the theories of Karl Marx and Friedrich Engels, but the direction of proposed reform was not always communistic. In general the liberals subscribed to the economic interpretation of history, and they supported trade unions, or the new Labor Party, or the Fabians of Webb-Shaw fame, or the Syndicalists (who flourished in France), or almost any group not allied with the old order. These rebels thought the world was approaching a crisis because the contrast between mounting profits to owners and inadequate standards of living for workers would have to precipitate conflict or concession. For them the cause of the eventual war was plainly economic, just as Carlyle and Dickens had thought the French Revolution was caused by economic distress among the peasants and ruthless use of economic and social privilege by the upper classes. Hobson and Orage were mainly concerned with the organization of industrial protest; they supported every strike.

Pound came into contact with the doctrines of Syndicalism at this time. This influence has serious significance, since Mussolini was once a Syndicalist and Pound's eventual admiration for the Italian leader stems from this early beginning. The Syndicalists sought to organize workers for revolt against exploitation, but their main contention was the establishment of a social or political order based on trade unions (or *syndicates*) in which each union would take charge of its respective industry. Orage's Guild Socialism sympathized with the aims of Syndicalism, although the French workers who listened to Sorel were told to be prepared to use violence, sabotage, and slow work to defeat owners and manufacturers in any conflict. The *New Age* group was more given to intellectual solutions, something like voluntary cooperation between management and labor, but the issues were discussed many times in Pound's hearing. Note that the Fabians, opposing any hint of violence, separated from this group early, as did H. G. Wells, and this may be the reason why Pound dismisses the Fabians so contemptuously. He has no time for George Bernard Shaw.

Orage wrote several books, one called *An Alphabet of Economics,* in which he says that the solution to economic problems is in Guild Socialism, defining guilds as self-governing associations of "mutually dependent people organized for a responsible discharge of a particular function of society."[4] A guild is conceived to have broad social and economic goals, to be more responsible than a trade union, although the difference is not always clear. Trade unions were obsessed with the practical matter of bargaining for higher wages. The National

Guilds League was formed in 1915, setting as its aims: "Abolition of the wage system . . . . Self-government in industry through a series of national guilds working in conjunction with the state . . . . A partnership with management, involving a full-time wage-salary agreement, sickness and accident insurance, unemployment benefits . . . ." The Italian Corporate State under Mussolini had its roots in somewhat similar goals, since each corporation combined management and labor in its organization. The state also worked "in conjunction" with the corporations, enforcing their cooperation within their divisions into management and labor, and setting price and wage standards if necessary.

It is interesting to note that Odon Por, the Italian economist and Syndicalist who later became Pound's closest associate in describing reform under the Mussolini regime, wrote a book (in 1923) entitled *Guilds and Cooperatives in Italy,* published in England with the blessing of Orage's group and an appendix by G. D. H. Cole. The thesis of this work was that Fascism would depart from violence and turn to the theories of Guild Socialism, setting up a constructive partnership in cooperation between labor and management for the good of the entire economy. From the earliest days of the Fascist Revolution in Italy, Pound's reaction was that any accompanying violence by Mussolini's cohorts was unfortunate, but not important in the long run.[5]

Accordingly Pound added to his intense interest in great art, music, and literature an absorbing attention to revolutionary economic theory. His sources were mainly the authorities who protested against the excesses of the Industrial Revolution. The standard economists never attracted him, and he shows few signs of acquaintance with any of them, Ricardo and Mill for example. His first conclusion was a strong conviction that most economic troubles derive from the difference between money made by production and fortunes made by manipulation at someone else's expense. He began to think of the manipulation of values by an evil class of businessmen or moneylenders as *Usury.* Pound is thus in the economic tradition explored in American scholarship by Thorstein Veblen.[6] The basic parallel in thinking comes from Veblen's contention that the surplus values of the private enterprise system create a leisure class which lives off the labor of the rest of the people. This class does not produce anything, but exists by means of coupons, dividends, stock-market gambling, and the kind of luck which discovers oil on the property one owns or leases. Pound collected examples of the rich men who made money from sharp practice, who preyed upon others rather than contributing to production, who exploited labor, the stock exchange, and dependent colonial nations. He also shared another thesis expounded by Veblen (as well as other economists, of course) that there is a difference between industry and wealth or money. For Pound this meant that working to produce something is admirable; working to make money at the expense of those who work or produce is not the same thing.

Just how early Usury became his main concern is uncertain. He did not meet Major Douglas till 1918, and Social Credit was a post-war development. But it is certain that he rebelled more and more against staid English society, its economic standards, its habit of muddling through every crisis, and its completely conservative standards of culture. The height of this revolt was the publication of two issues of *Blast* in 1914 and 1915. *Blast,* conceived by Wyndham Lewis, was a luridly printed and illustrated magazine which gave off the smoke of revolutionary art along with its vindictive blasting of everything traditionally British. Also involved was Gaudier-Brzeska, a young Polish-French sculptor who impressed Pound as the great and coming artist of our time. Gaudier did a huge block-statue of the poet, and generally contributed to his interest in the capabilities of the sculptor and artist in the twentieth century—always providing that the artist broke away from the conservative constrictions of decadent modern civilization. Gaudier was killed in the war not too long after the first publication of *Blast.* It is of passing interest that among the reproduced illustrations in the second issue is a print signed "Shakespear," showing that the woman who became Pound's wife had appeared upon the scene.

How did this blasting of England and Pound's mounting interest in the problem of economic evil affect the early Cantos? Generally speaking the influence is gradual. One is free to guess that Pound's primary interests were literary, but that the first thirty Cantos represent a balance among several purposes or themes. His disgust with the war, the economic reasons for international conflict, and eventually his support of the doctrines of social management by government for the good of all the people—all his serious public purposes ate into his predominantly literary motifs. The first emphatic appearance of economic considerations is in Canto 12, in which he presents three instances of financial malpractice. These are really rather peculiar anecdotes. Baldy Bacon is a man who got a start by cornering copper pennies in Cuba, then selling them at a premium. Baldy later made a small fortune in Wall Street, rapidly lost it, and when Pound knew him was doing fly-by-night insurance. The second incident deals with a Portuguese named Dos Santos who became a great landlord by first buying a ship-load of grain supposedly spoiled by salt-water, feeding it to pigs, pyramiding by mortgaging one lot of pigs to buy another, repeating, becoming rich. The last incident is the vulgar story of the Honest Sailor, told by Jim X in a banker's meeting:

> Bored with their proprieties,
>   as they sat, the ranked presbyterians,
> Directors, dealers through holding companies,
> Deacons in churches, owning slum properties,
> *Alias* usurers in excelsis,
>   the quintessential essence of usurers,
> The purveyors of employment, whining over their 20 p.c.
>   and the hard times,
> And the bust-up of Brazilian securities
>   (S.A. securities)
> And the general uncertainty of all investment
> Save investment in new bank buildings,
>   productive of bank buildings,
> And not likely to ease distribution . . . . (12/55)

These illustrations serve as an introduction to the posture of economic protest, but they surely need a great deal of background for illumination of Pound's eventual point. It is interesting that the poet, who had been concentrating his references and quotations, decided to tell the entire story of the Honest Sailor in the old-fashioned anecdotal manner. Only vulgar stories gain by being told in full. The theme of the Canto is that a certain kind of business practice is akin to perversion. Baldy Bacon contributes the idea of the "corner"; Dos Santos "pyramids." Bankers profit by excessive interest and investment in colonial markets. All these financial practices are abnormal and offensive, says Pound.

Cantos 14 and 15 are known as the "scatalogical" or "Hell Cantos." In them Pound expands some of the more lurid atmosphere and punishment from the model of Dante's *Inferno,* bringing the sinners up to date, summing up his opinion of blasted England particularly, citing politicians, profiteers, financiers, newspapermen, perverters of money, the murderers of Pearse, a few selected identifiable figures from the past for good measure, Verres, Calvin, St. Clement of Alexandria, vice-crusaders, usurers, scholars, orators, preachers, monopolists, "obstructors of knowledge, obstructors of distribution." USURIA is descibed as "the beast with a hundred legs," and the Fabians show up crying "for the petrifaction of putrefaction, for a new dung-flow cut in lozenges." These descriptions are notable for Pound's attempt to improve on Dante's stench, and since they have had to be printed with many of the names indicated by dots or asterisks, the reader can have stealthy fun trying to identify who the individuals are. A reading of *Blast* is occasionally of help. The first reference to Churchill is probably here, and the reformer Comstock affords an interesting example of appropriate eternal punishment.

The effect achieved is in the realm of name-calling, an expression of disgust which gains much of its literary emphasis from its parallel connections with Dante. The selected section of Hell is the place where Usury is punished. Pound's guide in getting out of this horrible place is, surprisingly, Plotinus, and it takes the student of *The Cantos* a long time to figure out the reason for this choice. Neo-Platonism is as undefined as the principles of economics in the epic. But the following Canto 16, after the escape from the usurers' Bolge, shows Pound encountering the first World War, cites a number of anecdotes about the people he knew and their experiences and conversations about war:

And Henri Gaudier went to it,
        and they killed him,
And killed a good deal of sculpture. . . . (16/71)

The other martyr whose death affected Pound personally was T. E. Hulme, but all the anecdotes center around disgust with a useless war, the same disgust he expressed so vividly in *Mauberley*. The Canto reaches its climax in a description of the Russian Bolshevik Revolution, and Pound says, "I told you so. Keep up the present economic policies, and look what happens." Some kind of revolt is bound to result from malpractice in the marketplace. Pound always expresses admiration for Lenin, but his eventual judgment on Communism will be that this was an opportunity which went badly astray. At the moment he looked with interest and hope at it because it represented a break with the stupid behavior of the old regimes in modern civilization.

The average reader and even the specialist must admit that up to this time he needs more information than Pound has suggested in *The Cantos* to assess the poet's reasons for protest against the prevailing economic system. But we find out more as he goes on to Cantos 18, 19, and 22. There is a helpful summation much later in Canto 40, and in 46 he manages to mention Orage while that oracle comments on Shaw and Wells. The theme of Canto 18 is suggested in its last lines: "War, one war after another,/Men start 'em who couldn't put up a good hen-roost" (18/83). Whoever starts a war has a wonderful opportunity to make a fortune, or even if he did not start it, why not capitalize on the chance?

After an opening quotation from Marco Polo, showing Kublai Khan's provocative and profitable use of paper money in the trade of China (one of the earliest uses of this medium in history), Pound presents a description of profiteers, introduces Zenos Metevsky (Zaharoff) and the international munitions-makers, describes the sales methods of somebody named Giddings (how he sold torpedo boats to Russia to keep up with rival nations), gets off on the rackets of the oil business, and comes to a mild climax with an anecdote about an adventurer named Hamish (or perhaps Fowler) who showed Menelik how to work machines for war efficiently in Ethiopia.

These incidents are intended to reinforce the main theme: that financial manipulations, selfish cupidity, and unbridled usurious competition cause wars, wars that make great profits for a special class only. Victims suffer and die, but not the usurers.

Canto 19 proceeds a little farther and gets more definite in explaining Pound's thesis against the traditional economic and political system. The exploited theme is in the line: "Those days are gone forever." The fact that those days are not gone must continue to rankle in Pound's mind now that he is old and looking back on his revolutionary hopes. Whenever Pound refers to "the cake shops in the Nevsky" (representative of the Czarist corrupt civilization before Communism), we know that he is recalling something that ought to be long gone. His idealistic hope is that there might be an opportunity for improvement in the Bolshevik change, but his central charge is against the economic and social evils of what is past. The old days cry out for change to something better.

The first node in Canto 19's vortex presents an instance of business sabotage. Pound is satiric about sabotage, since the Syndicalists urged this practice in their fight with management. Pound asserts that businessmen do this too when it suits their purpose, giving an illustration of an inventor whose new process was bought up and kept from the market because it would hurt the product already being manufactured at high profit. Odon Por later says that this kind of business sabotage was stopped by Mussolini.[7] The second part of the cluster is a little cluttered, but it apparently introduces two men, Spinder, a Marx enthusiast who "never had to rent any money," and someone else who did not have sense enough to finish reading Marx. As *The Cantos* proceed, Pound will contend that the businessman who makes money is likely to be the one who lends or manipulates it under the present economic system. Others can make decent profits if they are fortunate enough to be able to avoid borrowing from bankers.

The third ideogram introduces a conversation about economic reform and quotes a man we find elsewhere to be Arthur Griffith, founder of the Irish Sinn Fein movement and leader in the establishment of Irish independence. At some time or other Griffith expressed the opinion that it is politically valueless to explain economics because there is no demonstrated appeal to the voters in discussing reform of this kind. He said, "Can't move 'em with a cold thing like economics." This scrap of quotation Pound uses several times later with venom, for it is always hard for him to see why people and voters will not respond to measures which are intended to improve their financial position. The masses are likely to follow blindly the opinions of the wealthy classes and they look with suspicion on government subsidies, supports, and control of prices or fair dealing in industry, even when it is obvious that people in general would be better off under such conditions—or so Pound thinks.

The fourth node centers on the Russian Revolution and says that "the Russian boys didn't shoot 'em," contending that Russia supplied a refuge for many of those oppressed in other lands. Communism flourishes when the rest of the world is stagnant, and an insufficient remedy hardly excuses the rest of the world. Pound then leaps to an illustration supplied by Lincoln Steffens, the point of which is to show that a government leader can dictate economic practice in an emergency; he is implying that it is out of date to insist that business exists in a vacuum, or that personal rights are not subject to national needs.

Steffens' many articles, eventually his *Autobiography,* should have supplied Pound with a limitless number of examples of what he called the sickness of economic democracy in the United States. He selects one episode introducing Tommy Baymont, obviously the Morgan partner named Lamont, who told Steffens about his difficulty selling coal from a mine he had bought. Because of circumstances not exactly explained he had to make a deal with Diamond Jim Brady (a racketeer), a kind of blackmail payment, which Lamont collected by raising the price of coal to the consumer, the excess being Brady's cut. This resembles the gangster rake-off system or any profit exacted by a middleman, a "tax" on price which is always paid by the buyer, not the seller.

Then follows what is probably the key episode, buried in the rapidly flickering cluster of illustrations, coming out of a diplomatic meeting between representatives of Russia and Austria. Procedures were getting under way as usual when:

> ". . . my ole man
> Said it:
> Albert, and the rest of it.
> Those days are gone forever." (19/87)

Pound said that there is no intentional obscurity in the epic, but he does not avoid making it hard for us. His point here is hidden under the phrase "and the rest of it." Previously in the Canto the rest of it had been given fully: "Das thust du nicht, Albert?" We recall that Pound once claimed his quotations from a foreign language merely underlined his meaning, but this particular one has almost performed his underlining in invisible ink. The German means, approximately, "Don't *you* do that too, Albert?" He might have translated it as "Come off it; everybody does business this way, even if it is immoral or unethical." Now Pound is suggesting that such days are, or ought to be, gone forever—days when nations and international cartels exploited and took advantage of each other in striving for export markets, eventually building up enough animus so that some slight episode touched off a war. One notes that this is long before the days of the Common Market in Europe.

The final ideogram concerns a bawdy conversation in which someone boasts about the ten years he spent in the Indian army, particularly a time when he had fourteen girls in a fortnight (the girls are described as healthy but verminous); there was another place in Kashmir where you could buy anything with turquoise, which was dirt cheap by European standards. These are the advantages of the exploitation of a country, true colonialism. Everybody takes whatever advantage he can of those he meets, since this is the accepted law of competition and life. Make it the old life, says Pound. Probably most of us would be a little more pessimistic. The changes in our world have been in the direction of increased prices.

The argument of Canto 19 makes a better case than 18. Whether it is sufficient to convince many readers depends upon how much they read into it. In the history of the United States following the Civil War Pound could have quoted many cases of economic exploitation, for this is the era when wealthy men built great fortunes through the development of the frontier and new industry. Pound is all for the development; but too many developers cheated, bribed, and manipulated the game to their own extraordinary profit at the expense of what the entire society might properly have shared. Pound could have found —perhaps he meant to imply—hundreds of examples in the careers of spectacular capitalists like Rockefeller, Gould, Vanderbilt, Drew, Harriman, as well as Morgan. These are the promoters the rebels called "The Robber Barons," after their medieval forerunners who seized the connections separating production and distribution, levying heavy tribute by controlling the flow of commerce. Thus the medieval baron in—say, Switzerland—might possess a bridge across a river dividing farm and town market. All he did was charge a high toll for letting the product reach the market; he did not have to produce or sell in order to make more money than producer or seller. A Rockefeller might do this by controlling the refining of oil, a Vanderbilt by owning the only railroad, or a Morgan by building the bank which loaned the money for building a business.

Pound cites very few of the spectacular cases, but he does imply the charge against the robber baron or usurer. In Canto 22 he selects the railroad and lumber king Weyerhauser, a relatively small baron from the large collection available. This Canto's theme is stated most clearly in a late part of the ideogrammic collection. Yusuf says, down in Gibralter:

> . . . Yais? an' the reech man
> In youah countree, haowa they get their money;
> They no go rob some poor pairsons? (22/104)

One must remember, I think, that Pound is not calling *all* rich men robbers, just the usurers. If readers cannot distinguish between the two kinds, his point is being lost. The Weyerhauser incident is an example of cheating the general public by appropriating for private gain what ought to be public resources. Weyerhauser got legal permission to build a railway and to take the timber he cut in the process: "So he cut a road through the forest,/Two miles wide, an' perfectly legal" (22/101). Certainly, and any student of American history may add the Union Pacific manipulations, the Gould-Vanderbilt quarrels at the expense of the market, or the unbelievably excessive stock-watering done in the financing of American railroads. Many historians say rather passively that necessary industrial development of a continent would have been completed much more slowly by any other means, like national or public works in the interest of the whole country—works honestly administered by unselfish politicians. What politicians, says the practical historian?

The ideograms in this Canto expose a number of contrasts or sub-themes. At the very beginning is the tale of the man who built a railway and then suggested how much cheaper it would be to educate Indians rather than killing them off as the nation moved westward. An incident intended to emphasize the Weyerhauser (called Warenhausen) evidence tells of an army turbine contract which supplied extra profit through the private sale of a certain number of "rejects," the rejected pieces being really all right. This is another way of cheating the nation by intentional or pretended inefficiency.

Perhaps the most interesting private or personal excerpt is Pound's report of a conversation between Major Douglas and somebody called Bukos. It is generally supposed by Pound analysts that Bukos is a pseudonym for John Maynard Keynes[8] so that indeed an interesting scene is set: the most respected economist of our time, the most radical critic of banking and credit, and Ezra Pound. Douglas (C. H.) is represented as asking Keynes what causes the high cost of living; Keynes replies, "lack of labor." With two million men out of work, Pound and Douglas are exasperated. The conversation is unfortunately not pursued in detail except for Keynes' final remark, "I am an orthodox economist."

Since Keynes later furnished the logic behind Roosevelt's pump-priming, government expenditures to beat the depression, one would suppose that he was on Pound's side, but Pound usually insists that half-way measures are time-serving and hypocritical. He charges that "orthodox" economy is based on a system in which there must be no interference between rapacious competitors nor government regulation of private excesses. As a kind of postscript he shows Keynes (at this time a reader for Macmillan Book Company, called McNarpen here) refusing Douglas' manuscript for printing because it would make Keynes' own books "out of date." If this happened it sounds very much like Keynes' tongue-in-cheek idea of subtlety; Pound is remarkably impervious to subtlety in others.

Pound's disgust with Keynes sets him off, through what comes close to free association, on a folklore tale of the creation of woman ("Christ" takes the tail of the fox to make a female). The beast fable suggests a connection with his point, but one reaches for it. The moral apparently is that God can make something out of nothing. If the divinity can create a woman out of Adam's rib or a mate from a fox's bushy tail, what stops the forces of creation from supplying man with employment or money or credit out of nothing? Man needs things like this as much as he needs a woman. Note that the arguments of the Social Credit economists are based on the need and ability of the whole society to "create" credit in order to keep prosperity operative. Or you can say that divinity used something (a fox's tail), not nothing, so the point may be that the story illustrates orthodox economics of the closed system; that is, you rob the fox to pay Adam.

At this time Pound draws on an adventure of his own in Gibralter, an unusually rambling episode telling how natives "stick" tourists. Yusuf, a local guide, justifies this cheating as a law of life. Then Pound attends a service in a Jewish synagogue, picturesquely described. The only relevant purpose must be that "after all a chew ees a chew." Jews are the businessmen most likely to "stick" others? The insertion of this episode has an ominous ring, even though by itself it shows mild anti-Semitism. Finally Pound sheers off on a story about the girl who keeps correcting the judge, the point of which must be that an unenforceable law is pointless. The real issues of economic distribution are rarely allowed to come up for judgment. Pound is always talking about the "exact word," precise definition, or *ching ming*; business practices might ideally be investigated to find out exactly whether financiers observe the spirit of the law or not. At the end any reader can see that this Canto presents difficulties, even when you know where Pound is heading. If it were not for overwhelming evidence elsewhere this might be one of the Cantos that is "not about anything."

The arguments and materials cited in these early Cantos present part of the case Pound is beginning to make for an economic interpretation of the causes of the first World War. After Pound met Major Douglas in 1918, he and Orage were converted to many of the doctrines and arguments of Social Credit as the medicine which would ease the problem of distribution and prosperity in the modern world. The Cantos after 22 (really after 30, since 23 to 30 mainly develop the literary themes) are likely to involve larger problems of recurrent history, they will include data influenced by the doctrines of Social Credit, and they will also be more effectively organized around central themes. At the moment we can look at a later concentrated compilation in Canto 40 which might stand as a summation of the earlier evidence. Here he cites the exploits of J. P. Morgan, beginning with the disreputable episode of the condemned guns resold to a separate government agency, and ending with the Pujo Investigation which led to the passage of the Federal Reserve Act in 1913, a measure which was supposed to regulate banking enterprise in the public interest.

Canto 40's mélange of Morgan accomplishments supplies passing reference to the pressures put on Lincoln's greenbacks, introduces the Rothschild bankers, and continues with a résumé of Morgan successes in manipulating the credit of the country to his own profit. Some hints as to the methods of manipulation are supplied. Again the reader has to know a lot about what actually happened to fill in the hints; he also has to have a great deal of sympathy with Pound's point of view.

The formation of holding companies allowed many expanding business concerns to appropriate most of the rising profits of their produce through the superstructure of new stocks (it is now called stock-splitting[9]), so that the growth of the country and the advances of the machine age created gains which were siphoned off by management and by organizations like the Morgan banking groups. Bankers got in the act by selling the new stock issues at high premiums. Few of the profits of an expanding economy went to the working classes, almost all to the promoters. This is Pound's view, whether or not all authorities would agree in every detail.

Pound mentions Corey, president of U.S. Steel, and Morgan's partner, George Fisher Baker. Morgan's praise of Baker might remind the reader with background that the latter's chief claim to lasting fame was his remark to a reporter in a stock-market crisis when many little investors were being wiped out, "It is none of the public's damn business what I do." In any case the period from about 1890 to 1914 displayed bankers and stock gamblers in high gear, with results that often left the general economy in trouble. A profitable technique, if you could manage it, was to buy the controlling shares in a bank; then use these shares as collateral to borrow more money with which to buy another bank, and repeat as long as possible. If you control a bank it is easy to have the bank approve your loans; then you can buy into all kinds of other businesses or play the stock market. It should be recalled also that many banks organized subsidiary trust companies which were not bound by whatever banking laws existed and could lend up to or past their deposit resources without keeping any set fractional reserves to meet withdrawals.[10]

Other manipulations were common. Companies like U.S. Steel tended to combine and control prices in restraint of competitive conditions. Trusts were usual business structures. With the assistance of friendly banks, it was general custom to issue new stocks, invent holding companies, and generally create fortunes for the controllers or favored insiders. Almost all big business corporations began to name directors who were figureheads, some of them serving on other boards of directors. This interlocking custom was quite helpful in the establishment of business combinations which agreed upon mutually advantageous profit schemes and boosted prices beyond the pressures of supply and demand.

It looks today as if certain instances of widespread economic distress were induced by stock-market manipulations alone. For a time Morgan and Harriman fought for control of Wall Street, their conflict in 1901 over Northern Pacific Railroad stock producing a near corner which squeezed all those gamblers who had sold short, the panic spreading and bringing on a general business slump along with many business failures. Another more serious panic occurred in 1907, over-extended banks failed, and the public economy went into a pronounced decline. This depression can be traced to stock-market trading rather than to business conditions in general. At least, a lot of people thought so. In 1912 the Committee on Banking and Currency in Congress started out to expose what it called "The Money Trust," and the resultant hearings under Chairman Pujo disclosed the widespread "interlocking directorates" of the Morgan empire, through which the public perceived a pretty fair case for concluding that Morgan, not the government, controlled the finances of America. The old Adam Smith philosophy of competition producing a proper level of prices and profits was being nicely defeated. There seemed so much special privilege, so much economic mal-practice possible in our system that a number of talented writers began to explore the trickery of competitive greed. These writers came to be called *muckrakers,* the most prominent being Lincoln Steffens, but there were also Ida Tarbell, Ray Stannard Baker, Samuel Hopkins Adams, Thomas W. Lawson, and Upton Sinclair.

It is in the background of this period that Pound expresses the philosophy summed up by Cowley in his first two summary propositions:

> Western civilization is at the mercy of an international conspiracy of bankers, or, as he calls them, usurers.
>
> Wars are caused by this "usurocracy" in order to run nations into debt and create opportunities for manipulating the currency.[11]

Pound's charges go far beyond this kind of statement. Not only may wars be caused by special privilege, but also depressions. Pound suggests evidence for a great deal of public cheating for private advantage on the part of certain businessmen and bankers; he attacks the methods of stock-exchange manipulation, selling short, the acquisition of corners or monopolistic practices, trusts, pyramiding, international cartels, international munitions makers, investors who exploit colonial markets, the robber barons, the Morgans, the usurers. He contends that a combination of economic ills helped to create the reasons for World War I, making some such struggle inevitable. A number of business institutions made fortunes out of the war, including the Morgan interests (in most cases these fortunes added huge sums to what already existed), but Pound has not asserted (as Cowley seems to suggest) that the usurocracy entered into a formal conspiracy. The system produces the conditions dependent upon it. He attacks the men who deal in intangible wealth, who make fortunes out of deals or distortions of values, rather than the solid process of salable goods. He calls manipulation Usury and puts usurers in Hell. He thinks the very existence of Usury makes depressions and wars inevitable.

With Pound's conversion to Social Credit, his attention turned to banking procedures and credit manipulations. Perhaps Cowley's summary is intended to refer to this part of the Pound case. Investigation of Social Credit is the next step. At the moment it is important to ask whether the epic is effective in its development of the economic theme, or at least so far. If Pound's arguments had been clearer, Cowley would naturally have stated his conclusions more exactly. Part of the cloudy result depends upon the poet's ideogrammic choices. Suggestion in a series of concentrated bits may be extremely constructive in theory, but the point of Pound's attack shifts in flight, or connects itself with something that seems inconsequential. Eliot has complained because he said Pound wrote about economics as if the reader knew all about the subject but had not understood it.[12] The clues are not always in the poem up to this time, that is, through the first thirty Cantos. This result may have occurred because Pound was still feeling his way toward the analysis of history and economic sickness he would eventually adopt.

A salient comparison between the methods of epic poetry and epic fiction may easily be examined in this connection. Dos Passos' novel, *U.S.A.*, has an approach to American economics which parallels this part of the Pound contentions. In the novel Dos Passos presents a number of concentrated biographies intended to represent the key figures in the development of America between 1900 and 1929. Among the labor leaders are Big Bill Heywood, Jack Reed, Joe Hill, and Wesley Everest; the political figures include Eugene V. Debs, Bryan, LaFollette, Teddy Roosevelt, and Woodrow Wilson; there is Veblen, naturally, and the businessmen biographies climax a series of the most brilliantly written set pieces in provocative fiction. One expects to find Henry Ford (the man who actually produced, rather than manipulated production, but who kept away from the bankers and Wall Street; he was also anti-Semitic—how did Pound miss him as a hero?). Then there was William Randolph Hearst's career, a wonderful example of pyramiding; and Minor Keith, the banana king who furnished fine evidence in the exploitation of underdeveloped countries. It would indeed be more direct, appropriate, and not necessarily unpoetic if somewhere in the early Cantos we could find something like the ending of the Andrew Carnegie ideogram as Dos Passos wrote it:

> Andrew Carnegie gave millions for peace
> and libraries and scientific institutes and endowments
>   and thrift
> whenever he made a billion dollars he endowed an institution
>   to promote universal peace
> always
> except in time of war . . . .[13]

For our purposes the best of them all is "The House of Morgan"; one really needs to read this sketch alongside Pound's in Canto 40:

> The panic of 1907 and the death of Harriman, his great opponent in railroad financing, in 1909, had left him the undisputed ruler of Wall Street, most powerful private citizen in the world;
>
> an old man tired of the purple, suffering from gout, he had deigned to go to Washington to answer the questions of the Pujo Committee during the Money Trust Investigation: Yes, I did what seemed to me to be for the best interests of the country . . . .

> By 1917 the Allies had borrowed one billion, nine-hundred million dollars through the House of Morgan: we went overseas for democracy and the flag;
>
> and by the end of the Peace Conference the phrase *J. P. Morgan suggests* had compulsion over a power of seventy-four billion dollars . . . .
>
> (Wars and panics on the stock exchange,
> machinegunfire and arson,
> bankruptcies, warloans,
> starvation, lice, cholera and typhus:
> good growing weather for the House of Morgan.)[14]

There is usually something precise and exact about a Dos Passos biographical sketch, and the form in which he composed his descriptions has many of the values Pound attempts in his own concentrated and selective portraits of heroes like Sigismondo Malatesta, Thomas Jefferson, John Adams, Martin Van Buren, and a number of others. Is it better to tell or merely to suggest? Suggestion is more subtle, and its success depends upon the reader's compulsion to develop the point being made. There is no great matter if one does not see the concentration of a literary motif or the connection between Sordello and Browning. Search for solution may be fun, but not necessarily serious. The economic theme mattered so much to Pound that he would eventually dare the reputation of treason because of it.

Beginning with Canto 31 he got down to cases.

4 MONEY, CREDIT, AND DISTRIBUTION

Entered the Bros Watson's store in Clinton N.Y.
preceded by a crash, i.e. by a
huge gripsack or satchel
which fell and skidded along the 20 foot aisle-way
and ceased with a rumpus of glassware
(unbreakable as it proved)
and with the enquiry: WOT IZZA COMIN'?

"I'll tell you wot izza comin'
Sochy-lism is a-comin' . . . . (77/42)

"You called me your father, and I ain't.
"I ain't your dad, no,
"I am not your fader but your moder," quod he,
"Your fader was a rich merchant in Stambouli." (12/57)

From Canto 31 through Canto 51 the emphasis of Pound's epic is devoted to the development of his economic thesis. Only three Cantos, 36, 39, and 47, continue to explore his contrasting themes. The following Cantos, 52 through 71, containing the short analysis of the history of China and the accomplishments of John Adams, are almost completely dependent upon his theories of money and credit. It becomes vital to see what he is driving at, and from the very beginning we ought to note an important difference in the issues which are being presented. It is inaccurate, for example, to say: at this time Pound began to preach only the extreme doctrines of Social Credit, therefore all his argument is suspect. As a matter of fact, the material falls into two separate compartments. One corresponds to a diagnosis of history, an analysis of economic conditions and the circumstances which produce prosperity or depression; the other suggests theories of remedy or reform. The theories of reform are the ones which come under the fire of the average economist. But the diagnosis appears to be a different matter. The layman almost has to conclude that it is accepted in some degree by modern analysts, even though the implications are still arguable.

Pound's first contention is that any political organization, any government, has as its primary task the responsibility for insuring economic prosperity. He says in *The ABC of Economics:* "When the potential production (the possible production) of anything is sufficient to meet everyone's needs, it is the business of the government to see that both production *and* distribution are achieved."[1] His central premise is thus based on the idea of government direction or aid, not government ownership. Pound cites a great many instances of good and bad leadership to strengthen this thesis. From Confucius to Mussolini the road is a little bizarre, but the point becomes clear eventually. Jefferson and John Adams are his first examples of extreme good, and he adds several Italian princes to reinforce his American heroes. Pietro Leopoldo (Grand Duke of Tuscany, 1765-1790) is perhaps the clearest example of what Pound praises in the hero who directs the state in the interests of all the people:

> . . . Pietro Leopoldo
> that wished state debt brought to an end;
>   that put the guilds under common tribunal;
> that left names only as vestige of feudal chain;
> that lightened mortmain that princes and church be under
>   tax
> as were others; that ended gaolings for debt;
> that said thou shalt not sell public offices;
> that suppressed so many *gabelle;*
> that freed the printers of surveillance
>   and wiped out the crime of lèse majesty;
> that abolished death as a penalty and all tortures in prisons
> which he held were for segregation;
> that split common property among tillers;
> roads, trees, and the wool trade,
> the silk trade, and a set price, lower for salt . . . . (44/21-22)

As was stated earlier Pound's theory of history stems from the basic assumptions of Karl Marx. Economists are surely correct in seeing a major difference between Marx's analysis of economic forces and his program for reform. Almost every political thinker of the past century has been seriously influenced by Marx's diagnosis; his remedial medicine is generally rejected by democratic countries. It has apparently been rejected by Russia too. This argument can be documented from many sources, and it may have a great deal to do with the retreat from sympathy with Socialistic leanings experienced by so many intelligent people during and after the days of the Great Depression. It took a long time to dissociate Marx's economic analysis from what was happening in Russia, the diagnosis from the extraordinary application of the insufficient remedy. W. W. Rostow, a member of economic teams appointed by several presidents, says in *The Stages of Economic Growth, a Non-Communist Manifesto:*

> Marx belongs among the whole range of men of the west who, in different ways, reacted against the social and human costs of the drive to maturity and sought a better and more humane balance in society. Driven on . . . by a "demonic egoism," by an identification with the underdog and a hatred of those who were top-dog, but also disciplined to a degree by a passion to be "scientific" rather than sentimental, Marx created his remarkable system: a system full of flaws but also full of legitimate partial insights, a great formal contribution to social science, a monstrous guide to public policy.[2]

Pound absolutely rejected the Communist guide to public policy, but adopted a part of the diagnosis. What exactly was that diagnosis, as distinct from the Communist proposals for remedy? Marx's economic philosophy is not simple, but Pound's debt to Marxian diagnosis is uncomplicated. The points of influence are two: first, that the world's culture, health, and troubles are all caused by economic forces above all other causes; second, that the diseases of society rise from the fact that a favored class gets "surplus values" from the product of labor, leaving labor (and a majority of the population) exploited and cheated of its share of the returns of labor.

As Pound saw the problem, it could be explained by a simple mathematical formula. Reduce the whole discussion to terms of money, defining money as a vehicle of exchange. Let *V* equal the *value* of anything produced by work in terms of money; this means price, or what the commodity will sell for. Let *M* equal the *money* which the producer gives labor to make the commodity salable. If there is no other source of money, *V* must always equal *M,* or something will not be bought or exchanged. Marx's diagnosis contended that there was a gap between *V* and *M* under the capitalistic system. The gap could be called *profit* or *surplus value.* It was the fact that *profit,* call it *P,* is always substracted from *M,* the money in circulation, which brings the machinery of distribution to eventual halts and creates the "bust" periods of depression continually experienced by the economy under the capitalistic system. Marx's equation is thrown off if profits are used to buy products for sale; if *P* gets back into circulation, then there is no difference between *V* and *M.* Or, if there is from other sources a sufficient supply of money to equal profits withdrawn from circulation, Marx's formula will balance without eliminating *P,* profit. Alternately, not everything produced will be sold because it is either not needed or wanted.

This diagnosis, in whatever comparable terms it may be stated, is the basis for all Pound's reasoning. Does *V* really have to equal *M*? Obviously, even to one in the first degree of comprehension of economic theory, there must be sufficient money in circulation to buy what is sold if the country is to be prosperous. If the two quantities are absolutely equal, complete distribution will be assured. Every product will find a market. Pound's case is that on every transaction or sale, a profit, *P,* is subtracted from *M,* the wages paid to the worker. With every sale the gap between *V* and *M* grows a little wider. Finally the gap becomes so large on a national scale that too many products cannot be sold and the great economic crisis which ensues produces depression. While we are not for the moment concerned with the Marxian remedies, note that to the Communist "surplus value" is the right of labor appropriated by owners or capitalists. Therefore Marx wished to eliminate *P* entirely so that constant prosperity would have to follow, according to his reasoning. But Pound was not opposed to profit, nor did he argue that it should be eliminated. This is his point of complete divergence from Marx.

Major C. H. Douglas, the originator of Social Credit, made his own diagnosis from the Marxian beginning, and in the process somewhat complicated it. In terms of the above formula, Douglas derived his *A* plus *B* from *M* plus *P*. That is, he called wages and profits something a little different, added the costs of financing production from loans, making it all more accurate in his opinion. Douglas argued that the capitalist or producer makes two kinds of payments when he produces something for sale. "Group A—All payments made to individuals (wages, salaries, and dividends). Group B—All payments made to other organizations (raw materials, bank charges, and other external costs)."[3]

The price charged the purchaser (*V* in the Marxian formula) must be the sum of *A* plus *B*; but Douglas' contention is also that the purchasing power provided is always less than this combination. Somewhere, in bank charges or unspent dividends, or raw material charges, the gap between purchasing power and selling price will automatically be widened with each successive financial transaction. This is the diagnosis which Pound includes in Canto 38, where he argues all the above contentions, then says:

> and the power to purchase can never
> (under the present system) catch up with
> prices at large . . . . (38/40)

It is essential to emphasize for American readers the major difference between the Marxian and Douglas analyses, if only to ward off dismissal of all parts of the Social Credit philosophy because of its connections with the bogie of Communism. Douglas (Pound, too) always accepts the need for profit in economic exchange; his point is that the proper capitalistic system—managed by government which provides credit—ought to allow for reasonable profit but also supply somewhere the difference between selling and purchasing power. This amounts to subsidizing profit. In modern times he says that this has been done by extensive borrowing of money, on individual and national levels, and by the so-called "unbalanced budget." The Douglas interpretation proposes that nations can stop depressions by constantly overspending their budgets; if they are businesslike and balance things, then depressions are sure to happen. He remarks that nations overspend madly in wartime and always enjoy commercial prosperity while the national debt multiplies its deficit. He presents an interesting dilemma.

The "traditional wisdom" of orthodox economists (Galbraith's phrase) disputes Douglas' diagnosis by insisting that the *B* payments eventually do get back into the total purchasing power of the public. Whether they do or do not would appear to be the crux of the argument. Consider for the moment the relevance of the Marxian contention that selling and purchasing power do not meet because of the removal of profit from the purchasing potential. What does capital do with its surplus values, its profits, which in Marx's view it has appropriated unfairly? The capitalist can save some of his excess and spend some of it personally. If savings do not disappear permanently, this part of *P* will eventually provide power to purchase what is for sale. The classical explanation is that much of profit goes into reinvestment to create more business. To Marx this merely makes the gap eventually wider. When the capitalist runs out of places to put investment in his own country, he invests abroad, preferably in undeveloped countries where the labor is cheaper and the profits larger. This practice leads to international exploitation, colonization, and at the last—wars.

The Douglas diagnosis takes several factors into account in estimating causes of the possible differences between selling and purchasing power:

1. Profits (interest is profit on an intangible).
2. Savings, mere abstention from buying.
3. Investment of savings in new works, which create a new cost without fresh purchasing power.
4. Difference of circuit velocity between cost liquidation and price creation . . . timing . . . .
5. Deflation, i.e. sale of securities by banks and recall of loans.[4]

The Douglas proposals for remedy are in the opposite direction from those of Marx. He recommends putting into the economy sufficient purchasing power to make up for the legitimate difference between *A* plus *B* and the reasonable selling price. This would give rewards to the good businessman, defining such a person as a good *producer,* not a manipulator of values or a usurer who increases the distance between producer and buyer.

Several complications arise. Apart from the fact that an advanced economic system postpones differences between *V* and *M* (between money to buy and selling price) by deferred payments, installment purchasing, or borrowing, the traditional economist often argues that the capitalist system is not perfect but the best one which can be devised. For Adam Smith, Malthus, and Ricardo, prosperity depends upon competition. A small number of able people might acquire most of the money, but many people would be relatively prosperous. The difference Marx eventually pointed out between selling price and purchasing power—if it existed—would be made up by a certain number of business failures. Not everything produced would be sold, and some businessmen would make no profit or less than a profit, thus eventually balancing *V* and *M*. The economy as a whole would be prosperous over a reasonable period of time, and certain individuals would always be poor or unlucky or unsuccessful. Whether this condition is just or unjust, it is merely a law of life, argued Malthus, thus illustrating the rather cold eye of much economic wisdom. The standard economist is unlikely to be sentimental or humanitarian. This is the way things are; he is not concerned much with talking about how they *should* be. Arthur Kitson, one of Pound's sources who is not a radical or Social Credit man, complains bitterly about this tendency in his fellow economists: "Yet we find economic conduct to be utterly irreconcilable with any standard of right conduct. Not only so, but economists have not hesitated to proclaim economics and ethics as irreconcilable. 'Moral considerations have nothing to do with political economy,' says John Stuart Mill."[5]

Some or all of this exposition will be evident to many people. Much of it is taught in elementary economics courses. The more complex part remains to be developed. It should be clear that, whatever the importance or truth one finds in the Marxian and Douglas diagnoses, they depend absolutely upon their terms being stated in fixed concepts of value. That is, according to your opinion, *V* may or may not equal *M* minus *P*, or *A* plus *B* may or may not supply sufficient purchasing power to keep the economy moving and prosperous; but if the relative value of either *V* or *M* in terms of exchange varies, the whole equation is thrown off. This point refers particularly to the amount of money in circulation and to the variability of money itself in relation to price. If your money will buy something today at the parity of a dollar, but tomorrow will buy only eighty cents' worth of goods, you have lost and everybody has lost purchasing power. Pound's economic diagnosis depends therefore upon his acceptance of the Marx-Douglas propositions as to the difference between selling and purchasing power, but also upon his diagnosis of the causes for disastrous fluctuation in purchasing power itself. Pound says that because Marx ignored this second problem he missed the boat. The values of money are always going up or down. No real justice can be assumed in the workings of a system if what you have deservedly worked for loses value through the manipulations of others, no matter whether you got your fair share of wages or profits in the first place.

> "That an immigrant shd.set out with good banknotes
> and find 'em at the end of his voyage
> but waste paper . . . ." (37/31)

How can the purchasing power of workers keep pace with what they produce if inflation raises the prices and lowers the value of the pay check? All distribution in civilized countries depends upon money. Who or what controls the value of money? According to the orthodox economist, general economic and "natural" conditions control it—supply and demand. According to some economic historians, like Brooks Adams, the men who lend it control it to private advantage and public loss whenever they can. According to Major Douglas, it is the banker who has been given or who has assumed this power. According to the radical analyst of the history of money, Alexander del Mar, prosperity occurs only when kings or governments know enough to control the values of money.

Pound follows Brooks Adams, Douglas, and del Mar. Note that the modern economist hedges his dependence on supply and demand in the twentieth century. Keynes says that natural forces still operate, that bankers should supply credit, but that business and government will have to cooperate for their mutual benefit in stabilizing values and stimulating insufficient supply and demand. This philosophy is usually called "pump-priming." It is Pound's position that private individuals and bankers throughout history rarely cooperate with the public. Why should they when they have such a material advantage? Only the government can secure the gap between prices and purchasing power. Pound rejects Keynes as a man of compromise, still essentially on the side of the usurer.

The average individual thinks that money has value in itself. This judgment conditions his understanding. A coin is worth so much because it has some inherent value which would make it worth whatever it says it is worth whether it is in the form of money or metal. Gold and silver have been the most useful representatives of this concept of money. Pound says that if all trade and distribution take place in terms of gold and silver coins, then the amount of trade possible will depend upon the total amount of gold and/or silver in circulation. If you, a businessman or banker, control the gold and silver, you can force other people to pay you more than it cost in order to use it at all. If you, controlling the money, wished to be unselfish and to encourage business in general—to insure production, profits, and prosperity on a national basis—you would make coin available whenever it is needed—that is, if you have it. A king, an elected leader, or a dictator could do this. The banker is bound to use his monetary resources for his own business advantage; he makes more money when the general amount is in short supply and he controls the most of it. Therefore Pound concludes that banks ought to be controlled by the state, if the state wishes to be prosperous.

How accurate is the diagnosis? The Cantos from 31 through 51 document parts of it. It is a large and complex subject, but some attempt to assess it is not beyond ordinary powers of comprehension. Pound's case depends upon his quotations from the early history of America's fight with the

"National" bankers, Jefferson and Adams against Hamilton, Jackson and Van Buren against Biddle, Lincoln against the bankers who devaluated and eliminated the "greenbacks," the bankers like Morgan who put us on a restrictive gold standard before Bryan, the bankers who supposedly compromised with their ultimate powers through Federal Reserve controls, but who did much as they pleased anyway. Supplementary to this citation of American history is reference to what had previously happened in England, specifically the chartering of their National Bank (meaning a bank established and guaranteed by the government but run for private profit) in 1694. Pound says violently that private profit on public money or distribution is extreme Usury. Usury may be merely a matter of ethics to most people, but when the practices of Usury produce general depressions and wars, they become part of a question of survival for nations as a whole. Pound also insists that Usury strangles a nation's culture, its art, music, and literature along with its financial health.

The background for his historical documentation is somewhat complex. He assumes that most readers ought to know or be willing to look up the background, but his ideogrammic method complicates the readers' problems in attempting to use whatever knowledge is available. There are many people in the world besides readers of Pound's poetry who know little about theories of economics or money. Whenever one begins to investigate these theories, the proponents of the status quo, often interested proponents, always seem to suggest that advocates of change are crackpots, Socialists, or Communists. Sometimes the attack turns to ridicule, as in the summary of Malcolm Cowley for Pound's ideas in *The Cantos. Time Magazine,* for example, refers to Social Credit men as the "Funny-money boys."

Pound at various times recommends that the reader look for himself, and this appears to be a reasonable suggestion. He names Brooks Adams, Alexander del Mar, Christopher Hollis, Larrañaga, McNair Wilson, Soddy, Douglas, Gesell, Odon Por, Kitson, Butchart, and Gorham Munson as important sources for judging his own analysis. We recall one more time that Malcolm Cowley summed up Pound's economic ideas by saying:

> Western civilization is at the mercy of an international conspiracy of bankers, or, as he calls them, usurers.
>
> Wars are caused by this "usurocracy" in order to run nations into debt and create opportunities for manipulating the currency.[6]

We can now ask ourselves: Do bankers "run nations into debt?" How are wars financed? For that matter, how are deficits financed? Most of us think it is real money, "cash," which is borrowed from the nation's resources to finance wars. Pound says that the nation borrows "figures on the books" of banks, i.e., *credit.* The holders of this credit profit automatically from wars. Does this fact constitute a conspiracy?

The basis for Pound's economic point of view is thus his insistence that private individuals unfairly control public money, credit, and distribution in the world today. He never objects to the right of anyone to control his *own* money, just the money of other people or the nation. He is firmly opposed to any suggestions that the government take over business in general. Nothing but banks or banking privileges should be taken over. He wants effective encouragement for the producer, complete hindrance for the manipulator of credit.

A little more background is appropriate at this moment. A study of the history of money indicates that it is in the first place confined to coins made out of metal. It is indeed difficult to get past the popular illusion that the substance out of which the coin is made is worth what is stamped on it if the substance could be conveniently used for exchange in its original form. That is, we think we could buy the same thing with an ounce of gold in the form of dust or hardened into a coin and stamped with a specific value. Pound's position rejects this analysis. Money is worth what we think it is worth. His contention is that money is like a ticket. History shows that it must be based on something which guarantees its worth—popular confidence, backing by royal decree or government direction, even price controls. Pound suggests that the history of money can be most conveniently studied, in the beginning, through examination of what happened to distribution and commerce in the long history of China. China's experiences go through more centuries than those of any other present civilization, and we possess the records. This is his reason for devoting the ten Cantos (52-61) to Chinese history. Some rulers used the money in circulation for the prosperity of all the people, some did not. This statement is oversimplification, but Pound is zealous in praising the rulers who made sure there was enough money. There was even experimentation with paper money, backed by government or royal decree. This seems to have worked except when the amount was not strictly controlled. The emperors who stuck to the principles and ideals of Confucius were constantly dedicated to the philosophy of government concern for the welfare of the whole society. Basically this is the reason Pound praises Confucius. He certainly has no theological or religious interest in the great Chinese philosopher.

If the accepted medium of coinage is gold alone, then the total commerce and exchange of the state will depend upon the amount of gold in existence and in the form of money. Some of Pound's sources argue that states find themselves in economic trouble when they grow larger than their money supply, whenever they limit commerce and exchange to coins in short supply. It is the contention of Brooks Adams, in *The Law of Civilization and Decay,* that nations always deteriorate when there is not enough money over-all, or when a limited creditor class (the goldsmiths, the lenders, the usurers) gets control of the existing coinage and withdraws it from general circulation except upon its own terms. For Adams this is the real reason for the decline and fall of the Roman Empire. Gradually the money-man became too powerful, the needs of the economy exceeded the supply of money, and everything degenerated enough for the Goths to take over. Pound also argues that nations which have enough money need never decay, and *they can always create enough* with stable value for exchange if they wish. Hitler revived Germany by creating credit and established his powerful military machine in a country not far from bankruptcy through control of the currency and the value of money in the marketplace. So did Mussolini.

Alexander del Mar, the scholar who begins to influence the late *Cantos,* points out in his *History of Monetary Systems* that the Greeks and Romans originally reached their high state of civilization by establishing a limited and exclusive system of money issued and guaranteed by the state. Under such a system supply and demand can really set just prices. This general economic arrangement was eventually destroyed when enough states lost control of the amount and specific value of the coins or money in circulation. This situation developed gradually in various countries through the Middle Ages and came to climax in Europe in the last of the seventeenth century; del Mar insists that the economy of western civilization has been at the mercy of fluctuation beyond reasonable control ever since. Temporary relief came from the exploration and robbery of the immense treasures found in Mexico and Peru. Tremendous additions to the supply of coined money came into being from this lucky circumstance. For Brooks Adams, this new money caused the beginning of the Industrial Revolution, since mankind rapidly found ways to put money to work. When Clive conquered India, the gold of the Orient gravitated to England, stabilizing the power of the British Empire. The gold strikes in America and Australia in the middle of the nineteenth century produced enough additional money to stave off the revolutions urged by Marx and his comrades.

An additional point needs to be made. The entire question for Pound is not limited to the exact amount of gold in circulation, but includes silver. If there is not enough gold, silver is usually added to the potential store of coins. The problem of acceptable ratio in value between gold and silver was fixed by the Romans at 12 to 1. This ratio lasted down to the end of the twelfth century when it came in conflict with differing practices. The ratio in Moorish states was about 6.5 to 1, and in the Gothic states about 8 to 1. Anyone who could change gold for silver in England, then change the same silver for gold in India could approximately double his money. This became the main business of the East India Company in the seventeenth century, according to Brooks Adams, silver being drained out of England in order to be exchanged for more profitable ratios elsewhere.

Pound continually inserts data about the ratios in *The Cantos,* adding more and more instances in the ones which follow the Pisan section. The central argument is always that the prosperity of a nation depends upon the actual or fixed value of the money used for distribution. Ideally it must be adequate. Too little money strangles business; too much raises prices and produces inflation unless the state manages the details of distribution by instituting some form of price and wage controls.

At various times kings and governments have experimented with other metals than gold or silver. *The Cantos* are dotted with references to experiments with paper money too. As commerce becomes more widespread history shows that paper money is often substituted for gold or silver. Originally paper money was a replica of bullion or coin deposited somewhere for safe keeping and used as backing since it could be exchanged for paper on demand. But from the beginning paper money has been subject to manipulations which affect any measures to ensure an exact relationship to its backing. It has been based upon so many kinds of guarantees that modern banks have come into being to administer, regulation, and profit by this addition to the amount of money an economy needs.

Pound describes banks as of two kinds. A bank of exchange can hold your money for safety or convenience, and transfer it at your direction. Government banks, when they exist as separate institutions owned and run by the government, are often of this nature. They collect taxes and pay out government expenditures. Exchange banks need to charge a small fee for their services and pay their expenses in this way, almost like a cooperative enterprise. Strictly speaking a bank of exchange could also invest actual capital, say a set amount of coin or currency owned by the bank, in loans charging interest, thus making a profit as any business does on invested capital.

The second type of bank deals in the creation of credit, what Pound calls money "created out of nothing," perhaps out of the air. This process, as the poet sees it, is different from the kind of loan which occurs when someone takes money from his pocket and lends it to you. Bankers lend many times the amount of money their banks possess, since they have deposits and checking accounts and can therefore create credit. The ratio of lending to total deposits in the bank varies from country to country and age to age, but it is always far beyond the capital owned by the bank. This creation of credit is only possible with paper money, checking accounts, and bookkeeping figures. It could be done by governments as well as bankers. The fact that it is not done by governments is one of Pound's main areas of annoyance. Nor does he see why bankers have any possible right to their privilege except for the dullness of the class which has to pay for the bankers' privilege—you and me. Our disadvantage derives from ignorance of what is going on and lack of power to change the procedure. Pound insists that banking privilege in creating credit is completely different from freedom of business in all other matters of production and distribution. The idea that politicians would ruin the economy by using the government's right to print and issue money seems to him to be puerile. No politicians, he says, could hurt the general economy more than private unregulated money-creators have done throughout modern history. The thesis is argumentative, but it is worth examining.

As an illustration to get the discussion into figures, note that in 1942, a war year, the Federal Reserve Banks of the United States had a total capital of about 144 million dollars; their own reports indicate that they had outstanding "loans," including government securities, of more than 23 billion dollars. Somewhere between the two figures the amount of credit created seems to be about 160 times the capital the banks possessed in the first place. One can check the published financial reports of *any* bank and see that it lends many times the amount of capital it possesses. There is, of course, nothing evil or illegal about creating necessary credit. How could a modern nation's economy be carried on if this created credit were not thrown into circulation? Somebody has to create it, and banks perform an important service to the economy. Pound's point is: Who has the right to decide how much shall be created, and who has the unlimited privilege of profiting by the interest charged?

In actual practice the problem is even more complex. The banker, depending upon legal controls and his gambling spirit, can create much or little credit. If he creates too much, say beyond the total of deposits in his bank, the depositors might all decide to withdraw their money at the same time. Then the bank would fail, since it never has enough money to meet all possible wihdrawals. The soundness of the bank depends upon whether it can eventually turn its loans into the amounts involved in the loans, either by repayment or seizure of collateral. When banks call loans or restrict credit, the amount of real money in circulation goes down in proportion. Call enough loans and depression is a cinch. Pound's argument is that no business class has the right to expand or constrict a nation' credit deliberately. This right is the privilege of the nation as a whole, and nations should take back from the banking class the special privilege which is now theirs, the ability to control the flow of credit and the distribution of goods that depend upon the amount of money in circulation.

From Canto 31 to 51 Pound describes two types of banking procedures—discount not exchange procedures. He argues that one level is to aid prosperity and distribution on some broad social scale; the other works for its own profit to the disadvantage of the public in general. The Siena Bank in Italy is his chosen example of the "good" bank.

Apparently this bank was established by the Medici not to make a profit but to assist the prosperity of the community, the ruler providing the necessary capital or backing from a share of the customs and miscellaneous taxes. This happened in Italy in 1621, and Pound devotes Cantos 42 and 43 to describing how it all came about and how it worked. The idea was to provide whatever credit and money the community needed. Depositors received 5 per cent interest on their money; borrowers paid 5½ per cent. The small difference was used to pay expenses. In other words it was a cooperative bank whose reason for existence was to add to the usable money of the town. The government guaranteed the capital and the bank assisted the flow of commerce and business initiative. It was all done "on the whole people's credit/for public and private utility" (43/12). Profits above expenses were automatically put back into the bank, or used as a reserve in case a loss occurred. Pound says that the bank worked through the centuries and that you can open an account there today. The bank is called the "Mount," the Monte dei Paschi.

In one of Pound's Money Pamphlets, *Social Credit, an Impact,* the workings of this bank are described more fully than in the two Cantos. In contrast he refers to the Genoa Bank, Banca D. Giorgio, the type which was created "to prey on the people." In the centuries after 1252 this bank got the right to almost all important tax collecting, even church property taxes, as security for state loans. The community was constantly looted and the people in constant poverty.

There are more "hell-banks" in these Cantos (31-51). The central indictment is in Canto 46. Here his theme is the quotation from Paterson, the man who established The First Bank of England: "Hath benefit of interest on all/the moneys which it, the bank, creates out of nothing" (46/27). What happened in England was that the kings had been successively in more and more trouble finding enough cash to meet their expenses. Following the English Civil War, Parliament usually objected to providing enough money by taxation. Charles II attempted to issue his own money, that is, money based on royal authority rather than backed by gold, but met constant suspicion and failure. His power was limited and he could not control either prices or the moneylenders. When William and Mary came to the throne after the Revolution of 1688 the royal coffers were empty. Along came Paterson and his colleagues to propose the new Bank of England, an institution which has existed ever since. The plan was for the government to borrow £1,200,000 from the Bank instead of from the "goldsmiths" or lenders who had previously supplied money to the crown on demand, usually at extortionate interest. The Bank was given the right by Parliament to print that much money and to receive 8 per cent interest plus £4,000 each year "for expenses." The paper money was made safe by guaranteeing to supply from taxes whatever actual cash the Bank needed in order to satisfy depositors who wished to cash in their paper notes. While the Bank possessed capital, one begins to perceive that it needed no actual money of its own to perform this financial service, that it printed £1,200,000 "out of nothing," quoting Paterson himself, and received the interest and extra money for the privilege of doing what the government itself might reasonably have done in exactly the same manner. Pound points out that the people of England have been paying interest on the original and successive loans ever since. Technically the Bank was not supposed ever to issue more than £1,200,000, but in fact it went on to issue what it needed with successive loans to the Crown. The King did not dare to object, even if he had wanted to, since Parliament would not or could not give him enough money to pay off the Bank; that would take more taxation, and the Bank might recall its loan and go over to the opposition. This power resembles blackmail, and the English monarchy never escaped from the trap. Note that Pound apparently got much of this material from Christopher Hollis, who detailed the evidence in *The Two Nations*.[7]

The banking history of England since 1694 continues to provide Pound with examples of the power of the central bank to expand or contract credit at will. His case depends upon reading the worst possible construction into what happened. Various laws were passed through the years intended to control the power of the Bank to issue notes or charge "discounts," and since the Bank was naturally operated for its own rather than the national security and profit, it gained more and more power. Whether what happened was deliberately in opposition to the national welfare is not the question for Pound. He says that the system mortgaged the industry of the people to protect the special interest. The system did supply proper credit on many occasions. The Bank has been the main source for financing the government's need to borrow. Successive wars have sent the national debt higher and higher. Furthermore the Bank has always been able to supply whatever money is needed by writing figures on its books and printing the money. The legend is that money is worthless if the government issues it on its own backing; but the Bank's reputation makes printed money good. Most of us seem to believe this without question. Strangely enough we welcome the signature of the Secretary of the Treasury as an added guarantee of worth, having the general illusion that the country somehow stands behind money anyway. Pound remarks that money is always backed by the state, but we give the profit of creating and using this money to the banks, not the country.

When the American Republic was founded after the Revolutionary War, a National Bank was established by Alexander Hamilton in direct imitation of the English one. Pound first examined the reaction of Thomas Jefferson to Hamilton's financial manipulations, then later discovered that John Adams gave him material which so coincided with his own opinions that he devoted Cantos 62-71 to the life of our second President. Said Adams:

> Every bank of discount is downright corruption
> taxing the public for private individuals' gain.
> and if I say this in my will
> the American people wd/ pronounce I died crazy. (71/162)

And again:

> and as for Hamilton
> we may take it (my authority, ego scriptor cantilenae)
> that he was the Prime snot in ALL American hisory . . . . (62/96)

The second quotation is Pound's paraphrase of the opinions of Jefferson and Adams, a blunt conclusion.

The records concerning coins in the early colonial history of the United States show that English gold and silver was mainly used, with a sprinkling of Spanish coins added. There was not always enough for easy commerce, and eventually some of the colonies began to print their own paper money. New York and Pennsylvania arranged to lend money to settlers, amounts up to half the value of their property, to be repaid in from ten to twelve years plus nominal interest. When this was discovered in England, the practice was forbidden and the colonies forced to liquidate their loans. Pound and a smattering of historians suggest that it was the distress caused by this suppression which aroused as much resentment as stamp taxes on paper, tea, or what-have-you. In fact, this appears to be one of the causes of the Revolution. How important it was is hard to tell from this distance. Pound insists that it was of primary importance.

When the Revolution broke out, the Continental Congress was forced to print paper money to finance it, although various representatives, including Franklin and John Adams, went to France and Holland to attempt the arrangement of loans. Bonds were also sold to patriotic subscribers. The experiences of Adams in his missions abroad are explored in the Adams Cantos (62-71), and sufficient money and supplies were secured by our representatives to help finance the American victory. When the new government was established and Washington became our first President, Hamilton was made Secretary of the Treasury. He emerged as the man behind the executive. The national debt stood at $54,500,000, much of it in Continental bonds which were worth in the market about ten or fifteen cents on the dollar. Our history books have told us about the buying up of these bonds by speculators, since the new Constitution guaranteed full payment of national debts. John Adams says that only the insiders, some of them Congressmen or friends of Hamilton, knew that a new and guaranteed currency would be established and all bonds really redeemed at par.

The story, as Pound sees it, is all anti-Hamilton, since he and the First National Bank are equated with Usury and special privilege. The important result was that Hamilton established confidence along with the credit and money of the new nation. Something had to be done to create financial stability. He did it by setting up the National Bank, the system which prevails in some like form to the present. The system suffered setbacks from Adams, Jefferson, Jackson, Van Buren, Lincoln, and eventually Woodrow Wilson. Pound says that Bryan's suggestions for reform were wide of the mark, and Wilson's were ineffective. A failure also was the effort of Lincoln to pay for the North's part of the Civil War with the greenbacks, with what Pound calls piously "debt-free money." One may note that the poet associates himself with respected company. The weight of the evidence may not always be as he interprets it, but the facts are in some degree challenging.

Hamilton knew how the Bank of England worked, and he shows a complete knowledge of how banks create credit, how they utilize deposits and check-book systems to keep money flowing, and how they supplement the coin in circulation with the creation of paper money. The First National Bank received a charter for twenty years. It could accept deposits, receive public moneys, and act as fiscal agent for the national government. It could issue paper money which was legal tender for all debts, guaranteed by the government; it could make loans and charge discounts, including advances to the government so that it could operate. Of course it was privately owned (except for 20 per cent of the stock, for which the national government paid two million dollars, making the government a partner without control). The national debt was part of the guarantee of each share, the obligation of the people thus becoming security for the privately owned bank. All this was done in 1791.

Hamilton's reasoning has long been praised by the conservative American tradition, and it is firmly supported by many orthodox economists. Hamilton said, specifically: "Paper emissions [apparently those which might be made by the Government alone, not the Bank] . . . are of a nature so liable to abuse, and it may even be affirmed, so certain of being abused, that the wisdom of the government will be shown in never trusting itself with the use of so seducing and dangerous an expedient."[8] It is generally accepted today, much less then, that politicians would let money get out of hand if they could have anything to do with voting its creation. How to control government-created money was the rock on which the opposition of Jefferson, Jackson, and Lincoln split.

The National Bank's charter ran out in 1811, in the administration of Madison. Jefferson had embarked on a policy of strict frugality in order to get out of debt to the Bank, cutting the total from about 84 to 57 million dollars (despite the expense of the Louisiana Purchase) when he finished his second term. His position is historically exactly opposite to Hamilton's, and during the War of 1812 he showed signs of recommending that the government print what it needed, backed by taxes, instead of borrowing from any bank. But the crisis of the new war, the memory of the old Continental currency, the behavior of private banks which printed all kinds of money in the vacuum created by the lapse of the National Bank's charter, the need for finding large sums of money for military purposes, and the lack of information and understanding in a Congress which would have to vote the necessary measures—all these pressures finally led to the establishment of the Second National Bank in 1816. All the privileges of the First were renewed for another twenty-year period. Specifically the new Bank was given the right to issue paper money with no limitation except the signature of the Bank's president.

In Canto 37 Pound tells the story of the subsequent fight between Andrew Jackson and the Second Bank under the able leadership of Nicholas Biddle. Jackson thought the idea of the Bank was unconstitutional—this follows that part of the Constitution which gives Congress the right (and duty?) to control the money of the nation.[9] In Jackson's 1829 message to Congress there was suggested the study of a substitute method of financing the economy, "founded upon the credit of the government and its revenue." He considered government ownership of a new bank, doing what the old one did but for the profit of the public treasury. Jackson doubted whether the public would trust political appointees in bankers' chairs, and who could imagine a professional civil service which could be trained and hired to perform this service for the country?

The saga of Jackson's fight with the Bank has been told in every American history book, although most of us do not understand it very well. We usually interpret it as the effort of a great President to live within the nation's income. Or we say that this was the only time the country was out of debt. However we read it, it was an all-out battle. Pound is occasionally incensed because the behind-the-scenes story of Biddle's financial manipulations is best observed in Van Buren's *Autobiography,* a work which did not see print until 1918. Clay, Calhoun, and Webster led the fight for the Bank, Van Buren pointing out the discovery of the fact that Webster accepted substantial fees (expense accounts?) from the Bank for his legislative influence. Benton of Missouri was Jackson's best orator and Pound celebrates him later. Beyond the fact that the Bank put every possible pressure on Congress by monumental lobbying, Biddle finally deliberately inflated the currency by throwing vast sums of money into the economy in loans, particularly in the western states where Jackson's political strength was greatest.

> "30 million" said Mr Dan Wester "in states on the Mississippi
> "will all have to be called in, in three
> "years and nine months, if the charter be not extended . . .
> "I hesertate nawt tew say et will dee-precierate
> "everyman's prorperty from the etcetera
> "to the kepertal ov Missouri, affect the price of
> "crawps, leynd en the prordewce ov labour, to the
> "embarарsement . . . ."
> de mortuis wrote Mr Van Buren
> don't quite apply in a case of this character. (37/33-34)

Van Buren was obviously so incensed by what he considered Webster's prostitution of principle for pay that he was willing to "'speak ill of the dead"—writing after Webster had died. He charged that the Bank employed every means at its disposal to derange the country's credit, create panic and depression to force the continuation of its privileges:

> Bank president controlling the government's funds
> to the betrayal of the nation . . . .
> "on precedent that Mr Hamilton has
> never hesitated to jeopard the general
> for advance of particular interests." (37/34)

Jackson vetoed the Bill proposing to extend the charter, and won reelection to defeat the Bank and end its official term. Van Buren, following him as President, encountered a depression, which was caused by world crises as well as Biddle's manipulations of credit, and served only one term.

Jackson did not put any substitute for the National Bank into practice, depositing the government's tax collections in favored or "pet banks" (a practice still continued in many individual states for state taxes). These in Jackson's day seem to have used the deposits to create excessive credit and speculate wildly without effective control. Van Buren proposed the Independent Treasury, which was instituted in 1846. This arrangement lasted until the Federal Reserve Act of 1913, a measure which in effect established a multiple Third "National Bank" on the Hamiltonian model, the system which exists today. Its resources are many many times those of the first two banks. Note that the Independent Treasury was a bank of exchange owned by the government, that it collected and disbursed funds, issued money if it wished (new money was issued only once, the "greenbacks" under Lincoln in the Civil War) and helped ease credit if an emergency arose (it was never run ably enough to avoid economic panics). It did not attempt to compete with private banks in the lending of money. Probably the fact that it never had much to do with controlling the fluctuations of the economy can be attributed to default of intention as well as understanding. Private banks took over the credit and lending functions of the previous National Banks, and under financiers like Morgan managed currency and credit, even the Gold Standard, to considerable private profit through the years up till the first World War. It was one of Bryan's proposals that the government issue its own money, but this measure was lost in the "Cross of Gold" slogan and the campaign to ease depression by putting more silver coins into the economy. Pound assumes that Bryan never saw the points in dispute as clearly as his great predecessors had seen them. In any case the forces of special privilege managed to defeat him as they did not defeat Jackson.

To sum up Pound's position, then, after observing his version of American history, he insists that the government has the constitutional right through Congressional action to create and issue money, currency, credit as money—that it enjoys the right to add or subtract money in circulation—that it need not and should not borrow money from credit-creating sources at interest—and that these prerogatives are its supreme challenge and opportunity for creating business prosperity as well as cultural health.

> Independent use of our money . . . toward holding our bank.
> Mr Jefferson to Colonel Monroe . . . . (41/56)

> . . . nations were fools to pay rent for their credit . . . . (48/35)

State by creating riches shd. thereby get into debt?
This is infamy . . . . (49/39)

The greatest statement of his economic philosophy is the mock ode to Usury, Canto 35, and the Hymn to Light, Canto 51. For many readers these excursions into the traditional grand manner of impressive poetry are the highest levels of *The Cantos* before the Pisan section. In them the indignation, the concentration of all his theories against unfair privilege for the few reaches climax:

> with usura
> seeth no man Gonzaga his heirs and his concubines
> no picture is made to endure nor to live with
> but it is made to sell and sell quickly
> with usura, sin against nature,
> is thy bread ever more of stale rags
> is thy bread dry as paper,
> with no mountain wheat, no strong flour
> with usura the line grows thick
> with usura is no clear demarcation
> and no man can find site for his dwelling.
> Stone cutter is kept from his stone
> weaver is kept from his loom
> WITH USURA . . . . (45/23)

5 THE IDEOGRAMS OF ECONOMIC REFORM

> *you are right, Rush, our trouble is iggurunce*
> *of money especially (70/157)*

> *giving them easy market for merchandise*
> *and enlivening commerce*
> *by making to circulate the whole realm's abundance*
> *and said he knew how hard it wd/ be to find personnel*
> *to look after this . . . . (55/42)*

Diagnosis and remedial measures do not necessarily go hand in hand. In an epic like *The Cantos,* depending as it does on so many examples and on relatively few positive statements, Pound's specific ideas of economic reform defy easy comprehension and sometimes elude sympathy or support. The poetic method of *The Cantos* is not an ideal vehicle for explaining and arguing new nostrums. His ideograms are often full of stimulating single suggestions which may encourage the interested reader to investigate his recommendations. But persuasion is difficult because most people are committed to support of what they are accustomed to. The majority naturally suspects change. This attitude complicates the effect of the epic, for the accomplishment of *The Cantos* in developing Pound's economic theme depends naturally upon whether the reader acquires any rapport with Pound's conclusions.

It is also very easy to misunderstand Pound's remedies. For example, considering his reputation for advanced theories of radical economic reform, the average reader starts by thinking of him as pretty far out. So we are surprised to find that he is solidly on the side of the good businessman, at times talking like a conservative Manchester economist who believes in maximum profits for the deserving producer, but with the twist that such a producer will make more money by a kind of partnership with his workers. The competitive capitalistic system works successfully for Pound provided someone does not cheat its comparative values and enough extra money is somehow put into circulation for buying and selling to increase and multiply. Pound's main recommendations have to do with ways of getting the extra money into the economy. He thinks that the ordinary businessman is hurt by the usurer who constricts distribution, by the stock-market gambler, by the manipulator of values, by the representatives of unfair special privilege. Pound is on the side of the average producer and consumer, and he cannot understand why such people do not understand and support him for their own advantage.

Pound's eventual error is likely to be judged as seeing too much forward motion in the complex social programs of a Mussolini or a Hitler. Our problems in understanding his theoretical recommendations are tied to our difficulty in comprehending his position in the second World War. We note that his study of comparative history down through the centuries led him to believe that individuals with good intentions have never improved the world very much unless they possess enough political power to do something about their intentions. Like John Adams, he concluded that intelligent and benevolent leaders will have to do for the people what they cannot accomplish for themselves. Pound is not committed to benevolent dictatorship alone, since he believes that principles of improvement, progress, and reform in economic matters will eventually be obvious to an intelligent electorate. The eternal questions he investigates are: How can leadership in economic matters work on a national level? How can reforms be instituted? What reforms are possible, considering the lessons of history?

In Canto 109 there is a revealing exposure of his approach, a confession which should be set beside his many extreme statements: "Uncivil to judge a part in ignorance of the totality/nemo omnia novit" (109/123). No one knows it all? Many times in *The Cantos* Pound has given the impression that he thinks he knows it all and is too arrogant to explain it to us who either do not know or are not convinced.

Yet there is excessive misunderstanding about the reform notions he does suggest. One recalls that Cowley characteristically stated some of them thus:

> The usurocracy could be abolished by a simple reform of currency, namely, the issuance of stamped and dated script based on the goods available for consumption . . . .
>
> American culture, great in the days of John Adams and Jefferson, declined after 1830 and perished in the Civil War, also caused by bankers. "The United States were sold to the Rothschilds in 1863."[1]

These statements on their face leave out most of Pound's central contentions and recommendations, although they are fairly quoted as "a part in ignorance of the totality."

Let us state his central platform again. His reform program is based on his belief that it is the business of the state to insure and protect business prosperity, to supply intelligent leaderhip in economic matters, to regulate just prices and sufficient profits, to stimulate freedom in production and fair dealing in the market, and to check Usury and any other form of special privilege which interferes with the circulation of the money needed for buying and selling. The government of any nation has the power to stop depressions and to promote prosperity; it must be willing to use that power. If business is unable to take labor into partnership or is unable to employ everyone, the government must stimulate business or even fill the gap. Enough money and credit must be made available and not borrowed at interest from private banking institutions. He wanted an ideal New Deal.

A good example of this platform is supplied in his description of the reforms of a certain Ouang-Ngan-ché in the reign of Chin-Tsong in China in the eleventh century, A.D.:

> and at this time began Ngan
> (or more fully Ouang-Ngan-ché) to demand that they reset
> the market tribunals,
> posting every day what was on sale and what the right price of it
> as had been under TCHEOU emperors
> and that a market tax shd/ go to the emperor from this
> thereby relieving the poor of all douanes

giving them easy market for their merchandise
    and enlivening commerce
by making to circulate the whole realm's abundance . . . .
And Ngan saw land lying barren
    because peasants had nowt to sow there
whence said: Lend 'em grain in the spring time
    that they can pay back in autumn
with a bit of an increase, this wd/ augment the reserve,
This will need a tribunal
and the same tribunal shd/ seek
        equity
for all lands and all merchandise
    according to harvest and soil
so that the emperor's tithes shd/ be proportionate
        to the rarity or the abundance of merchandise
to make commerce more easy, that the folk be not overburdened
nor yet the imperial revenue be made less.
and Ngan made yet a third point
that was to fix the value of money
    and to coin *enough* denars
that shd/ stay always on the same footing. (55/42-43)

These ideas, simply stated as principles of economic direction, are equivalent to the standards of Confucius. The Chinese Cantos (52-61) are written to explain this ideal of social Utopia, and they come closest to the method illustrated by a Spengler or a Toynbee who cites the examples of history to indicate a trend or a movement which has meaning when one desires to profit by the trial and error of the past. Pound does not suggest a recurring pattern for the course of history; he merely attempts to identify the factors which produce depression or prosperity.

It is a contributory fact that general ignorance of Chinese history makes these Cantos more difficult to comprehend than usual. As poetry they suffer from simple lack of background in the typical reader, who really should have had a thorough course in the subject to understand Pound's presentation of the economic issues illustrated by his cryptic excerpts and comments.[2] Chinese names defy easy remembrance, the narrative omissions complicate communication, and the breezy colloquial notations include so many brief summations of social trends that these Cantos are alternately packed with meaning and spaced with serious gaps. The method of this section of the epic does not set parallel ideograms side by side, but rather proceeds chronologically to retell the whole story of known Chinese history, boiling it down to what Pound considers essential. The theme, the vortex of the examples, is an outline of the principles of Social Order, the methods of governing a state so that economic prosperity follows and depression is avoided. The counter-theme emphasizes what states should not do.

The reforms of Ouag-Ngan-ché may serve as a starting point for explaining what Pound is recommending in the way of reform. Ngan instituted price controls, a variety of sales tax (apparently the sole tax), loaned government money or seed to farmers in order to encourage more cultivation, attempted to manage the course of the economy so that "all merchandise" would achieve equity or proportion (sell at the Just Price) without inflation or deflation of prices, and put enough stable money into circulation to be sure there was no impediment to distribution because of lack of coin. Constantly emphasized is the fact that high taxes interfere with prosperity. "Call things by the names. Good sovereign by distribution/Evil king is known by his imposts" (52/7). Imposts are taxes, of course. The government must encourage "Goods that are needed": "And of the true base of credit, that is the abundance of nature/with the whole folk behind it" (52/3).

This sounds attractive in principle, but for many American readers it assumes a lot of government bureaucracy and controls. The reference to lowering taxes also introduces complications. Pound apparently thinks that prosperity increases revenue, and prosperity is more likely to occur when taxes are down. Presidents Kennedy and Johnson have said much the same thing in recent years. There are many examples in the Chinese Cantos of the "good" kings who reduced taxes in time of depression, or who limited taxing to a share of actual production. There is Tching Tang who

> . . . opened the cooper mine (ante Christum)
> made discs with square holes in their middles
> and gave these to the people
> wherewith they might buy grain . . . . (53/10)

Tcheou Kong said: "A good ruler keeps down taxes" (53/13). Li Wang added:

> 'A Prince who wd/ fulfill obligation, takes caution
> à ce que l'argent circule
> that cash move amongst the people . . . .' (53/16)

Hiao Ouen Ti is quoted:

> Earth is the nurse of all men
> I now cut off one half the taxes
> I wish to follow the sages, to honour Chang Ti by my furrow
> Let farm folk have tools for their labour it is
> for this I reduced the said taxes
> Gold is inedible . . . . (54/23)

In the days of Tchun-Tsong too much money had piled up in the national treasury and depression was rife because this money was unspent:

> If these [the coins] go to the national treasury
> they will go out of circulation
> the people thereby deprived,
> so HIEN-TSONG threw this into commerce . . . . (55/36)

A revolt started against Tai Tsong because taxes had made money so scarce that the people could not buy food:

> Therefore Ouang Siaopo of the people
> demanded just distribution . . . .
> Meanwhile Jelly Hugo
> the tartar, a Khitan, freed his people of taxes
> and started old age relief. (55/41)

Government subsidies, works financed by the government, relief by stimulus of employment—all strangely reminiscent of the American New Deal Pound sometimes denounces because it did not go far enough—are praised when they occur in China.

> YAO, CHUN, YU controller of waters
> Bridge builders, contrivers of roads
> gave grain to the people
> kept down the taxes . . . .
> And in Caï Fong they made a grain dividend
> and gave instruction in farming
> ploughs, money, ammassi . . . . (56/48-49)

Kang Hi spent three million a year on river embankments, also encouraging other public works (60/78), and Tong Tching set up a public kitchen in time of famine, public works for the unemployed, and a dole for relief (61/80).

> In time of common scarcity; to sell at the just price
> in extraordinary let it be lent to the people
> and in great calamities, give it free . . . . (61/81)

Again:

> Heaven has scattered riches and poverty
> but to profit on other men's loss is no better than banditry . . . .
> (61/84)

The idea of government stimulus for the economy is controversial in many countries. Still, Pound's reputation for unorthodox remedies stems not from recommendations of this nature but from his tendency to embrace theories which either have not been tried in the past or involve new proposals which are highly debatable. It is easy to say, as he does, that there must be money enough in circulation to supply distribution and prosperity. How do you really know how much is enough, and how does the government go about supplying the extra money? How do you stop inflation? What are the workable methods of putting responsibility for supplying credit under government control, and who guarantees that the government agencies will be efficient or honest? These questions are always asked, and Pound attempts some answers.

Part of his unorthodoxy depends upon the original Marxian-Douglas diagnosis, the idea that profits must either be used to purchase commodities, or eliminated, or else extra money must be supplied "beyond the balanced budget" to make up for the subtraction of profit from the purchasing potential. One of his remedies is the Douglas National Dividend; another is Gesell's stamp-scrip money. Naturally there are other ways in which an economy can manage to encourage or even guarantee distribution, and it is uncertain that the propositions of Douglas or Gesell would work unless very difficult conditions accompanied their adoption. They have never been tried, of course, unless the Alberta and Wörgl experiments can be considered trials.

According to Douglas the comparative value of money in relation to prices must be absolutely stable. Inflation or deflation would have to be avoided, and some form of state management seems necessary to make sure that money does not suddenly lose or gain too much purchasing power. Pound has the idea that stabilization would work naturally if the government either added or subtracted the amount of money in circulation as the economy needs it, without a complex system of price and wage controls. But nobody knows for sure. If prices do not find a "just" level, if there is extreme deflation or inflation, the government would *have* to interfere and establish controls. Apparently Pound's idea of just prices is akin to the conclusions advanced by the Douglas *A* plus *B* formula: that is, cost plus *reasonable* profit ought to make the price right. There is nothing frightening to business about this part of his case. In fact, quite the contrary, since profit would be more certain than now.

Pound's main remedy is for the government to own or direct credit in order to stimulate business. The first step must be to control banking privileges, in fact to change the way banks are organized now. There is in most countries some kind of control of banking privileges. Theoretically Pound is not opposed to banks' lending their own money and making a profit on invested capital; he is opposed to their lending what they create out of their monopoly of deposit resources and taking the interest out of circulation. One must remember that banks do not appropriate created credit or money; they make money in interest by using it. The interest charged is justified by the risk the bank assumes in getting back the principal loaned. All of Pound's references to the long fight in the United States between the National Banks and various presidents illustrate his belief that the government itself should create the credit and either eliminate or share the profit that results from the interest charged. In actual practice this would mean that a bank with a million dollars of capital could lend a million dollars and profit by whatever interest it secured. But the bank could not lend ten or twenty million dollars created out of nothing unless it shares the interest with the national treasury and on the government's own terms and control. Some Social Credit economists have suggested that the nation should own its own bank, have a monopoly on *all* money created beyond capital, and that properly qualified career bankers might be hired to do the government's distribution of credit in loans to business. The resulting profit in interest, a huge profit incidentally, could be used to lower or wipe out federal taxes. Alternately banks could become cooperative community enterprises (like the Siena Bank). The question is complicated by the obvious fact that the economy needs the created credit and that many modern banks fulfill community needs admirably. They are certainly likely to be less usurious than loan companies.

The other remedies Pound prefers narrow down to two methods: first, one must make sure that whatever money needed for the economy must be *added to,* not *subtracted from,* the total purchasing power of the public; second, there must be enough *new money* put into circulation to make up whatever gap there is between prices and purchasing power. Assuming some kind of price or credit control, Major Douglas proposed definite methods of getting the new money into circulation in order to keep distribution steady and normal. These methods would supply the difference between prices and purchasing power, according to his *A* plus *B* diagnosis. Douglas' proposals were originally of two kinds. You either subsidize the buyer or the seller, and the government *adds* the paper money which makes up the difference to either side of the equation. Subsidies have been used to some degree in the United States, mostly for agriculture, but the subsidies have come out of taxes or borrowing from banks on a national level.

Quite simply the Douglas proposal means a government bureau which would estimate the just profit on any article for sale, say a recognized fair percentage like 5, 10, or 15 per cent. Then a producer would keep records of his total sales and would be forced to charge a price which exactly equals his costs. Periodically the government would supply him with a subsidy to make up his agreed-upon profit needs. Or it could be done the other way. The producer charges a price which includes profit, as at present; but the buyer keeps proof of what he purchases, and eventually the government gives him a percentage of his cost of living to make up the excess between cost and cost-plus-profit charged by the seller. Either of these methods would keep the total of *V* (Value) equal to *M* (Money) in the original Marxian diagnosis, or *A* plus *B* equal to Money in the Douglas formula. The government could not create more money than is represented by the difference between *V* and *M*, and this restriction would halt inflation. This proposal is called "The National Dividend," not given automatically to every citizen but proportioned to labor, production, and individual initiative in the marketplace. This solution horrifies the modern Communist for it would theoretically make the capitalistic system invulnerable to depressions and keep the economy constantly prosperous. But it also horrifies the conservative economist who insists that it would not work because public utility is solidly based on individual competitive privilege, and all money would surely lose value.

These opinions and proposals of Pound's are not exactly "primer-book" examples of radical thinking, as has been charged, whether or not they are workable or desirable. Pound cites many historical instances where governments or leaders threw money into distribution in some way or other in order to promote prosperity. Whether the Douglas proposals would work would depend on several factors. The control of inflation looks difficult; the efficiency of government bookkeeping would be suspect and the amount of it staggering; a complex and probably frightening bureaucracy would be needed to manage the system. For most liberals this prospect envisages so much loss of individual responsibility and liberty that its weaknesses would tend to wipe out the possible advantages. Better bear the ills we have than fly to others we could reasonably expect.

But the theory might work without depending on the National Dividend. Pound's main point is that the government should not borrow from banks but should create what the economy needs. He dismisses the way governments finance themselves at present as being unbelievably stupid. Specifically he points out that all governments at present spend or have spent more than they are able to collect in taxes. The national debt of the United States is more than three hundred billions of dollars and steadily going up. The debt is backed by potential collection of taxes and credit "of the whole people," of the country. Do you know where this money comes from, he asks? That is, the money the government "owes"?

We are accustomed to say—since part of it does—that it comes from individuals who have bought bonds or lent their cash to the government. They naturally expect it back, plus interest, if and when they need it. However, this source is small in comparison with the total needs of the government. Much of the borrowed money is in the form of credit advances to purchase government securities, not capital or cash, but like any loan a bank makes "out of nothing," meaning out of credit rather than capital resources. Banks hold much of the debt of the country at the present time, and it is impossible to tell whether they have any actual capital invested in the government's debt or not. Banks can and do create the money they lend the government as they create all the credit they lend over and above their actual capital. Therefore, says Douglas, as well as Pound, Jefferson, Jackson, and Lincoln, there is no real reason why the government should not do likewise and borrow from itself (through its ownership, management or control of the banking system—or by any other appropriate means). It is of interest to note that the great orthodox economist, Ricardo, can be quoted directly about this problem:

> It is evident, therefore, that if the Government itself were to be the sole issuer of paper money, instead of borrowing it of the Bank, the only difference would be with respect to the interest—the Bank would no longer receive interest, and the Government would no longer pay it; but all other classes in the community would be exactly in the same position in which they now stand.[3]

One of Pound's suggestions is that the least the government could do, accepting the status quo and not going back on what has been previously done, would be to create the money to pay the interest on the government debt, thus in America relieving the taxpayer of the ten or more billions of dollars contributed each year to the "usurers." This would be one way of getting the differential in credit and purchasing power into the market without the complexities of the Douglas bookkeeping system. If the general public did not understand it, so much the better. Their confidence in values would not be shaken.

Other ways would be to supply without borrowing from banks the money or part of the money needed for old-age pensions, social security, job insurance, or any of the other social measures administered by the modern enlightened state. Stimulus for education could be furnished in this way without new taxes. Further, the present debt could be systematically retired, a little each year, by the careful feeding of the right amount of new money into the economy, taxes could be reduced and all kinds of public works encouraged and developed without new taxes. There would be no difference, theoretically, to the country's business system except that everybody would be more prosperous and the "unbalanced budget" would be financed by debt-free money. It is mostly a matter of bookkeeping, says Pound, and the knowledge necessary to do this without creating runaway inflation could be supplied by any of a number of competent bankers now working for themselves, if they wished to turn their knowledge to their country's needs or were paid to do so.

The Social Credit advocates have included all kinds of proposals in addition to the idea of a National Dividend. There are several historical phases in the movement. About 1918 Douglas converted Orage and many of his fellow National Guildsmen to his new principles of economic reform. This is when Pound joined too. In England Orage attempted to make Social Credit the motivating force in the British Labor Party, but was defeated by the Fabians and the organizers who were mainly interested in higher wages and a greater share of the profits of production. A split developed in the Labor Party and the Social Credit men spread their proposals overseas. South Africa, Canada, New Zealand, and Australia became involved, and some small impact was made on the United States. In England the Kindred of the Kibbo Kift adopted Social Credit in 1929. This group eventually became known as the "Green Shirts," giving a fascist impression to an organization which had originally grown out of the Boy Scout movement. In 1932 Orage returned from retirement to edit a Social

Credit magazine called *The New English Weekly*. The movement lost his great abilities when he died not too long afterwards. Pound contributed regularly to *The New English Weekly* until the war loomed on the horizon.

Douglas toured Australia and New Zealand in 1933. The depression focused more and more attention on any panacea which might restore prosperity. In Western Canada Douglas was received with what looks like wild acclaim, and eventually the Social Credit Party won control of the government in the state of Alberta. In 1934 Douglas visited the United States and was a guest of honor at a dinner given by Senator Bronson Cutting in Washington. Cutting is said to have been converted to Social Credit, but his death in an airplane crash shortly thereafter removed him from the councils of the New Deal. At the end of his world tour, Douglas decided to begin serious political action and formed a Social Credit Secretariat, urging the election of representatives who would put his ideas into action in the British Parliament. The Prince of Wales, shortly to be Edward VIII, gave the impression that he favored the new movement. This fact accounts for Pound's various favorable references to Edward as king, and to his insinuations that more than marriage to a divorced woman contributed to the pressures put upon him to abdicate.[4] But the Social Credit "Party" never elected a man to Parliament, even though it centered upon the give-away psychology of the National Dividend to attract voting support. Only in Canada has there been sporadic success at the polls. Douglas was not a good practical leader and showed few signs of political intelligence in action.

The prominent Americans originally interested appear to have been Archibald MacLeish, who wrote a play called *Panic* attacking the bankers or usurers, William Carlos Williams, James Laughlin IV (his New Directions Press has consistently published Pound in America), Gorham Munson, whose *Aladdin's Lamp* is the best and most informative book on the Social Credit point of view to be published, and there were a number of others. Pound keeps referring to Senator Cutting's estimate (in a letter to Pound) of only eleven *literate* congressmen, meaning those who knew anything about economic theory or were willing to assist real reform.[5] In *The Cantos*

Pound names only Senator Bankhead and Senator Borah among these literates. Wherever the Social Credit ideas made an impact, as in the British Commonwealth, the sponsors seem to have offered only a part of the essential Douglas program, or they became mired in compromise, and never accomplished much, if anything at all. This conclusion particularly applies to Alberta in Canada where Douglas himself had a historical opportunity to lead and showed clearly that he was incapable of seizing it. It is true that the cards were stacked against him in Alberta. Unlike the United States, a provincial government in Canada cannot constitutionally issue money. Social Credit became mixed in the public mind with extreme and rabid panaceas: religious revivalism; professional rabble-rousing; populist revolution against the established community because of the depression; the share-the-wealth slogans of Huey Long; Townsendism; even the diatribes of Father Coughlin, who attacked the bankers over the radio in the thirties and finally gave the impression of fanaticism.

When the second World War came along, all nations poured money and credit into the machinery of war-making, creating economic prosperity on a grand scale away from the battlefields, setting price and wage controls, and generally putting into practice much of what the Social Credit theorists had proposed for peacetime, except that they did this in every country by deficit financing with credit borrowed mainly from the resources of privately owned banks. In the meantime Social Credit as a movement was relegated to the background. The association of Pound's broadcasts with its principles did it no good in the Free World, and it has been ignored through most of post-war arguments about economic prosperity. It still exists in Canada and parts of the British Commonwealth, waiting around the corner in case another depression arrives. In the United States Presidents Kennedy and Johnson have apparently been influenced by what might be called Social Credit policies, but there has been no mention of the original movement, nor has there been an attempt to use any debt-free money.

A separate proposal for economic freedom has been stated by Silvio Gesell, the German iconoclast who made a fortune in South America, returned to Europe with his money and revolutionary ideas, wrote some books, and almost got the chance to try out his ideas in the hectic days following the end of the first World War. He was offered the post of Minister of Finance in the Bavarian government, a Socialist ministry which was almost immediately subverted by the Communists. After the reds were violently expelled, Gesell was arrested as a collaborator and had to stand trial for treason. Pound eventually felt some special sympathy for Gesell's predicament. The man of new money ideas defended himself in a speech that became famous, and even his enemies deduced that he was a genuine idealist. Anyway he was acquitted. He had accepted the post of minister because he wanted to try out his theories, not only of scrip money but also of land reform. In the latter respect he is a spiritual ally of Henry George and the old Single Tax Party.

Gesell's ideas are supposed to have worked later at isolated places called Wörgl and Schwanenkirchen in Central Europe. The experiments were stopped and abolished when they were discovered by the governments involved. Meanwhile Gesell heckled the German administrations which were in power after the days of the Versailles Treaty. Hitler ignored him, but he continued to write and gain followers around the world. He died in 1930, arguing to the last that "the right of the whole collective proceeds of labor implies the abolition of all *unearned* income, i.e., interest and rent."[6] He thought the capitalistic system would work nicely at all times and in all conditions if money and land were removed from the domain of special privilege and the opportunities for Usury. Note that Pound had no particular interest in Gesell's land reform theories.

In order to keep money moving Gesell evolved the idea of putting a tax on paper notes themselves. Metal coins practically disappear in this system. If you have a dollar bill you must on a set date—say the first of each month—attach a stamp to it to keep it up to its face value. Otherwise it loses value. Gesell suggested a penny or two-penny stamp, some of his followers up to five or ten cents. The idea makes it impossible to hoard paper money, since if you keep it long enough in your safety deposit box or your pockets, it will lose all value as money. So you spend it, if possible, before the date you have to put a stamp on it. The state issues the stamps, collects money for them, and eventually replaces used-up money by new notes. The secondary advantage of this system is that the stamps serve as a substitute for a sales tax, a very profitable source of income for the government itself. A sales tax operates when money is spent, but under the Gesell system somebody eventually pays the government for the money in use. The National Treasury collects in either case. Gesell assumed that this system would make so much money that it would supersede all other taxes. The business community would quit dealing in the manipulation of the value of money and would as rapidly as possible turn the money into something useful or productive in order to survive and profit. Production and distribution, along with state treasuries which would always be full, must naturally follow this system, he argued. There would be less need for financing a debt, and Usury would be immeasurably hampered—Usury again being defined as making a profit from money itself, not the uses to which money should be put.

Gesell's theories appealed to Pound because they seemed to him to furnish an alternate way of getting money away from the stranglehold of the banking community, besides reducing taxes for the general population. The Social Credit enthusiasts do not generally agree. They argue that this system would not do anything to put the extra money into circulation which they think is needed to keep $V{=}M$, or A plus $B{=}$Price. Mere motion of money, or so goes the argument, will not supply the gap between cost and selling price. Once in awhile a critic will ask how people will be stopped from doing all their business by checking accounts, or will these be taxed too? But stamp-scrip is only one of Pound's ideas, and it is treated by him as a kind of exciting experiment which ought to improve things if it worked—as he believed it would. Certainly he thought of it in the context of depression days, something to get money moving again.

Gesell's stamp money is anathema to all those who worship a Gold Standard for money, in whatever form the concept of the Gold Standard is supposed to operate. Nor would it be very easy to manage in international trade.

"No longer necessary," taxes are no longer necessary
in the old way if it (money) be based on work done
inside a system and measured and gauged to human
requirements
inside the nation or system
and cancelled in proportion
to what is used and worn out
à la Wörgl. (78/59-60)

Pound's reform ideograms thus run the gamut of old and new approaches to the problems of creating prosperity for the whole society.

"You damn sadist," said mr cummings
"You try to make people think." (89/63)

Sober examination of the Pound remedies may persuade the critic to put him in the company of the idealists rather than among the realists. Perhaps we can also put him in the company of Plato, whose Republic has possible flaws and has never exactly worked in real political circumstances. Sir Thomas More retains respect from a world which has never understood nor instituted his Utopia. Dean Swift castigated civilization and suggested that a race of horses could manage things better, an extreme position which does not invalidate many of his criticisms of the inequities and evils existing in our society.

Many people feel that Sir Thomas More was executed for an issue which in later years puts men of good will on his side. Religion, abstract philosophy, artistic detachment from a world which provides no lasting satisfaction for the idealist—these are qualities which can be praised if they do not actually touch us except in the realm of the spirit where their results can be ignored. Pound decided to abandon his own country for a kind of never-never land he thought he had found in Italy. This action is different from dying for your soul's survival, but it has points of contact. Practically speaking, Pound was wrong; but there is an argument for admiration in noting that he has not recanted nor whimpered.

But the lot of 'em, Yeats, Possum and Wyndham
had no ground beneath 'em.

Orage had. (98/37)

The comparison with *The Republic* and *The Utopia* is valid. Pound's reasoning is basically socialistic, even though it is not the kind of Socialism which creeps into Communism. We have to examine it carefully in order to find benefits separated in the average American mind from the extremes of the welfare state, *1984*, or the place where the government does everything for you and you eventually end in the camp of the slave state, minus individualism, freedom, and self-respect. But it is important to remember that Pound's main point has been to argue for the *perfect* capitalistic state. The government should control its economic system so that business will work better and we will end with more freedom after all. The stoppage of excesses, stock exchange variations, lack of sufficient capital to get into production, underpaid labor—all these evils would theoretically vanish under the vision of his reform ideals. Full employment and fair rewards follow, and freedom is supposed to come with a greater degree of economic satisfaction. The proper supply of credit would subsidize, not constrict industry and private incentive. The only class which would lose would be the very wealthy class which gets its money by taking our share, or so he says. The profit on invented money should be the possession of the whole society rather than just the usurers. Government control of banking prerogatives must supply debt-free cash and relieve the excess taxes which hamper us all. The difference, however large or small it may be, between cost and selling price must be made up by some supply of extra money put into the economy. This may be done by the Douglas devices, the increased speed of money under Gesell's stamp-scrip method, or merely by financing old-age pensions, social security, national hospitalization, job insurance, education, even relief if necessary, all through the credit of the nation as a whole, not by taxes or borrowing from the bankers. If the economy is run well enough, one may look forward to the day when there might be enough of a surplus to declare a dividend for every citizen. The government has the power and must exercise the right to keep prices steady so that an inflation spiral does not ruin any part of its advances in general prosperity. Controls do not ruin anyone's prosperity if proper wages and profits are guaranteed.

It would be convenient to say that Pound's concept of an ideal state is the great vision of *The Cantos*. Still, whatever our feelings about the workability or practicality of his proposals, other factors complicate our examination of his ideals. He associated something admirable with Mussolini, even with Hitler; he seems to have excluded Jews from participating in the pleasures of Utopia. His distortions undermine his vision as if the ideal were fleeing before him. His curious exaggeration of economic forces in all history makes him find a banker behind every evil face in the record. Despite the fact that an economist like Keynes also argued for government stimulus to the economy in time of need, Pound rejects Keynes because Keynes rejected debt-free financing of the government's needs. The similarities of the New Deal to some of the aims he proposes do not stop his scorn for the New Deal and distrust of Roosevelt's leadership. Because Woodrow Wilson was held responsible for the odious (in Pound's eyes) Federal Reserve Act and the Versailles Treaty, both giving bankers more control of the economy, he dismisses the rest of Wilson's record and his liberal intentions. The very mixed accomplishment of Mussolini he sees only through the rose-tinted glasses of the measures Mussolini adopted for economic reform.

The picture of a *flawed* idealist may be the answer. Pound's fugitive vision of paradise led him along a number of strange pathways. Perhaps he could have applied to himself the description he calls up in the *Pisan Cantos:* "ye spotted lambe/that is both blacke and white" (84/115). Or perhaps we can say, as he did: "Here error is all in the not done,/all in the diffidence that faltered" (81/100).

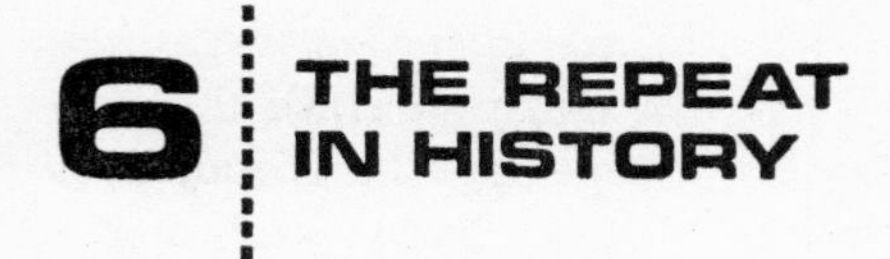

6 THE REPEAT IN HISTORY

"Can we take this into court?
"Will any jury convict on this evidence? (46/27)

and that Vandenberg has read Stalin, or Stalin, John Adams
is, at the mildest, unproven. (84/118)

After a long look at theory, at diagnoses and proposals for reform, it is appropriate to go back and see how well Pound stated his position in the epic itself. His most vivid Cantos are devoted to his conclusions, since he selects his data and occasionally lumps it into oversimplified formulae. But his judgments are exciting, unconventional, and often stimulating in their nonconformity. Chosen ideograms reflect national progress or decline, flickering back and forth to display comparative similarities. It is this intricate sampling and comparison which contributes to the bewildering effect of many Cantos on the reader who may not immediately guess what is being compared. One often needs to absorb the kind of detail likely to be known only to the meticulous scholar in order to see Pound's point. The experience is occasionally akin to attempting to understand something like five hundred pages of Toynbee in a dozen cryptic excerpts with all the explanations and connections omitted.

It is apparent that whatever exact long-range purpose was in the poet's mind when he began *The Cantos,* his directions changed through the years. The personal experiences which give depth to the Pisan section could hardly have been foreseen in any original prospectus, and it is fair to suggest that the full idea of the economic theme with all its references to the "repeat in history" materials did not strike him till well after the close of the first World War. The perceptive reader can find the growth of the economic theme in the first thirty Cantos (as we have seen) but the full statement was organized at the beginning of Canto 31. All the Cantos since then develop or intensify—with a very few exceptions—the propositions first stated in the fourth decad. It is true that he adds a new theme, the references to "Light," derived partially from his study of Scotus Erigena. Nor should we forget that he is still one with Odysseus and that he travels symbolically in Dante's afterworld.

The economic theme may now be stated formally:

1. The health, happiness, and prosperity of any nation or culture depend primarily upon the economic forces which control its production and distribution.

2. Good government encourages, arranges, or controls production and distribution so that the whole society has an opportunity to prosper.

3. The forces of special privilege or financial aristocracy must not be permitted to profit by manipulation of values or the means of production, particularly the money used by the nation. Alternate expansion or contraction of the currency eventually causes the decline of any nation.

4. The specific privilege of creating and controlling credit must be taken from banks of discount or usurers, the men who lend money not on capital or cash but from the presence of credit dependent upon deposits and book figures. The power of creating money "out of nothing" is the privilege of the government representing the whole of society. Abuse of the power of creating money contributes more than any other force to the decline of the nation.

5. Good governments make sure that the total money in circulation approximates the prices justly charged for necessary goods and services, this money being supplemented by national credit, not borrowed from private sources, if it is insufficient in amount to ensure distribution and prosperity.

6. The adoption of the Douglas Social Credit "dividend," the use of the Gesell stamp-scrip money, *or any other appropriate method of supplementing needed cash should be investigated and tried.*

7. History shows that the forces of special privilege are in vital conflict with the rest of society through the centuries. *Usury* is a convenient term for the practices of special privilege. *Usury* inevitably produces depressions, the general decay of vitality in a nation, and conflicts between nations which end in wars and the destruction of the best life for all the people.

8. Ignorance of the nature of money is the world's greatest sin, and the leaders who fight against Usury and special privilege are to be honored in the past and supported in the present. It is particularly important in the study of history to seek out and identify the usurious class—Jews have been notorious as belonging to it—and to establish a political economy in which the usurious aristocracy does not control society.

9. Political heroes in history can be identified because they have tried to lead their nations to prosperity and fair dealing. Confucius and his followers in China, the Medici and Malatesta in Italy, Pietro Leopoldo and Ferdinando in Tuscany, Jefferson, John Adams, Jackson, Van Buren, and Lincoln in America, Mussolini in modern Italy, all have tried to control the forces of special privilege. Civilization rose with these leaders; it falls when they fall.

As these judgments propelled themselves into Pound's mind, he began to visualize their application to the plan of *The Cantos*. The purpose of studying history was for him an attempt to profit by the experience of the past. The greatest influence on what he eventually chose to write was the thesis expounded by Brooks Adams in *The Law of Civilization and Decay*. Adams had used the perspective of a scientific interest in money to examine culture from the days of Rome down to 1896 when he first published his studies. He had concluded that Gibbon and other historians were inexact in their reasons for the rise and fall of cultures. The Roman Empire did not decay because it lost its moral fiber, but because its supply of money was gradually contracted and deflated through a number of centuries. This process was initiated by a commercial "special privilege" class whose financial practices vitiated the health and strength of the nation as a whole. A few wealthy men got most of the money and kept it out of circulation except on terms which gradually added to their possessions. Later

Constantinople had much the same experience, and when its currency became insufficient, gold coins were debased. But the usurers had too much of whatever coin there was, and so the center of civilization passed to the Northern Italian cities, Venice, Florence, and Genoa becoming the strongholds out of which the Renaissance flowered. Adams' case is dependent upon the evidence he cites to show that the same thing happened in each culture studied. Modern banking originated in the Italian cities, speeding up the process of rise and fall. France and Holland took over, and eventually it was England's turn.

> The important dates are 1694, when the Bank of England was incorporated and began to issue paper money, thus relieving the strain on the English currency; the Battle of Plassey in 1757, when Clive unlocked for England the immense hoarded moneys of India; the Battle of Waterloo in 1815, which crushed opposition to the banking interests in Europe; the passage of the Bank Charter Act in 1844, which fortified the English bankers in the commanding position in their national economy—which they have held from then to now.[1]

It is important to remember that Pound published his fourth decad of Cantos (31-41) in 1933. His interpretation of history is conditioned by what was happening to the modern world in the days immediately following the onset of the greatest modern economic depression. It was clear that the world had fallen on evil times. Surely there was good evidence that western civilization had declined. Probably Brooks Adams' theory of history applied to the present as well as the past. Possum Eliot's gloomy picture of a Waste Land had come true with a vengeance.

Pound's interpretation of American history was intended to supplement and develop the data which Brooks Adams had cited to explain what had happened to Europe's economy through the centuries. The thesis that Europe was going downhill was obvious; England, too. But there had been a great American surge in the days following the American Revolution and all through the nineteenth century. Pound dedicated his first attention to the story of what happened to American promises. We rose with Jefferson and the early leaders; we fought our way through the same hindrances suffered by other cultures up till the time of Lincoln and the Civil War. Then we came upon evil days, for the forces of special privilege began to win. After Lincoln the exploiters and bankers took over the economic development of the country. (No wonder someone assassinated Lincoln, says Pound, darkly.)[2] The Morgans and Harrimans, the Goulds and Vanderbilts and Rockefellers made great fortunes. The people fought ineffectually against the moneymen, never really possessing enough knowledge or power to protect themselves. Our leadership tailed off into mediocrity and frustration. Bryan was a pale follower in the tradition of Jefferson and Jackson. Wilson knuckled under to privilege, and what ideals he had crumbled before the political necessities of the Versailles Treaty. The nit-wit and the fat-face followed, if one uses Pound's insulting terms.[3] Roosevelt was on the horizon, but in 1933 all Pound had was the evidence of campaign oratory where Roosevelt promised to balance the budget and be frugal. Roosevelt certainly came from the class of special privilege and Pound thought could be counted on to share its attitudes and principles.[4]

Pound went on the compare the American story with what had happened in Europe. In the twentieth century the Communists took over Russia, the first great promise of a new day showing no signs of the paradise expected under Stalin. France and Spain were decaying rapidly. Germany was trying to get out from under the staggering economic retribution exacted by the Allies after 1918. Hindenburg represented stupidity and tradition. There was the potential rise of Hitler, with his original promises of economic and social reform in National Socialist principles, all of which were emphasized in the early days of the Nazis and displayed in approximately half of *Mein Kampf*. Pound's reactions to Hitler were all antagonistic at this time.[5]

Best promise of all—there was Benito Mussolini, with a new program and a new vision. Economic reform was working in Italy if nowhere else. Even the conservative capitalists were pleased with Mussolini, or so it seemed. The American ambassador, Richard Washburn Child, arranged to get Mussolini's *Autobiography* translated (with his own laudatory introduction) so that Americans could be informed and instructed. Eventually John Gunther, in the first of his "Inside" books, judged that Mussolini was the best of the dictators, a leader far superior to any of the English or French politicians, and by comparison with Stalin and Hitler a leader of some stature.[6] If the decay and decline of the modern world could be stopped or changed, surely the chance lay with someone like Mussolini, or so it seemed to Pound at this time.

Our judgment of the validity of this historical analysis is conditioned by what has happened *since* 1933. Whether we agree or not, most of us can understand how Pound came to his point of view if he is represented as interpreting conditions limited to that date. Certain truths, perhaps best described as partial truths, can be discerned. But other questions immediately arise. Did Mussolini fulfill his promise? Did Roosevelt stay with the privileged class he supposedly represented? Pound committed himself in 1933 and does not seem to have changed his conclusions materially thereafter.

All the historians who play the "repeat in history" game have a tendency toward interpreting everything according to their pet theories, usually bearing their own scholarly labels. Pound's label is extreme and has all the weaknesses of any interpretation which tries to explain absolutely everything in terms of a single thesis. His picture of American history deals in important truth, and our judgment of this truth depends upon how much weight we can give to what he selects without examining what he may have left out. Few of us like to accept the conclusion that everything is bad because some things are. When Pound says that America was "sold to the Rothschilds in 1863," we know we are in the presence of an opinion so extreme that we have to fight to keep from dismissing the rest of his analysis. The bright student said, "Maybe the Rothschilds just bought a little piece of America."

The easiest conclusion is that the Pound case is challenging because certain parts of his analysis must be true. A Spengler or a Toynbee may be partially right, partially wrong. Their reconstruction of the forces of history can be extraordinarily illuminating. The fact is, as Pound contends, that educated people have been too little accustomed to examine the movements which really explain history, particularly if they are economic movements. Consider how little we know of the basic opinions of Jefferson and John Adams about special privilege. Pound remarks, quite nostalgically, in Canto 84:

> and Mr Beard in his admirable condensation
> (Mr Chas. Beard) has given one line to the currency
> at about page 426 "The Republic"
> We will be about as popular as Mr John Adams
> and less widely perused . . . . (84/116)

This reference indicates the difficulty with Pound's hyperbolic expression. The great American historian Charles Beard is famous for his analysis of American history in terms of economic influences, and one would guess that Pound might refer to him often for assistance in his own evaluation. But Beard believes the currency issue to be one of many which caused the American Revolution, although he does mention it in more than one line. For example he quotes Franklin about the prohibition of paper money issues in the colonies: " 'On the slight complaint of a few Virginia merchants,' he lamented, 'nine colonies had been restrained from making paper money, become absolutely necessary to their internal commerce, from the constant remittance of their gold and silver to Britain.' "[7] Again Beard says: "Colonial populism was struck down in vetoes, warnings, and finally parliamentary action against paper money."[8] This action was made binding by Parliament upon the legislatures of all the colonies. Beard mentions many times the growth of depression because taxes and commercial pressures withdrew coin to the mother country, leaving too little in circulation in America, with the additional prohibition against the colonies' right to issue currency of their own.[9]

Pound's notion of the importance of these facts may exaggerate them, but he has not invented them. In the fourth decad of Cantos he begins the presentation of his case, the case for the American dream which was born, grew up, and—says Pound—has been defeated in our time. The fact that he is hoping the dream will not be lost forever remains as a primary purpose for writing *The Cantos.*

The revelation of the American heritage begins properly with concentration on Thomas Jefferson. Pound's various ideograms are intended to show an ideal leader, a man of tremendous capacity in knowledge of society, law, politics, business, economy, art, architecture, music, education, and philosophy. Fortune or destiny gave us Jefferson and John Adams both at the beginning of our national existence, and these leaders held that it was the privilege of the new government to aid, encourage, and direct the economic and social opportunity of all the people without reference to race, class, or creed. Jefferson and Adams differed, as we all know, about how much government direction might be needed, Jefferson believing optimistically that information and education would automatically aid the advance of the good life so that the government could gradually retire from interference with the economy. Pound's view is that under the brilliant leadership of a man like Jefferson the forces of historical decay were halted; a new world unlike Europe was born; a real civilization based on economic justice began to flourish. This was the great American opportunity.

The ideograms and examples selected to illustrate judgment of Jefferson (Cantos 31 and 32) show him interested in everything constructive; he encouraged the development of canals to stimulate trade; he was opposed to slavery. Pound assumes that we all know Jefferson's main record of accomplishments. What he does is select and comment on the record, emphasizing its importance. In later Cantos he adds extra ideograms which help fill in or remind us of some additional part of the Jefferson portrait. In Canto 65 Adams refers to the writing of the Decalaration of Independence:

> Cut about 1/4th and some of the best of it
> I have often wondered that J's first draft has not been
> published
> suppose the reason is the vehement philippic against
> negro slavery . . . . (65/113)

When Jefferson was in France he was impressed, even disgusted, with the inefficient management of the economy, the waste, the high cost of collecting taxes, the graft of special privilege and the stupidity of the monarchy. No wonder

France was on the eve of revolution (in cipher XTZBK49HT). He does not seem to have studied or understood the workings of the discount banking system at the beginning (Adams later found out at first hand when he arranged loans for the infant republic), but Jefferson observed with alarm the eventual adoption of the British system in the United States when Hamilton established the First National Bank. According to Pound this was what really set Jefferson off on forming a political "party" which opposed the Federalists, the group he felt to be dominated by wealth and special privilege. His opinions about the financing of our debt by the Bank are clear and positive:

> "But observe that the public were at the same time paying
> on it an interest of exactly the same amount [as they were
> paying on the principal]
> (four million dollars). Where then is the gain to either
> party which makes it a public blessing?"
> to Mr. Eppes, 1813 . . . (31/5)

Thus at the very beginning of the establishment of the new and better kind of government—one where liberty and justice for all were possible—the same cancer of unfair privilege began to endanger the health of the nation. The National Bank mortgaged public taxes for private gain, said Jefferson. Note that there is no question here but that everybody is devoted to private initiative; financing national needs to insure private profit on the credit of the whole nation is presented as something quite different, since productive management and labor are both losers. This was the disease which was undermining foreign political economy, the disease we should have known enough to avoid. Jefferson, Adams, Jackson, Van Buren, Lincoln (also Gallatin, Randolph of Roanoke, Benton—Pound will find many more)—all were opposed to a money system based on the private creation of national credit for the guaranteed profit of a privileged group.

In Canto 32 Pound manages to compare the ideal Jefferson with the reigning monarchs of Europe, Louis XVI, the King of Spain, the King of Naples, the King of Sardinia, the Portuguese Queen à Braganza, Frederic of Prussia's successor, Gustavus and Joseph of Austria, the mad George III—all are called fools or idiots. What kind of leadership could possibly be developed from such direction?

> a guisa de leon
> The cannibals of Europe are eating one another again
> quando si posa. (32/9)

Cantos 31 and 32 accordingly set the stage for Pound's analysis of all American history, the supreme and heroic Jefferson, the remarkable chance for a new country to start afresh free from the decline and decay of European models, the forces of Usury still being active, but nevertheless vulnerable to the ideals of the new democracy.

Canto 33 spreads its scope to John Adams, then takes a rapid look at the conflict between democracy and privilege down through the 150 years which followed the Revolution. The despotism Adams feared was rule by aristocracy which would seize power supposedly vested in the elective democratic process:

> . . . absolute power . . . unlimited sovereignty,
> is the same in a majority of a popular assembly,
> an aristocratical council, an oligarchical junto,
> and a single emperor, equally arbitrary, bloody,
> and in every respect diabolical. (33/10)

Here also are cross references to Napoleon which foreshadow Pound's later contention that the French emperor had some of the fine qualities of the American revolutionary leaders. But the French Revolution went astray, and after Waterloo the great bankers and industrialists were right back where they had been before it all started, even farther. The nineteenth century saw the excesses of industrial expansion growing so that the working classes fought to survive while the special privilege group made great fortunes. Pound's ideograms show Marx, sweatshops, inhuman working conditions, the vicious spread of child labor, all the evils which caused class conflict and the mortal struggles between capital and labor. What Pound considers unnoticed is that the banks, or the banks in alliance with industrial barons, continued to make the most money:

Bills discounted at exhorbitant rates, four times or three times
those offered by the Midland . . . .
150 millions
yearly, merely in usurious discounts . . . . (33/13-14)

The theme is now ready for further documentation. It is the historic battle between the people and the forces of Usury; Pound's position is that America was unfortunate in not being able to develop its resources in harmony with the opinions of Jefferson and Adams. Their words and councils have come to be ignored, although their reputations are revered and their names lauded. Note that Pound almost completely dismisses George Washington and refers slightingly to Benjamin Franklin.

The Adams family persisted in influence throughout the nineteenth century (John—John Quincy—Charles Francis—Henry and Brooks). Canto 34 is focused on John Quincy, another wise man who saw most political issues with his father's vision. But he had little success in persuading the country or the Congress to his views. His party was eventually led by Clay (whose ethics are described by Pound as "undigested"), by Calhoun ("half-educated"), and by the silver-tongued Webster (the paid representative of the moneyed interests). When the conflict about the Second National Bank developed, John Quincy showed a curious reaction to it. His political opponents were Jackson and Van Buren, but he could hardly stand against them on this issue.

I called upon Nicholas Biddle . . . and recd. two dividends
of my bank stock . . . . . as I might be called to take part in
public measures . . . . . I wished to divest myself
of all personal interest . . . . Nov. 9, '31. (34/19)

He does not indicate that he sold his stock, and Pound does not develop the point that he did not rise to his father's stature.

Canto 35 is concerned with Middle Europe, a comparison intended to develop Pound's thesis that special privilege was making a general mess of Europe. The kings and prime ministers apparently were allied with predatory aristocracy, or a part of it. The Austrian emperor, Franz Giuseppe (Josef), comes in for particular contempt ("in fact with the most patient research nothing good is recorded"), and at this point

Pound begins to blame the Jews for part of Europe's troubles. The Rothschilds gradually became his main targets—the family which established its branches in five major countries and played all the credit–stock-market–international-exchange rackets possible. Pound refers to the "intramural" warmth of Hebrew affections, an oblique reference to the Rothschild custom of marrying among themselves, cousins, or even uncles and nieces often being involved in their marital alliances.

Pound inserts, as a kind of counter-theme, examples of the rare moments when some variety of government direction interfered with the domination of special privilege. He looks in all directions. In Mantua there was established (centuries ago) a *fontego,* a kind of federal cooperative "bank" where money was loaned on cloth being prepared for sale, and where the selling price was equal to the wholesale price plus the tax needed to supply the return of the borrowed principal and interest. This practice encouraged production and distribution without recourse to private banks or usurious interest; it also put people to work for a living wage when private industry was unable to do so.

Before continuing his economic theme Pound now takes time out to go back to his contrasting literary materials. Canto 36 presents his great translation of Cavalcanti's "Donna mi priegha." The beautiful things which endure come not out of Usury. Pound mentions here, almost casually, the paradisaical concept of "Thrones," a condition which might be called a state of mind rather than of society, where authority comes from "right reason," and beauty lives on in spite of the forces gathered to destroy what never really decays.

Canto 37 concentrates on the high spot in the American struggle between privilege and the people. This is the era when special privilege, the Second National Bank, lost, when Andrew Jackson defeated Biddle. The Bank had been established in 1816 with a twenty-year charter, and Jackson felt that the country was able to pay off its "debt" and finance itself. Pound takes his illustrations and comments from Martin Van Buren's *Autobiography,* all of them vivid and challenging. Most of his contentions are assisted by reference to any standard historical account, perhaps Schlesinger's *Age of Jackson,* since Biddle descended to all the devices of manufacturing pressure on elected officials, lobbying, the buying of whatever Congressmen were vulnerable, and most of all the flooding of the country with easy credit which would have to be contracted if Congress did not vote renewal of the Bank's charter. Pound could have found no better example of the misuse of the nation's credit for private advantage and the artificial creation of depression by the hosts of Usury:

> "and men of wealth decrying government credit."
> ". . . in order to feed on the spoils." (37/31)

In the midst of many pregnant examples Pound manages to suggest some of the best evidence. This Canto is effective because the counterpoint reinforces Pound's indignation. In fact it is the best of the decad up to this point:

> "employing means at the bank's disposal
> in deranging the country's credits, obtaining by panic
> control over the public mind" said Van Buren
> "from the real committee of Bank's directors
> the government's directors have been excluded.
> Bank president controlling government funds
> to the betrayal of the nation . . . .
> government funds obstructing the government . . . . (37/34)

Because Pound is quoting Van Buren, the result is to place him in a more prominent position than Andrew Jackson, who vetoed the recharter bill, made his idealistic stand, never wavered, and deserves major credit for the victory. Yet Van Buren's part has not always been recognized, and he too refused to compromise. This quality is almost unexpected, since Van Buren's earlier record had not given any indication that he would take a stand on principle and hold fast. Somehow or other his *Autobiography* never came to public attention nor was it published at all until 1918. Pound ends this Canto by hailing him as the "liberator of the treasury." Apparently this accolade is given because Van Buren sponsored the bill to establish the Independent National Treasury.

Canto 37 is followed by the highly concentrated ideogrammic set piece of Canto 38 (it has been discussed in Chapter Two). The perverters of money are here represented on the international scale, forming cartels of all varieties, particularly in the field of war materials and munitions. Pound continues to hammer at the theme which asserts that usurious interests are likely in time of crisis to be loyal to themselves rather than to their country, even if as businessmen they pose as patriotic. Zaharoff, the international munitions king, is the perfect example of this type of villainy. There was also Schneider of Creusot in France, and Pound gets closer to the Rothschilds, whose activities were most successful when they played the economy of one country against another, without being loyal to anybody but themselves.

In contrast Pound inserts the example of Mussolini in modern Italy, and for the first time suggests the diagnosis of Major Douglas as a key to a new way of managing the economy to the advantage of the people as a whole. Here he begins to urge the adoption of any reasonable method which would reform the world's economy and produce prosperity. What Mussolini was doing in Italy represented a break with the usurious past, perhaps a new opportunity for a fresh start comparable to the chance Jefferson and Adams had in the United States. Pound implemented this contention in his prose *Jefferson and/or Mussolini.* Most Americans have had great difficulty in observing any close resemblance in the characters, capacities, or behavior of the two men, but it is possible to understand Pound's idea that Mussolini was attempting something new in government control, supervision, and encouragement of the economy of his country. By 1933 Mussolini's case was also at its most favorable moment for praise.

After the two striking Cantos, 37 and 38, Pound inserts thematic variation again, going back to the *Odyssey* and resolutely praising the men who had the courage to "go to hell in a boat," who loved largely, who gave everything for the sake of adventure, whose ideals were so supreme that they were willing to dare death for a cause, the ones who "have eaten the flame." Such excerpts are also evidence for Pound's getting into the psychological frame of mind where he too will dare everything for a cause.

Canto 40 returns to the theme of the great American opportunity. After Jackson and Van Buren came the Civil War. Lincoln talked Secretary Chase into attempting to finance the

North's part of the war by issuing government debt-free money: the so-called "greenbacks." There was no theoretical reason why this money should not have been as good as any other paper money, if the government guaranteed it. Lincoln said: "Issue treasury notes bearing no interest, printed on the best banking paper. Issue enough to pay off the army expenses, and declare it legal tender. Chase thought it a hazardous thing, but we finally accomplished it, and gave the people of this Republic the greatest blessing they ever had—their own paper to pay off their own debts."[10]

The exact facts about the greenbacks are still interpreted differently by authorities. The original bill made them full legal tender for *all* debts. But somebody—surely the banking interests, says Pound—got a "trick" exemption amendment which made a small exception. The greenbacks were made legally good for everything *except* duties on imports and interest on the public debt, payments which had to be made in gold. The banks had the gold and refused to give full value to the greenbacks which were offered in exchange for these two payments. General inflation occurred anyway, as it usually does in wartime, so that it was easy to charge all inflation to the presence of the greenbacks. Pound continues to belabor this episode, blaming a major part of what happened on the American representatives of the Rothschild banking cartel. So he says that from this time on the banking interests flourished more and more, eventually having a strangle hold on the economy of the country—at least by 1913.

Somewhat as Archibald MacLeish did in *Frescoes for Mr. Rockfefeller's City* (the pictures of predatory American capitalists hide the document which was originally on the wall behind: the records of the Lewis and Clark expedition reporting the glorious potentialities of the vast American frontier), Pound cites the odious exploits (in his eyes) of Morgan from the Civil War down to the Pujo investigation, a record which he submits as showing the insidious growth of Usury at the expense of the people, the use of banks for the manipulation of the supply of gold, the playing with stock exchange values, the devices of selling short, discounting stocks, the accumulation of corners in valuable goods, the dumping of vast sums into the credit pools of the nation and the alternate withdrawal of the same credit for the advantage of the few in foreclosures—all the economic manipulation possible he sets in contrast to the historical account of a great explorer, Hanno of Carthage, a hero who discovered new and "pure" worlds. Civilization which begins in a fresh setting has a special chance for perfection, and it always shows itself clean beside what usually happens later. MacLeish's choice of example, the Lewis-Clark expedition, appears more familiar to the American reader, but the contrast has a genuine ring. It is as if Pound says, "Look what America has done with her opportunities!" Other American poets besides Pound and MacLeish have emphasized "American promises." The tradition after Whitman extends to Stephen Vincent Benét with his *Burning City* poems, and there is Carl Sandburg who supplemented his celebration of the people with his prose *Remembrance Rock,* a clarion call to continue fighting for the American dream.

Canto 41 sums up the repeat in history theme, concentrating on the view Pound has been suggesting in the ten previous Cantos. He restates his picture of the American opportunity, the chances for a new social and economic structure under Jefferson, the battle between special privilege and the people joined, the forces of economic justice still keeping the upper hand until the Civil War, then America finding herself more and more at the mercy of predatory men. Europe too had vitiated its chances, settling into the slough of economic despond. And yet the possibility of paradise persists. Government control and encouragement of money, credit, and distribution are still possible. The positive forces are all in the tradition of Jefferson's opinions: "Independent use of our money . . . toward holding our bank./Mr Jefferson to Colonel Monroe" (41/56).

Pound now suggests that the forces for good in our time are best represented by leaders like Mussolini and economic revolutionaries like Major Douglas and Gesell. He sees no hope for England with her conservative prime ministers or with Winston Churchill, a man allied to the financiers and a friend of the Rothschilds. Nor is there a chance for Germany with a Hindenburg, a man also incapable of understanding the music of Mozart (for Pound such aesthetic idiocy exposes the entire lack of capacity in Hindenburg). Hitler is still around the corner at this point in Pound's thinking, and Roosevelt is not yet in focus. But Mussolini drained the marshes—public works for public benefit—and best of all, says Pound, he began effectively to control the bankers. In fact Pound represents him as reinstating the ideals shown when the cooperative bank was established in Siena in the seventeenth century, the bank whose purposes and profits go to the benefit of the community as a whole.

His argument is thus that what America had promised with Jefferson and Adams might in the twentieth century be realized in Italy under Mussolini. As a sign of this accomplishment, the new theories of Social Credit or even the stamp money used at Wörgl might be given a fair trial. Generally speaking the forces of special privilege are all-powerful elsewhere, and (in 1933) they controlled the economy of the United States. Pound uses as climax his citation of the evidence concerning the international munitions-makers in the first World War:

> 120 million german fuses used by the allies to kill Germans
> British gunsights from Jena
> Schneider Creusot armed Turkey
> Copper from England thru Sweden . . . Mr Hatfield
> Patented his new shell in eight countries. (41/56)

The fourth decad therefore states Pound's belief that country after country illustrates the basic conflict between privilege and the *people,* between Usury and the Good Society. Furthermore the moneymakers are not tied to the success of any particular country, just so they profit from the war. The plan of the next three sections of *The Cantos* builds on the foundation he has been setting. He does not share Spengler's thesis of steady rise and predictable fall of specific cultures. All nations show fluctuations, and it is Pound's belief that any culture would rise and flower rapidly if its economic prosperity were arranged, no matter how much it had previously gone down. America could return to the standards of the American dream if she wished, or if a new Jefferson or Adams appeared.

Accordingly in the fifth decad (42-51) he adds new data, builds on his previous ideograms and motifs, implements his general thesis of rise and fall dependent upon whether Usury or the People win their constant battles with each other. It is in this section that Pound reaches his greatest heights in presenting his economic contentions.

He begins Canto 42 with an attack on Lord Palmerston, the English Prime Minister who "sold out" to the English National Bank. Then he spends the rest of the Canto on a detailed description of the workings of the Siena cooperative bank, an example which was not generally imitated in Italian history. Pietro Leopoldo (Leopold II, 1747-1792) was Grand Duke of Tuscany till 1790 and Holy Roman Emperor for the last two years of his life; Ferdinand III (1769-1824) was Grand Duke of Tuscany after Leopold and eventually Archduke of Austria during the last ten years of his life. Canto 44 celebrates these two Italian princes. Both of them had ideals and principles which Pound compares to those of Jefferson and Adams. They were eventually defeated by the forces of special privilege. Nor did their countries offer them the same tremendous opportunity for reform which came to the new American republic. They could not start completely afresh.

Canto 45 is the great mock-ode to Usury, invoking the grand manner that borrows from the rhetoric of the King James version of the Old Testament prophets. Canto 46 presents the Douglas National Dividend:

> An' the fuzzy bloke sez (legs no pants wd. fit) 'IF
> that is so, any government worth a damn can
> pay dividends?'
> The major chewed it a bit and sez: 'Y—es, eh . . .
> You mean instead of collectin' taxes?'
> 'Instead of collecting taxes.' (46/25)

Pound also suggests that an important cause of the American Civil War may not have been the slavery issue, but the general discontent caused by the debts of the South to New York banks, "two hundred million." He also for the first time mentions Paterson, the original founder of the Bank of England, and the man who provided Pound with such a helpful slogan:

Hath benefit of interest on all
the moneys which it, the bank, created out of nothing. (46/27)

Linked to Paterson is a Rothschild ("Hell knows which Rothschild") who pointed out that the general public does not understand how banks make money against the public interest. This Canto, in fact, is Pound's clearest statement of his opinions about American history. He says that the money men stopped the colonies from creating and lending their own money. Continental bonds were made good by the establishment of Hamilton's National Bank, thus transferring the money of the people to the credit and profit of the few. Jackson and Van Buren fought against this class privilege and met its challenge in their time. The Civil War climaxed an essentially economic conflict. Pound then asks the question, saying: "This is the evidence; will any jury convict on it?" "Hic Geryon est. Hic hyperusura" (46/29). Geryon is a favorite symbol for his indignation. The three-headed monster served in Dante's Hell as guardian of the eighth circle where fraud, usury, and violence against nature and art are punished.

Following Pound's analysis of rise and fall in American economic history, the general decline of the American dream is chronicled. It culminated in the great market crash of 1929. The financial boom of the 20's, the stock-splitting, the holding companies, the wild speculation, the failure of the Federal Reserve System to check, manage, or control the credit supplied to the nation—all these forces had produced artificial and temporary prosperity. After three years of Roosevelt there was still depression and want. Whatever had been done to aid the unemployed and starving populace was insufficient. Here we were, says Pound, at the bottom of the eighth circle of Hell:

FIVE million youths without jobs
FOUR million adult illiterates
15 million 'vocational misfits', that is with small chance
for jobs
NINE million persons annual, injured in preventable
industrial accidents
One hundred thousand violent crimes . . . , signed F. Delano,
his uncle.
CASE for the prosecution . . . . (46/29)

What Roosevelt had done to relieve depression was not enough.

After this explosion the next Canto allows Pound to return to Odysseus to get the literary contrast which incidentally shows the state of mind of those who are making a journey to Hell. This theme had been first stated in Canto 1. What wisdom can one find in the land of the shades, where Tiresias knows all, where knowledge will tell us how to return to the promised land of Ithaca? "Yet must thou sail after knowledge" (47/30). The contrast is pleasant in style and mood. There is also the satisfaction which accompanies the old Eleusinian ceremonies, the worship of the gods that have the gift of healing, "the power over wild beasts."

Cantos 48 and 49 are contemplative, as if Pound's passion required relief. We still find references to details of the economic theme, that Bismarck blamed the American Civil War on the Jews, that a Rothschild remarked to Disraeli that nations were fools to pay rent for their credit, that certain emperors in China had managed to rule the state so that the people were well fed and happy.

Canto 50 provides the great cumulative statement of theme, the piling up of more details which illustrate the sins of Usury throughout history. In a sense this Canto documents the attack made poetically in Canto 45. Interest on the public debt eventually overturned the Medici. In Tuscany Leopoldo was a good man stymied by the forces of Usury:

> and Leopoldo meant to cut off two thirds of state debt
> to abolish it
>   and then they sent him off to be Emperor
> in hell's bog, in the slough of Vienna, in
>   the midden of Europe in the black hole of all
> mental vileness, in the privvy that stank Franz Josef,
> in Metternich's merdery in the absolute rottennness,
> among embastardized cross-breeds . . . . (50/41)

Pound implies that Leopold's successor, Ferdinando, helped stave off revolutions outside France. Then Waterloo reestablished the old regime, the Georges, the latrine out of which came Metternich—how the Rothschilds (the cross-breeds?) loved Metternich—everything which permitted the triumph of commercial usury in the nineteenth century at the expense of the public:

'Not'
said Napoleon 'because of that league of lice
but for opposing the Zeitgeist! That was my ruin,
That I ran against my own time, turning backward' . . . . (50/43)

The cumulative statement of his main thesis is intended to be constructed in Canto 51. Some of the material serves as an echo of the Usury Canto, some of it is a Hymn to Light, the ideal Light which should shine on a good world, but which sees misery, greed, want, fraud, and special privilege in the midst of plenty. The big lines ought to be a real climax, but we come to them with a sense of distraction and perplexity. It was so hard for Pound to make a big point plainly, so hard that his ideogram seems to obscure his point: "Time was of the League of Cambrai:" [followed by the Chinese *ching ming* characters, implying "this is a true definition"] (51/46). Probably the point intended is that in 1508 various rulers joined together at Cambrai to combat and suppress the economic superiority of Venice. Civilization is presumed to have had a chance (like the American chance? This is the first time this parallel has been brought up) in Venice too. Special and selfish privilege crushed it. Does Usury always win? Surely Pound is still hoping that the forces of justice will overcome Usury, in the United States as well as in Italy.

The high-spot brings *The Cantos* to the end of 51 and 1935. Between that time and the opening of the second World War Pound composed twenty more Cantos, designed to continue his case against Usury, but centered on materials which outwardly do not connect themselves with the main theme. From 52 through 61 he presents the Chinese parallel for his repeat in history motif; from 62 through 71 he celebrates the greatest of his ideal historical heroes, John Adams.

The inclusion of the Chinese historical data has puzzled many readers, probably most of them. It is as if Pound eccentrically decided to tell us about China for no particular reason except that he liked Confucius and had a lot of information the usual reader does not have. But the solution to the puzzle is that these Cantos provide detailed evidence for the same conclusions he has been examining through the facts of Italian and American history. He shows by a fairly lengthy and complete commentary the alternate rise and fall of economic prosperity in China; some rulers were benevolent, some completely stupid or tyrannical. Out of early Chinese history came Confucius, and all the rulers who later followed the essential principles of government laid down by Confucius contributed to the greatness of China.

Pound begins the first of these Cantos, 52, with a restatement of his creed that the great need of the world is to find out about the influence of money policies on political health. Somehow or other his anti-Semitism achieves heights of vituperation, and his bitter attack on Jewish moneymen was more or less censored when it was sent to the printers. Pound insisted upon black lines to indicate exactly how much was suppressed, and it is fair to point out that this blacked-out material was about the Rothschilds.[11]

The case for "Order" in Chinese history we have examined previously. It may be noted here that Pound refers to *ammassi* in several places, and to the *fontego*.[12] These are specific economic devices practiced in Italy, designed to furnish government stimulus, aid and control for agriculture and industry, the ammassi under Mussolini. Generally speaking Pound confines himself entirely to Chinese history and avoids flickering back and forth to display comparative ideograms. His intention is to set his analysis squarely beside the previous pictures he had drawn of the United States, Italy, and Europe in general.

The following Cantos, 62-71, celebrate the hero who is now presented as the great example of what a ruler or leader should be: John Adams. The choice is natural when we consider the background of Pound's ideas and habits of poetic composition. He followed Joseph Anne Marie Moyriac de Mailla's thirteen volume *Histoire Générale de la Chine* for his Chinese Cantos. He had the twenty volumes of Jefferson's *Works* for his various references to that president. He possessed Van Buren's *Autobiography* for Canto 37. He read John Quincy Adams' *Diary* for Canto 33. Antonini Zobi's *History of Tuscany* gave him Leopoldo and Ferdinando for Cantos 44 and 50. Frobenius, Major Douglas, Gesell, Brooks Adams, and Alexander del Mar provide definite source material for quotation. But none of these originals fascinated him more than the ten volume edition of the *Works* of John Adams, printed with a biography written by his grandson, Charles Francis, and published from 1852-1865. The ten Adams Cantos confine themselves almost entirely to this source and attempt to select and emphasize the important conclusions which can be deduced from the life and opinions of the great American president. Pound intends to say that Adams is the greatest of all the political geniuses he has found in the past history of any country. The fact that John Adams' opinions support Pound's main ideas about politics, economics, and the repeat in history theme makes him an ideal, if coincidental choice for celebration. Besides, Adams was isolated in the past and his record was available after it was finished. Mussolini, in contrast, was making history which was in progress, and Pound did not have the same kind of source materials at hand. It may be that Pound intended to treat Mussolini in more detail later, then changed his mind because of the outcome of World War II. He never attempted to draw on Mussolini's *Autobiography,* and anyone who reads it is free to guess why.

The beginning of Canto 62 sets the mood for all the Adams Cantos. It quotes John as saying America should profit by the mistakes of Europe:

> *'Acquit of evil intention*
> *or inclination to perseverance in error*
> *to correct it with cheerfulness*
> *particularly as to the motives of actions*
> *of the great nations of Europe.'* (62/87)

All through the Chinese Cantos Pound had been praising the "Order" of the Confucian heritage; now he praises Adams for equating Order with "Liberty." One should be blood for the other's bones.

The traditional record of John Adams in American history is often restricted to the impression that he was a staunch force in organizing the early American Revolution, that he was solid in his views, conservative, a Federalist, that he served his country well in many capacities although he tended to be a "natural aristocrat" with defects of pride and ego, that he was probably half-way between Jefferson and Hamilton in viewpoint, that he followed George Washington as President, that he was ousted by Jefferson and the people's party (a party claimed by the Democrats through the following years), and that he carried on a long post-presidential correspondence with Jefferson discussing most of the issues of democratic government and politics in remarkable letters which serve as essential sources for all students of American history. Pound accepts much of this traditional view, but points up the lesser-known data, the experiences and opinions which to him are more important and illuminate the real Adams. Particularly interesting to Pound are the days when Adams went to France (two missions) during the Revolutionary War, eventually negotiating important loans from the Dutch bankers in Holland, but also checking on the major loans France made us through the negotiations of Franklin, Lee, and Deane, the early commissioners. Since Adams was supported by the Federalist faction, we would expect him to be allied with the measures of Hamilton, the man who stood for the business class in our early political history. Pound must have been surprised initially to find that Adams was as opposed to the National Bank as Jefferson was, and that his opposition began with the experiences gained while he was negotiating with European bankers. Pound was fascinated by his study of how this knowledge grew on Adams, how wise and just this solid man was, how honest and forthright his judgments, how completely uncompromising with evil as he saw it. The poet decided to make Adams the great hero of his epic and worth the most space.

The man who helped Jefferson with the Declaration of Independence was also the statesman who aided the creation of the Continental currency, who sponsored the bill to establish a navy, who was responsible for many state constitutions through his advice, who guided the states in measures to avoid jurisdictional disputes among themselves:

> republican jealousy which seeks to cut off all power
> from fear of abuses does
> quite as much harm as a despotism . . . . (62/90)

This is the leader who was for proportional representation, "the clearest head in the Congress," the ambassador who managed the foreign relations of the rebellious nation in France and Holland without intrigue, flattery, or corruption, the man who rapidly understood that an accumulative national debt was likely to be perpetual and that such debts lead to more revolutions, the scholar whose love of law, science, and letters made him encourage schools and academies as the "only means to preserve our Constitution."

All of Canto 62 forms a set piece outlining the accomplishments and capacities of John Adams, the final statement contrasting him with Hamilton (called the "Prime snot"):

> the man who at certain points
> made us
> at certain points
> saved us
> by fairness, honesty and straight moving
> ARRIBA ADAMS (62/96)

Arriba is, of course, Spanish for "Hail!" or "'Up with . . . ." Pound may have selected it because it was alliterative.

The next nine Cantos develop the initial picture of the great leader and how he grew. The emphasis upon Adams' views of money and special privilege appears gradual. Sometimes the ideograms are obscured by the relative fascination of the total portrait, the biography piling up details which depict a man of extraordinary perception in so many matters that his financial and economic opinions may be glossed over. Adams is not certain of the individual capacity of the average American in understanding or self-reliance:

> STOOD by the people much longer than they wd/ stand
> by themselves. (64/107)

And again he says:

> One party for wealth and power
> at expense
> of the liberty of their country
> wars, carnage, confusion
> not interested in their servitude
> I am, for all I can see, left quite alone. . . . (64/107)

When he went to France to assist and in effect rescue Franklin and the other American representatives, he was appalled at the condition of Europe. The haphazard way in which our first representatives did business also disgusted him, although he speaks softly about it:

Enormous
sums have been expended, no book of
accounts, no documents wherefrom
able to learn what has been rec'd in America
Wrong in having three commissioners one is enough
in leaving salaries at uncertainty
in mingling public minister and commercial agent
Mr Deane never succeeded in throwing much light on
his mode of doing business in France.
Many other qualities I cd/ not distinguish from virtues. (65/119)

He saw the alternate luxury and squalor of France, deriving from his observations contempt for the economic structure of European nations:

A national debt of
274 million stg/
accumulated by jobs contracts salaries pensions in
the course of a century
might easily produce all this magnificence .... (66/126-127)

He began to see that the original rights of man must be backed by the economic opportunity to live comfortably in a political system which supplied sufficient money for distribution or trade:

OB PECUNIAE SCARSITATEM
this act, the Stamp Act, wd/drain cash out of the country
and is, further, UNconstitutional
yr/ humanity counterfeit
yr/ liberty cankered with simulation .... (66/128)

This opinion dates back to the early days before the Revolution. Now he was able to add more details and understand the larger needs of the national economy.

The original grievances of the Colonies had been financial, for the Stamp Act had been only the beginning of the measures designed by Parliament to drain money from America back to England. How could this kind of practice be avoided or mitigated when the new independent government was established?

Adams suggested several measures to keep one part of the people from exploiting the rest. He was early attracted to the division of responsibility among the executive, legislative, and judicial powers:

> The colonies under such triple government wd/ be
> Unconquerable by all the monarchs of Europe
> ▌few of the human race have had opportunity like this . . . . (67/137)

For him there was no more agreeable employment than to study the best kind of government, and Pound is particularly attracted by Adams' inserting in the Constitution of Massachusetts the opinion that it was the duty of legislatures to "cherish the interest of literature." Adams added the idea that "good humour" was also imperative, something Pound found less exciting. The main thing was to avoid allowing special privilege—a cunning aristocracy—to gain so much power that most of the common folk would be deprived of their opportunities and rights:

> Whole history of Geneva:
> the people have given up all balances
> betraying their own rights and those of the magistrates
> into the hands of a few prominent families . . . . (67/140)

America must never allow this.

But, according to Adams and Pound, America rapidly *did* allow it, in minor degree at first, to an extreme later. The financial establishment of the new republic was admittedly difficult. It is hard for us today to see how it could have been done unselfishly or without concession to privilege. There had to be unbacked Continental paper currency to pay for the rebellion in the first place. This paper money fluctuated in value according to the respect the public had for the course of the war, since the money existed only by the backing of a revolutionary junto. Its value could have been revived with great difficulty after the war was won.

We had to borrow in France and Holland to get needed supplies and credit from the Continent. This would have to be paid back by something which had value in international exchange. Adams felt that the security of the new country was ample and that we could rapidly pay off whatever we needed to borrow in establishing ourselves:

when England borrows each year a sum equal
to all her exports
shd/ we be laughed at for
wanting to borrow up to 1/12th (one twelfth)
of our exports? (68/146)

Adams saw early that the depreciation of the Continental currency was a tax on the people "paid in advance," but he felt that such injustice was necessary to win the war:

England has increased her debt 60 million
ours is not over 6 million
who can hold out the longer?
the depreciation has not tended to make the people
submit to Britain .... (69/149)

When he finally succeeded in arranging the needed loans abroad, the terms were not exorbitant as terms went in those days. The Amsterdam bankers did not decide to help America until the war was won, but they must have found Adams to be a good bargainer and a reliable representative, a man of business they could trust. Consider how shocked Adams was after the war's end to see the establishment of American financial affairs on the same basis as those of Europe—a basis he had accepted because he could not help himself abroad, but which he felt to be part of the system America ought to avoid. Special privilege raising its ugly head in the new land: "To T. Jefferson:/'You fear the one, I the few' " (69/153).

With the charter of Hamilton's National Bank the country's money was made stable. Stability was certainly an important advantage, one which has blurred the picture considerably for Americans since that time. Pound charges that it was accompanied by all the possibilities for private manipulation or fraud which can be observed in the history of European credit practices. There was *no* legislative check on the National Bank. Adams was also horrified at the bill in Congress which paid off the Continental bonds. It was Madison who proposed that the *original* bond holders should get their face value of the bonds, but naturally this amendment was defeated—with major assistance from Congressmen who had bought up some of the bonds themselves. "Traitors blacker than Arnold," says Canto 69.

What should the new government have done? Alas, so few people know enough to propose fair remedies, and if they do know, how can they be elected? Adams is rueful about the problem:

> aim of my life has been to be useful, how small in
> any nation the number who comprehend ANY
> system of constitution or administration
> and these few do not unite . . . .
> I am for balance
> [here the Chinese character for the unwobbling pivot,
> or strong center balance]
> and know not how it is but mankind have an aversion
> to any study of government . . . . (70/158-159)

Adams continued to fight against special privilege, as did Jefferson, and between them Pound feels that great progress was made, even if Usury was not wiped out. The First National Bank became the prime aversion of both men, and Adams' final opinions about government began to concentrate more and more on the need to control manipulations of credit:

> depreciated by the swindling banks, a multitude
> of such swindling banks have ruin'd our medium
> Their issues are against gold or on nothing. (71/160)

The most important of Pound's conclusions is quoted in the last Adams Canto. It is Pound's case in essence, and it marks the frame of mind which was his during the last days of the 1930's, the days before the second World War broke out:

> Funds and Banks I
> never approved I abhorred even our whole banking system
> but an attempt to abolish all funding in the
> present state of the world wd/ be as romantic
> as any adventure in Oberon or Don Quixote.
> Every bank of discount is downright corruption
> taxing the public for private individuals' gain.
> and if I say this in my will
> the American people wd/ pronounce I died crazy. (71/162)

One can hardly miss the fact that the poet who quoted Adams was considered crazy too. Still, Adams made a record of complete loyalty, fighting evils from within, not without. Both the hero and the poet join in lamenting that the great social and political weaknesses of the people are "Ignorance of coin, credit, and circulation!" Pound ends his study of Adams by giving him a salutation, this time in Greek. Adams ought to be the most honored of the immortals!

Whether Pound has exaggerated the position of Adams by isolating his various remarks about banks and credit is a matter for the specialist. Any of us who have examined the Charles Adams volumes which serve as Pound's source note that at least his quotations are not distorted, even when they are shortened and run together. The original of the last quotation, for example, is taken from a letter Adams wrote to Benjamin Rush in 1811. It reads:

> A national bank of deposit I believe to be wise, just, prudent, economical, and necessary. But every bank of discount, every bank by which interest is to be paid or profit of any kind made by the deponent, is downright corruption. It is taxing the public for the benefit and profit of individuals; it is worse than the old tenor, continental currency, or any other paper money.
>
> Now, Sir, if I should talk in this strain, after I am dead, you know the people of America would pronounce that I had died mad.[13]

Pound felt that mentioning Adams' objections to paper money would distract attention from what he considered to be the main point, and he is probably right.

What should be our conclusion as to the effectiveness of Pound's economic theme, after following it from Cantos 31 to 71? The poet has referred to a horrifying number of sources. The main emphasis has been upon the historical development of his own country compared with Italy and China. He has found admirable similarities in Jefferson, Adams, Confucius, and Mussolini; he has set up the ideal leader in terms which derive from the measures which were supported against Usury. He says America has declined, has fallen from her promise since the days of our Civil War; he says that Italy has the new opportunity. And so he cast his lot with Italy when the war broke out. Mussolini was the new Jefferson, or, alternately, the new John Adams. Roosevelt was not.

Americans are predisposed to be on the side of Jefferson and Adams, even if we interpret their record a little differently from Pound. We may be surprised to find out about some things they said and did. We will assuredly have trouble agreeing that America has decayed completely since the days of Lincoln, even in Pound's special interpretation. We are more likely to agree that special privilege is evil, but Pound's portrayal of the forces of good and bad has been put in extremely narrow compartments. A still small voice may ask how much of his case is correct. Amazingly enough, if Pound has any appeal to Americans in the presentation of his economic theme, the attraction must be to the class which represents the culture he says he could not find in his homeland.

At the end we come up against Mussolini himself. What about his record? Can he be assessed and judged on the basis of Pound's picture of his economic accomplishments? Did not the United States adopt many of the welfare measures Pound praises in parts of the New Deal program? Where in the world can one find the "forward" economic progress Pound admired so much? Did it really happen in Italy?

Some of the answers to these questions are suggested in the Pisan Cantos.

7 MUSSOLINI AND/OR EZRA

> *"I believe in the resurrection of Italy   quia impossible est*
> *4 times to the song of Gassir*
> *now in the mind indestructible* (74/20)
>
> *"I am noman, my name is noman"*
> *but Wanjina is, shall we say, Ouan Jin*
> *or the man with an education ....* (74/4)

The Pisan Cantos begin with a disturbing phrase: "The enormous tragedy of the dream." Pound compares the hanging of the Duce and Clara by the heels to the crucifixion (not of Christ) of the Persian sage Manes, who also—by implication—died for his ideals and was "twice crucified." The American poet had dared the reputation of treason for his dream; he had taken sides against his own country because of his intense belief in what he saw as an ideal. He had ended in the symbolic hell of his poem. His tragedy encompasses the dream and the real world. Surely it is necessary and proper to examine the connection between his ideal and reality, to consider the evidence of the epic in support of facts which transpose poetry from words to sense.

First, for the sake of argument, let us suppose that we are willing to suspend judgment, to give Pound the benefit of some modicum of doubt or disbelief in examining his economic and political contentions. Say that we have found stimulus in his condensed comments on leaders like Thomas Jefferson and John Adams. We note almost immediately that his references to Mussolini are scanty in comparison. No ten Cantos devoted to the accomplishments of this present-day "hero" are available, as there are for Adams. Not even one or two Cantos. If the materials are not in order, why not? It is true that Pound's historical method works best when he has books and sources from which to quote and comment. Still, one wonders, even without our automatic rejection of Mussolini because he was a hated wartime enemy, whether there is not an occasional separation of actuality from Pound's dream, that the record would not uphold what the poet was talking about. There has been at least a serious attempt to document Pound's opinions about Confucius, Pietro Leopoldo, and the great American presidents. Does Mussolini's record fulfill the poet's own picture of his ideal? Consider the possible tragedy of a dream which cannot be anything but a dream.

Before the second World War began, *The Cantos* supply only a reference or two to Mussolini. Canto 38 mentions the inevitable draining of the Italian marshes; Canto 41 talks about the dictator in some greater detail. Pound centers on a quotation: "'Ma qvesto,' said the Boss, 'è divertente'" (41/52). "That's diverting," Mussolini says, talking about the Malatesta Cantos and apparently catching Pound's point "before the aesthetes had got there." It seems clear that Pound was comparing Mussolini to Malatesta, a leader who made many compromises in order to further the culture of his country. Several bits of evidence follow: the draining of the marshes must always come first, and the point is that cultivatable land and new jobs were provided for the unemployed, public works instituted by a benevolent government. Mussolini is said to have jailed the businessmen who wanted to subtract their customary cuts from government contracts. The total implication of this Canto, if other ideograms are set beside these two examples of Mussolini's tactics, is that the Italian leader stood out against the forces of special privilege, and that the usurers could not control him. He is the man who tries to do today what Jefferson and Adams had tried to do and had partially accomplished in their own day. We note that these cited references are absolutely all there is in *The Cantos* about Mussolini before the Pisan reminiscences.

The two Cantos which have not been published (72 and 73) may have further mention of the dictator. Also one may legitimately suggest that Pound intended to say more in the epic, but kept his celebration of Mussolini to a minimum after the war was lost—that is, after Canto 71—and he was in danger of trial for treason anyway. One can even imagine that the next planned decad after Canto 71 was to explain and praise Mussolini, to fill out the data presented about China and John Adams. As the epic stands, however, little is said about Pound's ideal modern hero, the man who stood for part of the dream. Let us look at all there is in the Pisan Cantos.

After praising Mussolini for going out with a bang, not a whimper, Pound says that he transmitted "a precise definition." (Does this suggest an exact description of the ideal economic state?) The following comment on the mistakes of Stalin signifies his belief in the *correct* policies of Mussolini: "and but one point needed for Stalin/you need not, i.e. need not take over the means of production" (74/4). Mussolini stands for the encouragement of distribution in production without seizing private enterprise (as Stalin had done), without government ownership or absolute dictation. Canto 76 (76/30) insists that the ideal political system of Mussolini may be broken, but the economic system will remain.

Canto 77 says that Mussolini made some mistakes. He should have rid himself of people like Ciano: "and the dogdamn wop is not, save by exception,/honest in administration any more than the briton is truthful" (77/48). Canto 78 supplies several additional hints. The Jewish representative of Imperial Chemicals (an example of a cartel, probably a Rothschild) is supposed to have said lispingly that it took twenty years to crush Napoleon, but that Mussolini would be crushed faster (78/55). Apparently this threat occurred because the dictator was interfering with profitable monoplies, and also: "Put down the slave trade, made the desert to yield/and menaced the loan swine" (78/57). This comment connects with the Ethiopian conquest; and whatever improvements might be needed in that African country, the conquest still smacks of colonialism and aggression.

The only actual discussion of Mussolini's money policies is also in Canto 78. Pound mentions Odon Por for the first time (78/59), calling attention to a book by Por for details. Since Pound translated this book into English, this brief notice legitimately calls for further research. After Por comes his main plug for the Gesell money-scrip:

"No longer necessary," taxes are no longer necessary
in the old way if it (money) be based on work done
inside a system and measured and gauged to human requirements
inside the nation or system
and cancelled in proportion
to what is used and worn out
à la Wörgl . . . . (78/59-60)

Mussolini is not praised for adopting this monetary reform, but Pound reports that the Duce said he would "have to think about this," and was hanged dead before "his thought in proposito came into action efficiently." This statement is almost surely wish-fulfillment.

Canto 80 returns to a defense of the Duce against some of his followers. The argument is that if the dictator erred it was by "excess of emphasis": "the problem after any revolution is what to do with/your gunmen" (80/74). Also repeated is the reference to the man who said it would not take twenty years to crush Mussolini (80/75). This completes the Pisan Cantos as far as the ideal leader is concerned.

It is unlikely to be enough for most of us; nor do the later Cantos add much. In the Rock-Drill sections, generally devoted to contrapuntal emphasis and more historical comparisons, Pound sets forth two main points for special attention. These suggest that Mussolini's main accomplishments were his system for making labor and capital work together (87/31) and his many acts in the interest of what Pound calls "distributive justice" (93/87). There is also a rather interesting ideogram on the idea of a government charge for the use of money or credit, Pound's favorite thesis which insists that a nation should use its own credit and not pay interest on something it owns itself. Exactly what act of Mussolini is referred to is not clear. Then Pound recalls 1932 and the time Mussolini is represented as saying to Pound, "Why do you want to [put] your ideas in order?" (87/29). This perception intrigues the poet, and he says, with a touch of wistfulness: "If I had known more then,/ cd/ have asked him" (87/29). Apparently Mussolini could have been asked about the proper use of money, but there is no fact mentioned which helps us see the direction of Pound's efforts to put his ideas in order.

The Thrones Cantos furnish only a footnote or two. Canto 98 reads: "said the Consigliere, 'we thought we could control Mussolini' " (98/38). The dictator made a sarcastic comment about Russia (103/85), and it is later asserted that he saved what was savable in Spain, an elliptical defense for the Fascist part in the Spanish Civil War (105/98).

It must be remembered that by the implications of his counterpoint Pound intends to equate Mussolini with the positive aspects of his economic theme, so that we are supposed to read into the record much of what is parallel by comparison with some other significant fact from history. Still, it would be helpful to have some more direct mention of subjects like the corporate state ideal, or *autarchy,* the self-sufficient concept which is Odon Por's main object of praise in explaining Mussolini's accomplishments. Pound does refer to *guilds* and we know that he believes the corporate state to be an extension of the National Guilds program which had first been urged by Orage. On three occasions (all in the Chinese Cantos) he mentions the *ammassi,*[1] the grain pools which represent one of the measures for just price and fair dealing in agriculture credited to Mussolini. In all these cases he tends to assume that any informed person would know what he is talking about, an assumption which is occasionally irritating when the facts are in dispute or hard to come by.

There are four main sources which may fruitfully be examined in order to explain what Pound must have intended in his exaltation of Mussolini. These are: his book, *Jefferson and/or Mussolini;* his six *Money Pamphlets;* the records of his wartime broadcasts from Rome; and his translation of the Odon Por book called *Italy's Policy of Social Economics.* There is additional incidental information in some of his letters and his essays, also in his contributions to various magazines like *The New English Weekly,* but the best records are in these four named sources. *The ABC of Economics* is strangely unhelpful; nor do I find *Guide to Kulchur* of much assistance to the economic theme or the case for Mussolini.

The text for Pound's dream of Mussolini may be taken from the sentence he printed on his personal stationery, a quotation from Mussolini: "Liberty is not a right but a duty."

This cryptic statement, which surely might imply many things, is perhaps close to President Kennedy's remarks about what you can do for your country rather than the opposite. Mussolini made a number of speeches in which he described his social and economic goals. The most forthright is probably the following:

> The present crisis means the end of liberal capitalism, the economic system which emphasized the individual profit motive, and marks the beginning of a new economy which stresses collective interests. These collective interests will be achieved . . . through the corporate system which is based on the self-regulation of production under the aegis of the producers . . . When I say producers, I do not mean only employers, I mean workers also . . . Speaking to the people of Bari I said that the economic objective of the Fascist regime is greater social justice for the Italian people. What do I mean by greater social justice? I mean the guarantee of work, a fair wage, a decorous home, I mean the possibility of evolution and betterment . . . If modern science, spurred on by the state, has solved the problem of multiplying wealth, science must now solve the other great problem, that of the distribution of wealth, so that the illogical, paradoxical, and cruel phenomenon of want in the midst of plenty shall not be repeated. Toward this great goal all our energies and all our efforts must be bent.[2]

These particular words are dated October 4, 1934, but they might easily serve as the starting point for Pound's *Jefferson and/or Mussolini*. At least they are evidence that Mussolini said he would *try* to solve the problem of distribution. Under his regime, says Pound, "scarcity economics died."[3] Only in Italy did honest legislation leave the airy field of talk so that a decent monetary system can take on "legal and concrete existence."[4]

Some puzzlement remains. Whatever Mussolini was doing about distribution, no one has presented any *concrete* evidence that he did anything about the monetary system which is different from what is done in other countries. Mussolini may have spent the money for good things—at times, anyway—but he financed government expenses just as the United States did and does. Pound becomes extreme at the drop of an adjective, and this tendency obscures proper judgment of his arguments. If Mussolini's aims are taken from the speech noted, one can easily see virtue in his intentions. Many politicians promise pie in the sky. In any case Pound uses the intentions of Mussolini as the basis for his comparison between the Italian leader and Jefferson.

When one reads Pound's book about his two heroes, it is difficult to restrain a strong feeling that any reaction depends upon how one feels in the first place. If you are in sympathy with Mussolini, what Pound says is likely to be convincing. If not, the whole argument is suspect. The central information includes attacks on American stupidity in economic affairs, and presents the case for Mussolini's making labor and capital cooperate. Celebration of compulsory arbitration, laws that make strikes illegal, even a kind of partnership that Pound asserts works out to the advantage of both sides—all this material has little to do with Jefferson, but is presented as something *similar* to what Jefferson would have done had he been presented with the modern world and its problems in capital-labor relationships.

I do not find the purpose of the book very persuasive. Perhaps the most illuminating statement in it explains much of Pound's subsequent behavior, his willingness to award accomplishment to what he hopes is happening in the Italian economy, whether or not it really does:

> Any thorough judgment of Mussolini will be in a measure an *act of faith* [my italics], it will depend on what you *believe* the man means, what you believe he wants to accomplish . . . I don't believe any estimate of Mussolini will be valid unless it *starts* from his passion for construction. Treat him as *artifex* and all the details fall into place. Take him as anything save the artist and you will get muddled with contradictions. Or you will waste a lot of time finding that he don't fit your particular preconceptions or your particular theories.[5]

And there we are left, a little muddled, but holding an artifex. Mussolini means well, he made capital and labor lie down together, and you must believe in him because he says he is against the old system of special privilege. You may not know exactly how he is going to get distribution to everybody, but he is trying. Keep the faith.

Evidence is not necessarily something which should be avoided in Pound's poetic style. Even his prose escapes any regular method of presenting deduction or the substance of logic. The six *Money Pamphlets* are sketchy when it comes to mentioning exactly what Mussolini is doing which merits so much devotion and support. Pound spends most of his pages in attacking economic deterioration in other countries, usually beginning with America. He restates the need for a decent social system where money is stable, prices are just, and men are not permitted to prey upon each other by manipulating values or appropriating the credit of the people as a whole. It is Pamphlet Number Two, *Gold and Work,* which says that the United States were sold to the Rothschilds in 1863, the charge which gives the illusion of violent distortion to the other parts of Pound's thesis which may not be so distorted. For example he says over and over that the state "can LEND." The evidence he always cites is the ancient occasion when the state of Athens lent the money to build the fleet which was victorious at Salamis. At this distance it is difficult to see how this applies exactly to later economies or whether Athens "created" or guaranteed "debt-free" money to shipbuilders. Maybe the state just ordered ships out of taxes the way any modern state buys a ship. Wonderful evidence for Pound's thesis would be proof that Mussolini's state lent the money to finance something important, perhaps the social security program. Many states borrow by deficit financing to inaugurate programs they feel to be important. There does not seem to be any evidence that Italy ever used any debt-free money, unless lowering the gold backing of the lira may be so construed. In fact Mussolini borrowed money he needed from credit organizations like the Morgan banks; he built his great armed forces as other countries do. He kept his Italian economy on what he called the gold standard.

Pamphlet Three, *What Is Money For?,* sets forth the best material for our present study. Pound insists that Mussolini enforced "just prices," a model which resembles the price controls almost always imposed in time of war or crisis in many other countries too. "Only the STATE can effectively fix the JUST PRICE of any commodity by means of state-controlled pools of raw products and the restoration of guild organisation in industry."[6] This principle seems to include wage controls: "Mussolini and Hitler wasted very little time PROPOSING. They started and DO distribute BOTH tickets and actual goods on various graduated scales according to the virtues and activities of Italians and Germans . . . . The goods are getting distributed."[7]

Pound says that this method is completely different from the dole, from relief which is not dependent upon work. Whether or not this kind of control included any signs of the slave state can hardly be told either. Mussolini is quoted: "DISCIPLINE THE ECONOMIC FORCES AND EQUATE THEM TO THE NEEDS OF THE NATION."[8]

A natural question arises. Did Pound suggest that Italy instituted any of the principles of Social Credit or the devices of Gesell to insure his economic ideals? Apparently not. In Pamphlet Number Four, *A Visiting Card,* he mentions Rossoni, the Italian Minister of Agriculture, as an adherent of the Gesell stamp-scrip device, but it is impossible to say whether Rossoni merely expressed interest and thought the experiment might work, or whether Pound is again exaggerating his case.

In Pamphlet Five, *Social Credit: An Impact,* the general theories of Douglas are concentrated in praise for the cooperative banking system in contrast to the predatory bank of discount. Pound argues that the American New Deal has not tried any steps to relate the credit of the nation to its purchasing power. There has to be enough money in circulation to purchase WANTED goods. Mussolini is claimed to be doing this, and his price controls stop inflation: "Japan and Italy, the two really alert, active nations are both engaged in proving fragments of the Douglas analysis, and in putting bits of his scheme into practice."[9] Then he admits: "The foregoing does not mean that Italy has 'gone Social Credit.' "[10]

Pound does not at this point include Germany in his "alert, active nations." Places can be found where he refers sarcastically to Schacht, the big banker Hitler put in charge of Nazi finances. Whether Pound knew how Hitler was manipulating the German economy is problematical here. The early Nazi propaganda included theories of reform which outlined broad social planning and a campaign against social privilege. Gottfried Feder was Hitler's first financial expert, a heretic who might have cooperated nicely with some of Douglas' theories about Social Credit. To us it looks as if Hitler rapidly got rid of Feder as well as Gregor Strasser and most of the other early Nazis who could possibly have been more interested in social betterment than power politics and military expansion. In Feder's place came Schacht, and the extraordinary financial growth of Germany under Hitler, the building of the great war machine, was done by orthodox book figures, deficit financing. The unbalanced budget was extended to extreme proportions. Schacht wangled the figures as he pleased, and Germany's debt to the bankers must have been astronomical. Since the debt is a numerical myth if you control prices, wages, and money in circulation, Hitler merely proceeded to make his money stable by force and decree. He never expected to pay off the debt, of course, but the bankers got interest on paper records and taxes were high. There is no theoretical resemblance to Social Credit ideals in the Nazi policies, and special privilege turned out to be an Aryan or Gestapo matter. There is overwhelming evidence that there is no connection between what Pound was ideally urging and supposedly finding in Italy with what was happening in Germany. How much of this should Pound have known? Certainly he had little information about Japan, which also paid for its military expansion in the orthodox method of deficit financing.

Just what could Pound have meant when he said that Italy was putting bits of the Douglas Social Credit program into practice? This assertion is of major importance in explaining his decision to support Italy against America in the forthcoming war. Since few of the details are really spelled out in *The Cantos,* it is helpful to look at the statements of Odon Por, *Italy's Policy of Social Economics, 1939-40,* translated into English by Pound under the dateline of September, 1941. Por was a theorist, originally a Syndicalist, and apparently never held any very important political post under the Italian regime. His role was to explain and justify what Fascism did, and he served as a scholarly propagandist for the corporate state. How friendly he and Pound were is not clear, but Por is the main influence on Pound's ideas as to the intention and execution of Mussolini's program.

Por outlines the economic accomplishments of the Italian regime thus:

1. Mussolini invented and applied a new technique of social peace, as opposed to class war, encouraging cooperation between capital and labor. This means collaboration, no strikes, arbitration, and mutual benefits for owners and workers arranged by the government.

2. Mussolini applied the new principle of *autarchy* to the Italian economic system. Autarchy means national economic self-sufficiency, the building up of every means of production within the country so that it can exist without foreign imports; it means the absolute control of all foreign trade in the interest of the whole state, directed by the government. Por carries this principle into many phases of production:

> An autarchic regime like ours does not permit new inventions and processes of working to be blocked by vested interests. In Italy anyone, of however modest condition, can submit his inventions to the Central Commission for examination of inventions, an organ of the National Council of Research; if the result of the examinations is favourable the invention is brought to the notice of the State boards and of industries which it might interest. When it appears that the invention has an immediate utility for the public, its use is recommended, and if it meets resistance, it is imposed by authority. Products due to new inventions and processes receive a ruling re/price and consumption that guarantees their marketing at a profit.[11]

National planning, no confiscation of industry or government ownership, regulation which guarantees reasonable profit in theory, and consistent policies of business expansion which builds self-sufficient production and supplies purchasing power through new jobs to stimulate the economy. More business, more jobs, more money to purchase what is produced—all these units of policy fit theoretically into the Social Credit recommendations of Douglas and Pound.

3. Mussolini introduced the management of increased production in agriculture through obligatory pools called *ammassi*. The guilds, the farmers, and the Minister of Agri-

culture finance and control the whole process of planting, harvesting, and marketing grain. Each ammasso in theory buys and sells at a price set so that the farmer can produce profitably. Payment is made on delivery to the pool; at every stage which follows in getting the grain to the consumer the price is regulated so that no middleman can raise prices unfairly and no speculation can occur; salaries are fixed all along the way; the final price of a staple like bread may even be reduced and supported by the government in order to keep living costs down. Agriculture in Italy is claimed to have increased by leaps and bounds under Mussolini, and this principle is the opposite of regulation which restricts farm production to avoid surpluses. Italy never reached a surplus beyond her needs, of course. Whether the farmers were really better off is now disputed, but they worked harder.

4. Mussolini pump-primed the economy by a government-financed program of reclamation, opening up the cultivation of new lands, reforestation, and the draining of swampland. Big non-productive estates were broken up and forced into production; they were not expropriated by the state, which on the contrary helped to finance their development.

5. Mussolini instituted social security measures, pensions, and various types of job insurance. This program included the controversial "family salary," which gave extra money to workers in proportion to the number of children in the family. Employers paid for this partially before 1939 and entirely thereafter. Wages also were adjusted so that increased profits in any industry automatically raised labor's share. The books were open to both management and labor so that theoretically neither could take advantage of the other. Prices of staple commodities were fixed with regard to the consumer's ability to pay; this principle was particularly applied so that creeping inflation (the wage-price spiral) would not destroy the workers' advantage in salary increases. The advantage to the owner is that he operates with a sure profit; to the worker the advantage is that he gets his share in wages and profits if the business makes money. Holding companies and stock-splitting could not exist.

Certain resemblances to parts of the American New Deal emerge, although Pound in his broadcasts later asserted that the United States took over measures originated by Mussolini in a program which is "two-thirds fascist, missing the essential one-third" (February 26, 1942). The accomplishments listed by Por are liberal in a socialistic sense, and on their face constitute economic and political vision of dynamic force. Por is a propagandist and probably overstates the case. Like Pound he is subject to the suspicion of citing intentions as things actually done. Still, there is a case for idealism. Por's book indicates the intellectual background for Pound's decision to side with Mussolini in time of war.

When the reader comes to look at the records of Pound's broadcasts, he must be struck more and more by the variability of the poet's judgment. No writer of reputation is more likely to set persuasive materials beside exaggerated or distorted reasoning. It is hard, also, to remember that this is a great poet from the evidence of what he says over the air. The broadcasts are an unholy mixture of ambiguity, obscurity, inappropriate subject matter, vituperation, and a few pearls of unexpected wisdom. Most of the magic of his great writing vanishes.

Pound generally attacks or gloats, especially in the first programs. He rarely persuades or gives evidence which might persuade. Despite the fact that his general point of view is to "tell us" what is right, he has too little to say in explanation or defense of Mussolini's economic miracles—the argument which might explain much of what he is intending to say. In the February 17th broadcast (1942) he recommends the reading of Odon Por and says Americans are not aware of the accomplishments of Mussolini during the previous twenty years. But he does not detail those accomplishments or tell us where to get the book (it was unavailable to 99 per cent of his listeners). In the March 6th broadcast he says that labor is better off in Italy than elsewhere and recommends examination of Mussolini's new code for labor. But he does not explain the code or how it aids the worker. In his April 20th broadcast he takes issue with an article in the London *Daily Mail,* finally getting down to part of his case. The newspaper had said that Pound's sympathy with Fascism was an "aberration." Accordingly he attempts for the first time on the air to explain why he had endorsed Mussolini's brand of Fascism. He mentions the draining of the swamplands (an issue which by now has had most of the moisture drained out of it), the encouragement of agriculture, the improvement of housing and living conditions for the workers, the increase of water resources and electric power, the development of the railway system, and finally he defends the corporate state concept, claiming that it makes sure every man is represented in his government because his vote goes to someone who stands for the voter's own economic interests, his business or profession. Voting because you live in a particular district means that elected representatives may not represent anything except place of origin or the money it takes to run and get elected. The Italian system made sure that there was always someone who stood for your own economic section or division or interest, your own corporation or guild.

This is one of Pound's rare broadcasts which presents any kind of reasonable evidence. The April 27th one extends this theme a little, mostly by reverse reasoning. He says that in England and America legal rights have become less than our Constitutions intended. The trades, the artisans, the farmers, the small landowners all are less and less likely to have members of their own groups representing their interests in legislative bodies: "Now there is a new revolution, and in Italy and Germany governments are fulfilling the wills of the people, taking first what the people want first, and second what they want second."[12] This has to be examined in an unusual context to keep it separate from nonsense.

Pound's fixation about the Jews deserves some mention. Considering all that was happening to the Jews in Germany, it is hard to look at any Pound reference to them without experiencing some kind of nausea. Nor does it help much to say that he did not know about the extermination ovens or the death camps, but merely supposed that the Jews were losing property, money, freedom, and influence. The May 31st broadcast is an example.

> Mussolini has aimed to discipline the economic forces and equip them to the needs of the nation, and from him

> you are learning: economic discipline is a consequence of the assertion that man is over matter; money and machines are the servant of man, not his master. But you are still dodging Hitler's basic text. Very few of you have read the writings of either Hitler or Mussolini; you don't get any news from Italy. If Mussolini stands for social justice, for breaking Usury, the Nazi revolution is based on good breeding, eugenics.[13]

Several broadcasts imply that something had to be done about Jewish Usury. He does say that small Jews are unjustly suffering for the sins of certain big Jews. He also connects Usury with the earlier Spanish Civil War, in the July 20th broadcast asserting that it was "the financial gang that brought Civil War to Spain."

The offensive side of the broadcasts would have sounded bad had they been introduced in an American court in a trial for treason. But it is fair to point out that the radio records do contain certain exegesis for the positive ideas he had always embraced, incidentally explaining what he had suggested in the economic sections of *The Cantos,* even clarifying small parts of his creed which might previously have been sketchy. For example, in explanation of a difficult ideogram, the perceptive critic may recall that in the great Canto 38 the second reference is to the Pope's interview with Marconi:

> His Holiness expressed a polite curiosity
> as to how his Excellency had chased those
> electric shakes through the a'mosphere. (38/37)

In the June 19th broadcast Pound says that all economic distribution used to take place with metal counters, probably gold or silver coins. Then somebody discovered you could do without the counters and use credit. Pound compares this to the fact that we all used to know that lightning could travel through the air because we could see it. But we did not do anything about using the lightning until Marconi came along and discovered the potential inherent in electric power which could be harnessed and controlled. This discovery changed the world in a material way; so should the proper harnessing of credit. He implies that such discoveries ought to be used for the benefit of the entire nation, not just the special interests.

At any rate, one who knows the first instance from Canto 38 now sees why Pound inserted it there. It would have helped if he had given a hint in the poem as well as over the air. For this and other reasons the June 19th broadcast comes close to being the one which is most illuminating in terms of his idealistic purpose.

This summary brings us to the end of the prose sources which may legitimately be cited in explaining Pound's support of Mussolini. How does the case compare with the record as far as we can determine it? Did Mussolini actually do what Pound claimed, and can we understand how the poet came to take him for an ideal?

Direct and complete answers to these questions are hard to come by. The records are not easily examined, nor can any reporting of Italian economic measures attain satisfactory accuracy as far as I can determine. Some judgments may be attempted. For instance, it is possible to suggest that Mussolini and Hitler were not necessarily quite the same pair of devils, that Mussolini really did attempt many political, social, and economic measures which might be praised if separated from some other things he did, assuming that separation is possible. In terms of Pound's ideal case, his dream of economic paradise, the picture has a number of flaws. The flaws do not invalidate Pound's dream, but they do little for our judgment of his perception in connecting it with Italy and Germany. It would be simpler to say that all nations are combinations of good and evil accomplishments. It is human to concentrate on the good in our own nation and the evil in our enemies. Ranting against the Rothschilds and their like may have possible point; the violent castigation of Jews in general is unforgivable. How much his vital errors affect the ideal economic vision of Pound is a matter for every individual reader to judge for himself. Let us examine as many facts as we can find, reserving absolute judgment for some intensive reporting on what happened under Mussolini.

First, note that the essentials of Fascist doctrine have been based upon the idea that the individual exists for society, not society for the individual. Economic freedom is a matter of state health and must not conflict with the interests of the social group as a whole. Uncontrolled individual competition and lack of national planning cause depressions. Therefore the structure of the state, which means its elective regulatory bodies, must be based upon economic divisions rather than population or geographic locations. The Fascists in Italy organized the so-called Corporate State to implement these principles.

The following facts are in all the records. In 1926 there was established a National Council of Corporations which theoretically became the regulatory body for the Italian economy. It had thirteen national confederations, six representing employers, six labor, and one for professional men and artists. The six divisions were Industry, Agriculture, Commerce, Land Transportation and Internal Navigation, Credit and Insurance, and Maritime and Air Transportation. These divisions constituted "syndicates" or "guilds," and the opposite approach to the communistic one was established: collaboration within each confederation in the interest of the whole nation. Management and labor were eventually concentrated in the same guild, not in deadly competition with each other, and the state expected to enforce their working together—no strikes, no class struggle. The Charter of Labor, Declaration IX, says that the state will intervene only when private initiative fails or becomes antagonistic to the interests of society. "Such intervention may take the form of encouragement, regulation, or direct management."[14]

How well this system worked is not really clear. More power was gradually given to the Corporate structure. In 1928 the system of political representation was changed to an occupational basis. In 1930 a supreme economic council was established to direct the economic life of the nation. In 1934 twenty-two boards of economic control, each concerned with a separate corporation, were given advisory functions in order to aid needed reforms and help speed up the economy in the face of world depression and the rising storm which was growing over Ethiopia. After the League of Nations voted economic sanctions against trade with Italy, it was simple for Mussolini to retaliate by attempting complete economic independence, what Odon Por would call *autarchy*. The nation, perforce, assumed more and more direct power over all parts of the economy, establishing controls and dictation of production and consumption.

How much did this policy aid in creating better social conditions? Was business better off? Were the workers more prosperous? Some authorities say yes, some say no. Part of the system worked, and the condition of Italy could always be compared favorably to what it was before the Fascists came to power in 1922. Italy was one of the first nations to put into its economy a great number of social security and welfare state measures. The Charter of Labor says that wages must provide a "fair standard of living." If wages are below subsistence or reasonable comfort, the state steps in and corrects the inequity. Naturally this is fine in theory. The records show continued unemployment. But the employed were forced by law to carry accident, sickness, old-age, tuberculosis, and unemployment insurance. Some parts of the economy were definitely encouraged. If other things, like the war and power politics, had not intervened, or we can say that if Mussolini's entire attention had been devoted to economic and social matters alone, maybe the picture would be bright.

If you interpret what happened according to the rosiest of intentions, Pound's analysis is not all distortion of fact. Less helpful is the story of how Mussolini financed all his government-instituted measures, his pump-priming, his encouragement of industry, and eventually the building of his military machine. When the Fascist regime was first established, it attempted to carry out some of its revolutionary reform proposals. De Stefani, the original Finance Minister, tried to regulate banks and credit issue, and also attempted to stop stock speculation. He was forced out of office, and Mussolini appointed a representative of big banking, Count Volpi, Pound's usurious class, to succeed De Stefani. This man was an efficient and typical banker who seems to have supported a liberal credit policy to the right people like any capitalistic system. Mussolini himself stepped in after a crisis in 1926 and ordered the economy stabilized. This included rigid economy in government budgets, setting Italy on the same road urged by orthodox economists in all non-Communist countries.

Loans had to be recalled, and banking issuance of credit was put in the Bank of Italy, the only bank which was permitted to issue paper money. The procedure resembles England's centralization of monetary management in the Bank of England, and the only difference would be in a question of who owned the Bank. There is no evidence that Italy owned its bank either. Despite Pound's stories about Mussolini's control of the forces of special privilege, the Bank apparently operated as any large bank of discount operated elsewhere, for its own profit, not the nation's. Mussolini had more direct say about how much credit should be thrown into business, a kind of control that the United States does not have directly under the Federal Reserve Act. At any rate Mussolini's policy was hailed internationally as establishing the soundness of Italy's credit with the rest of the world, and it coincidentally resulted in starting the depression in Italy before it happened elsewhere in 1926. Mussolini had power to survive his first serious economic troubles, and he immediately learned to pump-prime the economy, just as many other nations eventually did, just as the American New Deal did. By 1929 things were a little better in Italy, just when they were suddenly beginning to get very black in the rest of the world.

One thing can be said. Pump-priming is easier when you have a dictatorship. Measures do not have to pass legislative bodies. Deficit financing is also easier; you just order the National Bank to print the needed money or supply the credit and put the debt on the books. You also control wages and prices if inflation rears its traditional head. Whatever loans the government wanted were ordered, and the Bank complied. The banking interests received interest on their government loans, the procedure Pound always attacks.

There was also a private national bank for lending to business, called the *Instituto Mobilaire Italiano,* which could lend on bonds up to ten times its capital and in practice supply whatever business needed, something like the Federal Reserve System in America. For large-scale national investment and development there was formed in 1933 the *Instituto di Ricostruzione Industriale* to handle long-term loans which were backed through bonds guaranteed by government decree, but which also guaranteed the interest to private ownership. This measure resembles the Reconstruction Finance Corporation established later in the United States, except that the government here got the advantage of the interest and did most of its business on a kind of cooperative basis. Government spending helped beat the depression in Italy, but the whole program seems to have been financed exactly as the United States financed its own pump-priming, by the unbalanced budget, deficit borrowing, and spending from the credit created on the books of the private bankers. The national debt rose spectacularly, as did taxes, and regulation of private business and individual initiative increased in proportion. Mussolini, like Hitler, gradually discovered unlimited national credit, and the question of meeting the huge debt he contracted could always be deferred to later generations. If you consider that the book figures were meaningless and ignore the mounting problems of interest, Mussolini's fiscal policies meet some of the Social Credit program, but it is hard to ignore the central foundation of the theory which Pound consistently mentions in discussing the failings of other nations like England and the United States.

Eventually the major part of Italian spending was devoted to military budgets. The campaigns in Ethiopia and Spain demanded a lot of money. Pound's concept of debt-free money and all his exaltation of the theories of Adams, Jefferson, Jackson, and Lincoln show little reference to what Mussolini did in this area. Perhaps this is the reason Pound keeps saying that Mussolini *intended* to do many positive things, either put in debt-free financing or attempt the stamp-scrip of Gesell. We recall that Pound says Mussolini died before what he intended could come into being. But Mussolini had been in power from 1922 on; most of us think that he had time for what he wanted to do badly enough. "The enormous tragedy of the dream," Pound said.

Technically Italy remained on the gold standard, the economic base for money which Pound consistently attacked. Probably the reason was that Mussolini needed foreign credit in financing his program; his printed money was good only inside Italy. Through the twenties Italy was always in difficulty with the difference between her imports and exports, the balance being consistently against Italy. This condition causes gold to flow out of the country when national accounts are settled yearly. Accordingly Mussolini took over all foreign trade. Imports could only be made by government authority; there was no export or import of money, the Italian *lira* being the unit; all gold owned by individuals was called in. This also eventually happened in the United States, which like Italy lowered the backing of its currency. Mussolini reduced gold backing of the lira by 40 per cent after the Ethiopian campaign. This decision was his only gesture in the direction of debt-free money, for the decreased backing added more currency to the government's assets, the only money Mussolini seems not to have borrowed from private banks. He also increased taxation severely after June 30, 1936, forced the buying of government bonds from workers, decreed that Italians must sell all foreign securities, and used the called-in gold to keep the international exchange satisfied with Italy's credit position. All this was practical, considering the circumstances, but it has no resemblance to Pound's Social Credit principles.

We still need more years for a proper perspective on Mussolini's economic accomplishments. The Italian authorities since the war interpret him in violently contradictory fashion according to their political prejudices. The viewpoint of international labor is generally antagonistic. If one investigates a few samples, George Seldes usually turns up. An American labor analyst, Seldes wrote a muckraking book about Mussolini called *Sawdust Caesar*. He also published a furious attack on Italian economic aims in *Facts and Fascism*, 1943. There is a certain Gaetano Salvemini, who wrote *The Fascist Dictatorship*, a study which makes a detailed comparison between American big business and Mussolini's program. Both Hitler and Mussolini are charged with making deals with the biggest businessmen, particularly with Fritz Thyssen and the Farbeinindustrie, prime examples of the cartels Pound attacks. The deals were for control of government contracts, war business, money expansion, and credit manipulation to the advantage of the big bankers. Pound insists that these "big boys" never controlled Mussolini, but one wonders if he made necessary concessions. In the early days he abolished taxes on inheritances, a social measure which had been intended to contract large fortunes. The much-discussed assassination of Matteotti, the Socialist leader, came after Matteotti had denounced in the Italian Parliament a law which would have given a monopoly in Italian oil to the Sinclair firm. Pound never, so far as I can discover, mentions Matteotti. Seldes sums his case up: "The significant facts to hang on to are these: if you were an early Fascist, or contributed generously to the March on Rome, you are likely to enjoy the business benefits that accrue to a high position within the Fascist Party."[15]

The Luce magazines, *Fortune, Life,* and *Time,* generally supported Mussolini before World War II, and the normal attitude of American conservative business was pro-Mussolini in the thirties. *Fortune* even printed, in its July 1934 issue, an enthusiastic account of the prosperity of the great Italian corporations under Mussolini. If you wanted sure returns for your money, put it in an Italian corporation. General Motors, Du Pont, Ford, and many American firms stretched their operations to Germany and Italy. The great sentimental business propagandist, Bruce Barton, consistently praised Mussolini for recreating "the sense of national obligation in the soul of Italy." Seldes comes to an interesting conclusion. He charges that Hitler and Mussolini ruined most businessmen, but the upper thousand profited tremendously. How about the bankers?

The Morgans were certainly involved in some of Mussolini's financial ventures. The largest loan to Italy was $100,000,000. The "Jewish" banker, Clarence Dillon, of New York's Dillon, Read and Company, helped finance Thyssen and also issued loans to Italian Fascist cities. Details and figures are sometimes hard to locate, particularly after the war broke out.

The conclusion must be that there are two sides to the coin. William G. Welk, in a Harvard economic study of Fascism, says:

> Disregarding such benefits as are implied in extended social insurance and the social welfare activities of the regime, our general conclusion about the condition of

> Italian labor under Fascism as measured by prevailing wage and employment conditions must be that on the whole it has not only failed of improvement but has been made worse—certainly in agriculture and most probably in industry.[16]

This conclusion may be conservative or distorted, but judgment must remain in doubt. Some of the signs of the slave state are apparent; not all the slaves suffered. Surely there were some benefits, as Pound and Por insist. The stated economic aims of Mussolini sound like those of a man sincerely devoted to social progress, but he was a politician and you must select your evidence with care, as Pound did. There was undoubted advance in the realm of social security and job insurance. Wherever he got the money, Mussolini devoted some of it to public works and social improvement, a record not consistently duplicated by Hitler in Germany. Unlike some of the Nazi leaders, he did not pile up a personal fortune to be carefully deposited in a Swiss bank in a numbered account.

Even though the picture is a mixed one, I suggest that the facts do not bear out the major contentions advanced by Pound. Considering Mussolini's alliances with big banking and certain kinds of big business, why was he superior to Franklin D. Roosevelt in improving economic conditions? Pound equates Roosevelt, not Mussolini, with the kind of big business called special privilege, with the usurers. This surprises many Americans who are naturally confused about Pound's ideals. Roosevelt's record was eventually on the side of establishing many of the same measures Pound praises. The ideal and the dream must be a long way ahead of what happened. The ideal also has to contend with all the ignored offensive characteristics of the Fascist state.

Yet *The Cantos* were intended to represent the case for economic paradise. They stand for a carefully constructed historical illusion, even a remarkable dream. Pound's attempt to interpret his dream in terms of current history led him on to tragedy. How poignant is the record of the Pisan Cantos! He had fallen back into his idea of Hell! " 'I am noman, my name is noman' " (74/4). His only possible comfort through the long years in St. Elizabeths Hospital must have been that he still thought the dream was defendable. Whatever was unreal could always be referred to what he thought should be. Like the ideal but mythical city of Dioce, it was "now in the mind indestructible" (74/8). Vision, or illusion?

8 THE TRAGIC FLAW

a man on whom the sun has gone down . . . . (74/8)

As a lone ant from a broken ant-hill
from the wreckage of Europe, ego scriptor. (76/36)

The enigma of Ezra Pound is a geunine one. The man is a poet of great stature. To say he commands words but not ideas is an insufficient judgment. *The Cantos* cannot be dismissed because they are not completely acceptable in a political or economic context. There is too much extraordinary erudition, too much real poetic grandeur, too much far-reaching vision to allow rejection of his noblest intentions. Yet the vision does not always fix itself upon identifiable horizons. Nor is it competely satisfactory to label him an idealist and let it go at that. Idealism is a form of maladjustment to the real world. Many idealists have been able to estimate the past and future with perception; the present baffles them.

The form and structure of *The Cantos* complicate the enigma. The epic is a great mosaic, composed of variable fragments. Perhaps in some imaginary world T. S. Eliot before he died might have performed for Pound the service Pound did for Eliot in looking at the manuscript of *The Waste Land.* As it stands now, with all its proliferation, the critic can select certain fragments and prove almost anything he likes about the poem. Ideograms even change in appeal and conviction within each Canto, ringing all the changes on literary background, but shifting abnormally in their power of suggestion or stimulus. Pound's extremes are most noticeable in the development of his economic theme, and his interpretation of the conflicts of history is no exception to this rule. If you repeat, in or out of context, what he appears to be saying, separate the excerpt from the rest of the pattern of the accompanying ideograms, you may find an appalling exaggeration which repels you. Closer examination and comparison may moderate your reaction, even if you never accept the exaggeration.

We must take into account the fact that Pound's economic opinions are all deliberately stated in an extreme form in order to startle and surprise the reader. This artistic technique is related to the manner of great satire, Rabelaisian hyperbole, the Swiftian excess of dissent, the cynical exaggeration of a Voltaire. The reader who enjoys satire does not expect to join Gulliver in living with the horses in real life, nor will he shiver in the lettuce while Gargantua prepares a salad. Pound has been so busy making himself a modern Homer that he has usually neglected to mention his relationship to Voltaire, the kind of observer who views the awfulness of his world and presents it through slanted spectacles which never reflect the ordinary, the half-good, or the tolerant. If this technique, transferred to poetry, is ever effective, it results in your being made angry enough to debate the issues. If any of the implications stand up to the light of reason, emphasized in some degree by planned distortion, you may return to the original poem with a feeling of respect which you cannot completely defend or clearly explain. If you grudgingly conclude that some of it is convincing, you may be willing to accept the method while you reject the absolute satiric hyperbole, the frenetic overstatement, the occasionally brilliant excess which is stated obliquely. "'I cannot possibly believe this," you say, and then examine it again to see whether there is some important element of truth mixed in. The technique is forceful and infuriating. So is Pound.

For example, look at Pound's extreme statements about the Jews. For any man of good will they include indefensible and hysterical components. Only the ignorant or the psychotic can hold that racial or religious characteristics are exclusive. Pound is not ignorant, and his art denies the refuge of irresponsible psychosis. If he is merely using the worst examples of Jewish Usury to illustrate his diagnosis of economic malpractice, he is in a distinguished tradition. Shakespeare produced an extreme portrait of the Jewish moneylender in Shylock; Marlowe gave us the impossible Jew of Malta; Dickens selected the nauseatingly comic Fagin.

But Pound's position is not exactly the same as that of these authors. His attacks on the Jews are all related to their part in the economic hell he hates.[1] Several of the most extreme examples of everything he dislikes are furnished by Jews. He never says that only the Jews are usurious. Other creeds, races, or nations supply the Hamiltons, the Biddles, the Morgans, the Patersons, the Churchills, the evil kings and rulers of China, Italy, Europe—anyone can collect an imposing list, whether or not one agrees with Pound's estimates. But of them all Pound is most infuriated by the Rothschilds. The Rothschilds are obviously Jews.

There is a sense in which the Rothschild story attracts admiration rather than fury. In a world dominated by the Adam Smith doctrine of laissez-faire competition, this family added to an exceptional business sense of acquisitive accomplishment the knowledge and practice of international banking manipulations. They were spectacular operators, and if they were pirates, their piracies can be considered relative; that is, they contended with others like them and were more able in their progress to extreme wealth and power. Most biographies or accounts of the Rothschilds are respectful or laudatory, and their march to fortune is considered to be a kind of noble adventure story where the hero makes good because he makes money on a grand scale. If their procedure is ever ethically doubtful, one can always say that the Rothschilds merely beat other businessmen at their own game. Like other men of great wealth they have occasionally been charitable; their money was a major factor in establishing the modern state of Israel.

Old Mayer Amschel, the founder of the dynasty, lived in Frankfort from 1774 to 1812. He started in a second-hand shop on Jew Street in the restricted ghetto. The local prince was William of Hesse-Hanau, a financial wizard who sold Europe everything from spare cash to hired soldiers (the "Hessians"). Mayer gradually became the main business agent for this very wealthy lord, used his connections and credit to establish an enterprise which grew larger and larger, eventually turned it all into the banking or loan business, then stretched it to the other capitals of Europe, sending out his five remarkable sons to form an international cartel with tentacles that reached everywhere. The operation required tremendous ability and capacity. "Meyer Anselm, a rrromance, yes, yes certainly/ but more fool you if you fall for it two centuries later" (74/17). This is Pound's comment in the first of the Pisan Cantos.

The five sons were Amschel, who stayed mostly with his father and eventually was treasurer of the German Confederation of States; Salomon, who rose to be the most powerful man in Vienna, the Titan who worked hand in glove with the tricky Prime Minister Metternich; Nathan, who became the wealthiest financier in London, perhaps the most powerful banker in the world; Kalmann, who took Italy for his territory; and Jacob, who started young in Paris and ended managing the finances of the French Republic and Empire. The confederation worked amazingly. Since the Rothschilds owned their bank entirely, they manipulated credit without red tape or consultation with boards of directors. They generally bought whatever needed more capital. They usually outbid other banks for the floating of important loans. They often forced the stock market up or down, as the situation demanded for their own profit. Any differences in exchange values of currencies between nations were exploited to their own advantage. Their communication system was as complicated and efficient as any modern intelligence organization of spies and secret agents. In time of war they played every end against the middle. The story of Nathan's coup on the stock exchange after the Battle of Waterloo is typical. He had early secret information (by carrier pigeons?) that the British had won, but few people really expected the victory. The first news indicated that the Allies would probably lose. Nathan sold consols and other stocks in great quantities, dumping his holdings on the exchange. Everyone panicked and sold too. He forced prices down to the lowest depths, then suddenly, just before the news of the great victory broke, he bought everything in sight. Values rose to startling heights immediately. How many hundreds of millions did he make? Any guess is good since the Rothschild Bank never published a financial statement. All we know is rumors like the one which estimates that any new Rothschild baby is worth approximately $150,000,000 at birth. There have been a lot of Rothschild babies. Surely this is the wealthiest family the world has ever seen, at least if you measure wealth by banking credit.

One of the late books about the Rothschilds, a best-seller by Frederic Morton, begins with an interesting conclusion: "For the last 150 years the history of the House of Rothschild has been to an amazing extent the backstage history of Western Europe."[2] The Rothschilds have been given titles, have entertained kings and queens (Edward VIII fled from publicity after his abdication to a Rothschild castle), have dealt honestly and profitably with prime ministers and state treasurers, have bought the most magnificent chateaus, castles, and manor houses in Europe, and have accumulated railroads, mines, and shares in every kind of business which needed capital and borrowed it from the Rothschilds. Pound thinks of them as the prime villains in his case against private banks of discount. If you accept any part of his thesis, they look like the biggest of usurers. They were Jews.

There are three important instances of extraordinary Rothschild manipulation which he quotes as prime examples of Usury. These three examples present simple problems in ethical practice. The first concerns the manner in which Pound charges that Napoleon was defeated, and he associates this story with the modern Jew, a Rothschild representative, who says that it would take less than twenty years to crush Mussolini ("We got Napoleon; we'll get Mussolini too!"): "gold through France into Spain" (86/24); "Sodom on Thames sold out Napoleon" (105/99).

The facts referred to appear to be that the Duke of Wellington, fighting the Peninsular Campaign in Spain against Napoleon, had to be financed when communications were hazardous. The British had trouble getting supplies or money to him. Nathan in London managed to corner the available gold (£800,000 from the East India Company) and then sold it at a handsome profit to the government, undertaking to get it to Wellington. In Paris, Jacob, now called James, talked the French into letting Nathan transfer the gold to France (as if it were still Rothschild gold), suggesting that taking gold out of England might embarrass British finances. Thereafter James smuggled it all, or the equivalent, over the French border through French territory to the British Army, a complicated maneuver which contributed mightily to Napoleon's eventual defeat, since it saved Wellington to fight again. In fact, whenever England needed to transfer money to her allies, Austria, Russia, and Prussia, she did it through the Rothschild branches, depositing gold in London to be drawn upon in Vienna or Frankfort. Napoleon did likewise. Anyone can see that this was the perfect international banking cartel, a business which operated completely for its own advantage in time of war, with no necessary patriotic ties to the country in which it happened to be.

The second instance concerns the British purchase of the Suez Canal. This occurred during the period when Disraeli was Prime Minister, and the purchase was considered by Englishmen to be a great boon to English finance and commerce. Pound asks abrasively if anyone knows how much the purchase cost and what was paid to whom. He always looks at Disraeli through jaundiced eyes, since the Jewish Prime Minister was a great friend of Baron Lionel, the son of Nathan Rothschild. Note that in contrast Pound's source, Christopher Hollis, considers Disraeli to be on the side of the angels.[3] Disraeli was at the Rothschild mansion eating dinner when Lionel, at a psychological moment, received news from his private grapevine to France that the shares controlling the Suez were available in Paris. Why they were available is not usually explained, since the Rothschilds had some dealings with the Egyptian Khedive too. Parliament was not in session, so Disraeli made a deal with the Rothschild international credit service to transfer the necessary 4 million pounds to the Khedive's accounts. Three per cent interest is all that appears on the records for the service. What else the British government paid, or how much the Khedive contributed, can hardly be traced in the history books.

question? England not yet sold for the Suez—
That would have been 20 years later,
or was it '74?
At any rate, sold down the river,
passed over Parliament,
"whatever else he believed in,
it was not representative government"
Nor visible responsibilities. (86/24)

In Canto 89/59 Pound repeats that Disraeli sold the Brit fools down the river. In Canto 104/90 he says Disraeli bitched England and by-passed Parliament. The final reference is repetitive since it (108/118) charges Disraeli with "bitching" Cap. VI of the English Charter, presumably the one against Usury too. The charge is that England had no right to the Suez anyway, and that Disraeli bailed the Rothschilds out of an uncollectable debt owed by the Khedive. Whatever the extreme it is probable that the Rothschilds considered the deal to be to their material advantage. What the Bank of England could do, they could do better, because they were not confined to England.

What connections did the Rothschilds have with the United States? They invested vast quantities of money in the business expansion of the continent after the Civil War. (This investment is usually identified in the history books as "English money.") They maintained alliances with a number of bankers in New York. They also got to the ranch lands of Canada, the iron and coal mines of Vitkovitz in Czecho-Slovakia (the ones Hitler took from them as ransom), the railroads of Austria, the diamond mines of South Africa, almost everything in South America. But it is a shock to find Pound asserting that the United States were "sold" to the Rothschilds in 1863, even if much Rothschild money was invested in the expanding American economy.

> The whole history of the United States oscillates between these two camps [Usury and the Good of the People]. The people rebelled against London usurers and instituted a government in America. This government fell prey to the resident usurers who kept in touch with the arch-usurers in the mother-country. Belmont used to represent the Rothschild, etc. Today the Main Office is in New York, the Branch Office is in London.[4]

What happened to fix the year 1863 in Pound's mind? This is his third instance. Specifically it was the National Bank Act. The North was in need of money to pay for the conduct of the War. The government wanted to ask private banks to take a large amount of bonds; there was no chartered national bank from which to borrow. Under the Constitution the Treasury could theoretically have printed the money needed (as it could have in the twentieth-century world wars) as it did the greenbacks. The Bank Act proposed to pay interest (6 per cent) to the subscribers, but an additional lure was to permit the bank which deposited its bonds with the government to issue money up to 90 per cent of the face value of the same bonds. On this money they could also collect 6 per cent or more by lending it. Even if the bookkeeping details are hazy, one can deduce that banks could easily collect interest at least twice on the same investment. Many Wall Street fortunes date back to the privileges made legal by this Act. Who thought it up? Lincoln opposed it, but signed it under the pressures of war.

The historians have usally called this Act of 1863 progressive. The law provided charters and regulations, required minimum reserves against deposits and the issue of notes. It stabilized banking practices. It also permitted banks to make a lot of money in legal interest rates. In Canto 46 Pound says:

> Semi-private inducement
> Said Mr RothSchild, hell knows which Roth-schild
> 1861, '64 or there sometime, "Very few people
> "will understand this. Those who do will be occupied
> "getting profits. The general public will probably not
> "see it's against their interest." (46/27)

Pound amplified this statement in his second Money Pamphlet, *Gold and Work,* dating the letter 25 June, 1863, and noting that it was from Senator John Sherman of Ohio (not a Rothschild), later Secretary of the Treasury, written to a New York bank, agents of the Rothschilds, called Ikleheimer, Morton & Van der Gould. Canto 40 had said that the "Belmont" firm represented the Rothschilds at this time. Pound implies that the Rothschilds can be credited with conjuring up the National Bank Act as well as suggesting the device which devaluated the greenbacks.

Canto 48 adds another bit of argument:

> . . . Bismarck
> blamed american civil war on the jews;
> particularly on the Rothschild
> one of whom remarked to Disraeli
> that nations were fools to pay rent for their credit . . . . (48/34-35)

There is little point in carrying the issue farther. Pound's argument is excessive. He used evidence which meant something and said it meant everything. Any of us can say that the causes of the Civil War were various, slavery remaining paramount. The economic difficulties which had root in the debts of the South, owed to Northern financial firms, may have contributed to the tensions leading to strife. How much money was supplied by the Rothschild agents, whether they thought up the National Bank Act or the devaluation of the greenbacks, can hardly be told for certain now. Many private firms made money out of the Civil War; the Rothschilds presumably got a large share. We can easily see that Pound's position is extreme. But it is not manufactured out of thin air.

If we concede any part of Pound's case against the arch-usurers, can we understand his transference of it to Jews in general? "Poor yitts paying for [the Rothschilds?]/paying for a few big jews' vendetta on goyim" (52/3). The 52nd Canto begins the series on Chinese history, and its prelude contains Pound's most violent diatribe on Jewish Usury. The five censored lines[5] must have been more offensive than usual. If they had been printed, would the Rothschilds have sued? Surely they would not have bothered. The poetry could have been offensive for its four-letter words, but Pound must have known words like *coprophilia*. It is this prelude which includes a quotation from Benjamin Franklin about the Jews:

> Remarked Ben: better keep out the jews
> or yr/ grand children will curse you
> jews, real jews, chazims, and *neschek*
> also super-neschek or the international racket
> ________________________________
> __________________________
> _____________________________
> _______________________________
> ____________________________
> (52/3)

It has been charged that the first part of this quotation is pure invention, although it was consistently repeated by the anti-Semites and found its place in the Nazi propaganda which attempted to justify the annihilation of the German Jews. Theodore Fritsch, in his *Handbuch der Judenfrage,* says that Franklin made this statement at the Constitutional Convention, arguing for the exclusion of the Jews from the United States in our Constitution. The evidence is supposed to be in a diary kept by Pinckney recording his part in the Convention. Search of all American historical materials reveals no diary or any other evidence that Franklin made any such statement or had such views.[6]

The exaggerated satiric posture is on shaky legs when it derives from an unexaggerated fact which is inaccurate or nonexistent. No Pound critic can justify his extremes by the reduction of his subjective correlatives. Plainly speaking, you cannot assume that a small part of what he violently expands or overemphasizes is necessarily convincing or even true. It sometimes is, but he made some inexplicable falsifications in exaggeration.

For example there is the really puzzling case of Pound versus Franklin Delano Roosevelt. If we refer his rejection of Roosevelt's position in American history to the "repeat in history" theme, if we assume that Roosevelt is representative of Pound's belief that America degenerated after the Civil War, letting the special interests take over development and management of the economy and our culture, then Roosevelt becomes the lowest point on the curve, below the line of presidents who started with Grant, fell farther with Cleveland, Harrison, and McKinley, got nowhere with Theodore Roosevelt, Taft, and Wilson, reached the depths with Harding, Coolidge, and Hoover, then struck the absolute bottom with F.D.R.[7] This position, on Pound's own terms, is a misconception of the New Deal and all the liberal acts which have been associated with the Rooseveltian image. It was the usurers (to use Pound's language) who fought Roosevelt, and this circumstance ought to put Pound on Roosevelt's side at least a part of the time. It is possible to say that Pound thought Roosevelt did not go far enough in economic reform, but the student of history must be somewhat mystified to find Pound consistently attacking the man who was more for his ideals than against them. American opposition to Roosevelt politically has been allied with the conservative Hamiltonian position, and Pound found himself with strange bedfellows as he, like big business, castigated the New Deal. It is at the least a confusing position, needing explanation.

Apparently Pound's reaction against Roosevelt began with his feeling that the depression illuminated his general economic interpretation of history. Usury had exploited the country up to the twenties, and after 1929 we had reached disaster. Surely this was a remarkable opportunity to make a complete economic change in the American system. What Jefferson, Adams, and Jackson had wanted could be done now. Pound from afar watched the 1932 campaign and read accounts of election speeches, all of them representing a conservative position. Roosevelt was very firm about his plans to balance the budget. After the election came the day when the banks all closed. Pound said to himself, "What an opportunity!" The government could take control of its money, escape from the Federal Reserve System, issue enough new currency to get the economy moving again, and start a new world. But instead Roosevelt reestablished and tried to improve the old ways. He put in voluntary NRA, began some simple unimaginative pump-priming with deficit financing, borrowed more money from the banks, and generally showed little awareness of his theoretical opportunity.

Compared with Mussolini, Roosevelt looked weak to Pound. In *Jefferson and/or Mussolini* he explains this comparison:

> DISTINGUISH between fascism which is organization, with the organizer at its head, to whom the power has not been GIVEN, but who has organized the power, and the state of America, where the Press howls that we should GIVE power to Roosevelt, i.e., to a weak man, or a man generally supposed to be weak, a man who has shown NO UNDERSTANDING whatsoever, and no knowledge whatsoever of contemporary actuality.[8]

By "contemporary actuality" Pound means modern economic opportunity for the state to take over and guarantee prosperity.

He is overemphasizing his belief that some sensible move might have been made to change the old system, if Roosevelt had really understood economic theory and had known how to free downtrodden starving or poverty-stricken millions of Americans from the clutches of special privilege. Pound ignores the fact that some of the special privilege class were in trouble too, but his opinion is that Roosevelt made a few gestures because he had to, began social reforms which were forced on him, played politics, but generally moved nowhere except by accident. For example there was the Federal Reserve System. It had failed up to 1933. Would not a great president have wiped it out, as Jackson did, but have gone further to put the government completely in control of the issue of its own money and credit, and generally begun the establishment of the kind of democracy our founding fathers had stood for? Jefferson, Jackson, and Lincoln had not been able to do this either, but Pound seems to have expected it from Roosevelt.

It should be remembered that Pound's estimate of American history makes much of the fight made by the early American presidents against the National Banks. According to this view, the first and second banks lost out to the forces of social good. Although the Independent Treasury Act theoretically gave the government control of its own credit, private banks after the Civil War had appropriated the privileges of the original national banks. The 1863 Act had allowed banks to issue money if they bought government securities. From the death of Lincoln to the administration of Woodrow Wilson the great banking combinations had seized more and more power, particularly Morgan. The revolt against special privilege in controlling money was especially strong in the Middle West, where a number of Populist leaders grew up with ideas about social protection, Bryan at first, then independents like Norris, LaFollette, Lindberg (Senior), Brookhart, and many others who preached the doctrines of money reform. This mounting tide of opinion, according to Pound's view, forced a compromise like the Federal Reserve System, inaugurated after 1913 and the Pujo Congressional Investigation of the Morgan interests and banking practices in opposition to the public interest.

The Federal Reserve System was a good idea, said many people, conservatives, liberals, even radicals. Most Americans still say so. But not Pound. In effect it was the third formal attempt at a national bank, with private bankers being given the uses of public money and credit. It regulated private control, outlawed wildcat banks, but none of its positive features outweighed Pound's feelings that it was the monster Jefferson fought against and Jackson defeated. Did Roosevelt fight against it? The answer seems to be that he thought he did, and that he went as far as his Congress would go in improving the system. Pound quotes Jefferson consistently, and perhaps he might have recalled the occasion when Jefferson suggested that no reform can proceed much faster than public understanding will support. Pound is sure that public understanding is too slow. Our greatest fault as a nation is: "Ignorance of coin, credit, and circulation"!

To see Pound's point at all we should be aware of the outlines of the argument. The Federal Reserve Act of 1913 was intended to create a stable banking system with power over the creation and regulation of the nation's money and credit. Woodrow Wilson's idea was that it would assist the proper needs of the national economy, taking such operations away from the Money Trust, expanding money nationally when it was needed, contracting the supply when prices began to rise because there was too much money in circulation. Wilson explained his position thus:

> The great monopoly in this country is the money monopoly. So long as that exists, our old variety of freedom and individual energy of development are out of the question. A great industrial nation is controlled by its system of credit. Our system of credit is concentrated. The growth of the nation, therefore, and all our activities are in the hands of a few men, who, even if their actions are honest and intended for the public interest, are necessarily concentrated upon the great undertakings in which their own money is involved and who, necessarily, by every reason of their own limitations, chill and check and destroy genuine economic freedom. This is the greatest question of all; and to this, statesmen must address themselves with an earnest determination to serve the long future and the true liberties of men.[9]

It might have been Pound speaking.

The technical organization of the Federal Reserve System set up reserve banks in twelve regions of the nation, each of these twelve "banks" becoming a corporation created by Congress. The U.S. government owns no part of the banks, which are euphemistically called "Federal" or "National." The President appoints a seven-man Board of Governors, but there is no other formal connection between the government and the banks. The relationship is therefore supposed to be cooperative and benevolent, and this relationship is one of the points at issue. The Governors are, for example, paid by the Banks and are responsible only to the financial agencies (specifically the six thousand banks in the System) which are private, not public. Congress has no check on what they do.[10]

It is difficult for the public at large to understand exactly how the Federal Reserve System contracts or expands the economy. But it does theoretically control how much money and credit is in national circulation, nobody apparently being absolutely sure how exact the control is. It has power to vary the ratio of cash reserves to demand deposits, to raise or lower the rediscount rate (these measures supply more or less money or credit for loans), to purchase government bonds to expand credit generally, to sell them in the open market to contract credit, and to issue money directly. Incidentally, these powers do not seem to be in doubt, no matter who is describing the system. The control of the nation's economy is, to an important degree, in the hands of the Governors, who are responsible to the banks, not to the Congress or to the Executive or to the people.

Pound implies that the System sometimes has worked in opposition to the health and prosperity of the nation. Loans have been expanded when there was already too much money in circulation on a national basis; money has been contracted (particulraly following 1929) when it was desperately needed by the economy. He cites what he thinks is the most flagrant example of the Federal Reserve Board acting in opposition to the needs of the country immediately after World War I. The Chairman was W. P. G. Harding (not the President of the United States), a man who believed that inflation should be controlled by severe measures and national business forced back to the normal level after all the wild expansion of the war. His statement was: "The fact must be recognized that, however desirable on general principles continuous expansion of trade and industry may be, such developments must accommodate themselves to the actual supply of capital and credit available."[11]

What the Board did was make sure the actual supply was low. It raised the rediscount rate sharply so that outstanding loans had to be called all over the country. Interest on loans was jumped to 7 per cent. This deflated the economy in a hurry, and many commentators believe the Board was directly responsible for the depression of 1920. The farmers of the Midwest were hit particularly. This temporary depression was lightened by the following extreme relaxation of credit which encouraged the great speculative boom of the twenties. Pound says that the easiest way to ruin a country is to contract and expand its credit in rapid alternation.

There are other instances of Federal Reserve control which operated to the advantage of the bankers themselves, but certainly not to the country at large. There was no attempt on a national level to slow down the speculative extremes of the post-war period, some Federal Reserve Banks themselves joining in the orgy of stock-buying which forced prices to false heights. After the crash the surviving banks took about eight billion dollars out of circulation by foreclosing loans between 1929 and 1933.

Among all the problems faced by Roosevelt, this one was of first importance. He did what he often did, played both ends against the middle. He kept Morgenthau, a conservative Secretary of the Treasury, but he then appointed a liberal banker to be Chairman of the Federal Reserve Board, Marriner Eccles, a man who took the job on condition that the whole System be reformed, and whose economic philosophy was modelled on the theories of Keynes. These theories including priming the economy with subsidies and government-paid work programs, but they also assumed a kind of benevolent Hamiltonian philosophy: banks and businessmen can be depended upon in an emergency to work for the good of the nation. "Don't take control away from us; that would be radical and irresponsible. We'll show you we can use our power for the creation of better times." Many bankers thought Eccles was a traitor to his own profession, rejecting the humanitarian pose. Pound is not impressed with Eccles and calls him "a bank tout."[12]

Pound charges that the new Federal Reserve Bill sponsored by Roosevelt and Eccles was futile. But Eccles' philosophy resembles some of Pound's criticism, since Eccles aimed at effective government control of the entire economy. Pound bases his rejection on the same reasoning he used to attack Keynes. What Eccles said was:

> Over the years, practices had grown up inside the System which had reduced the Reserve Board in Washington to impotence. The System had originally been designed to represent a blend of private and public interest and of decentralized and centralized authorities, but this arrangement had become unbalanced. Private interests, acting through the Reserve Banks, had made the System an effective instrument by which private interests alone could be served. *The Board in Washington, on the other hand, which was supposed to represent and safeguard the public interest, was powerless to do so under the existing law and in the face of the opposition offered by the men who ran the Reserve Banks throughout the country* [my italics].[13]

Roosevelt and Eccles had a difficult time getting their bill through Congress. Senator Glass, who had engineered the original 1913 Bill, led the fight against the changes, and while Glass may be considered a liberal in comparison to Senator Byrd of later years (a little to the left of the Neanderthal Man), Glass also stood with the banking interests who fought violently as if their entire privilege were at stake. The struggle was hard enough that Roosevelt is reported to have thought he was repeating the battle waged a century before by Andrew Jackson. The Roosevelt-Eccles intention was to put the regulation of national monetary policy under effective government control. The details that mattered made three changes: (1) Power over open-market operations was given to the National Open Market Committee of the Federal Reserve Board in Washington. This made the supply of reserves and volume of money and credit subject to a national, not regional, credit policy. (2) Separate offices of chairman and governor of the Federal Reserve Boards were abolished. This made the Federal Reserve appointees the men who actually ran the banks and supposedly stopped local bankers from doing pretty much as they pleased in issuing credit. (3) "Eligible paper" used as backing for credit was changed to "sound assets," so that much more credit could be easily released if the national authority thought it necessary to promote distribution or ward off depression.

It is difficult for the average observer to see what all the smoke was about, or why these proposals were considered so radical. One begins to wonder if perhaps Pound was right. Eccles later said that he really wanted a completely unified banking system for the nation. Roosevelt never supported this extreme, nor did Truman. However Roosevelt backed other Eccles proposals, measures which most of the Brain Trust also suggested or supported, government spending through unemployment relief, public works, and the domestic allotment plan in agriculture. To get out of the depression, said Eccles, there must be "an increase of purchasing power on the part of all the people."[14] If the money had been supplied from debt-free sources, this would be Social Credit.

To many of the liberals Roosevelt seemed as conservative as he seemed extremely liberal to the conservatives. When Keynes made his visit to America and talked with Roosevelt about economic pump-priming, a great boost was given to the theories of putting more money into action. Keynes urged that private initiative be retained at all costs, but he also proposed to manage capitalism by some form of collective action, by a larger measure of public control over currency, credit, and investment. Private initiative running wild left too much to chance in time of severe crisis. In his conversation with Roosevelt Keynes pointed out that direction and regulation were always installed in time of war. Why not in an emergency in peace time? But Keynes found Roosevelt singularly lacking in theoretical perception. He said to Alvin Johnson, "I don't think your President Roosevelt knows anything about economics."[15]

Schlesinger records a final observation about Roosevelt's views on economic theory:

> "I brought down several books by English economists and leading American economists," he once told a press conference . . . . "I suppose I must have read different articles by fifteen different experts. Two things stand out: The first of them is that no two of them agree, and the other thing is that they are so foggy in what they say that it is almost impossible to figure out what they mean. It is jargon, absolute jargon." . . . Roosevelt dealt proficiently with practical questions of government finance, as he showed in his press conferences on the budget; but abstract theory left him cold.[16]

It is important to note that Pound examined the American scene in a continuous series of articles printed in *The New English Weekly,* beginning September, 1932, and continuing to June 6, 1940. Between 1933 and 1937 he wrote a great deal about how the New Deal was coming along. He often called it "The Nude Eel." During this period he said many things about Roosevelt, not all of them derogatory. There are moments when he makes critical remarks about Hitler, where he denies anti-Semitism, where he praises America for positive acts like the bill restricting holding companies, even to the point of saying that the choice of Roosevelt over Landon was a great victory for the forces of good in our country. He had some small hope that the United States would institute a "newer deal," that Roosevelt would come around to putting more money in circulation after he tried out measures which would be false or insufficient. Most of his references to reformers like Father Coughlin are complimentary, and he expresses the hope that the Coughlin radio talks would rouse American opinion to the point of supporting more effective control of Usury, bankers, and special privilege. He hoped the candidacy of Lemke's third party would make more headway than it did, and while he has some words of praise for Huey Long, he says that Long's "Share the Wealth" slogan reminded him of the man who cut up the cow to increase milk production.[17]

As the second World War loomed on the horizon, Pound's articles become more and more partisan and shrill. From saying that Hitler was owned by the great usurer Thyssen, that he was a pathetic hysteric,[18] he begins to change his perspective, finding great forward steps in Germany as well as Italy. He praises the Munich pact and Chamberlain, and he never falters in his support of Mussolini and Italian Fascism. Roosevelt's economic measures after 1936 do not receive any support from Pound's articles, and he gives every indication of having lost all hope for the New Deal by 1939. His extremes eventually embarrassed his old British friends and the magazine which had sponsored him for years.

In the last of the Pisan Cantos the poet reports his impression of Washington just before the outbreak of the second World War (he came back for a quick visit). One suspects a little *hubris* here. Roosevelt had no time to waste visiting with an eccentric American poet who had lived most of his life abroad and who was an apologist for Fascism. Pound was always treated respectfully by Mussolini.

> "an' doan you think he chop an' change all the time
> stubborn az a mule, sah, stubborn as a MULE,
> got th' eastern idea about money"
> Thus Senator Bankhead
> "am sure I don't know what a man like you
> would find to *do* here"
> said Senator Borah
> Thus the solons, in Washington,
> on the executive, and on the country, a.d. 1939 . . . . (84/115)

Pound had gone to see Senator Bankhead because he had written to him previously. Pound's correspondence with Americans interested in economic reform must have been widespread. Little of it has been made available to critics. Senator Bronson Cutting, the liberal from New Mexico, was the legislator most interested in the Douglas Social Credit theories, and Pound quotes him several times in *The Cantos* (86/28, 98/37, 102/80), particularly about the eleven literate Congressmen who alone knew anything about economics. The others are never named, although they probably include Senator Wheeler and Senator Key Pittman. Astonishingly enough they seem to include Senator Byrd. Cutting died early, and the liberals did not have much influence with Roosevelt. One may say that some of them supported peculiar interpretations of the new money policies, Bankhead once proposing a bill modelled on the Gesell stamp-scrip idea, but distorting it so much that it could not possibly have worked. Pound comments on this in his *Money Pamphlets:*

> Senator Bankhead proposed an emission of dollar-bills up to a limit of a milliard dollars (Bankhead-Pettingill Bill, 17 February, 1933), but the stamps were to be affixed at the insane rate of two cents per week, equal to an interest of 104 percent per annum. Incomprehension of the principle of the just price could not have been carried to absurder lengths.[19]

Bankhead did get a bill through Congress in 1937 which helped tenants and farm laborers become farm owners through government loans at low interest with long terms for repayment. This act took over some of the aims of the Resettlement Administration which, under Tugwell, had tried to put families back on the land, a measure which Odon Por had praised highly when Mussolini attempted it too.

The American economist who might reasonably have been hailed as an ally by Pound was Irving Fisher, the Yale professor whose ideas resemble those of Professor Frederick Soddy of Oxford, a Nobel Prize winner.[20] Fisher is in the tradition of American divergence from orthodoxy, perhaps the most brilliant of his school. His book *100% Money* urged dollar-for-dollar reserves in banks to cover demand deposits. The proposals of Soddy and Fisher are a little hard for the average person to understand, which may be the reason they have never been understood by many legislators either. Soddy's idea is that the government should issue newly printed money for what banks actually create and lend from their deposit credit. Banks would be given this money by the government and not permitted to lend on credit created out of nothing unless they had the cash in hand. But they *would* be encouraged to supply "necessary" credit. Then when anybody repaid his loan, the bank would send the principal back to the government, which would use it to pay off the national debt. Eventually after the debt was paid off, one could use this credit money in place of taxes to finance expenditures of the nation.

This is slick reasoning, economic sleight-of-hand. No one has really been able to say why this plan would not work, but it is so daring that nobody has tried it.

Roosevelt adopted only one of the basic Social Credit schemes, and this trial was more or less forced on him by the emergency he inherited on his inauguration. Fisher consistently urged devaluation of the gold backing of the dollar, or some other kind of monetary expansion to beat the depression. Roosevelt, after abrogating the gold standard and calling in all gold in the country, like Mussolini, finally decided to cooperate with the European nations, particularly France and Italy, which wanted a solid international gold standard. In 1934 he stabilized the dollar with a lower gold backing, 59.06 per cent of its original value. The devaluation is just like printing almost as many "greenbacks" as had been in circulation, the United States Treasury getting the advantage of the new money.

The Roosevelt story has other assets in the realm of social reform. Those who believe in some aspect of the welfare state can mention a host of measures: The T.V.A., the bill which curbed the formation of holding companies, social security acts of various kinds, all follow a pattern which Pound liked in the Italian system. Furthermore the forces opposed to Roosevelt were almost constantly the forces which Pound describes elsewhere as those of special privilege, reaction, and the old regime which he said had taken over the economic development of the country after the Civil War. The best explanation for Pound's censure of Roosevelt is that he believed the American President to be a reluctant and reactionary progressive, meaning a political hypocrite who had liberal measures forced upon him by circumstance and who did only what he felt would win votes and gain power and prestige. This is a difficult view to accept, although it is possible to say that it has some elements of truth if you also dislike Roosevelt. By the time of the outbreak of the war Pound had committed himself irrevocably to Italy, so that all his opposition to Roosevelt became hardened, vituperative, and generally unrestrained. The broadcasts attack Roosevelt blindly. Pound suggests that he is really working for the special interests while he pretends the opposite (December

7th), that Roosevelt's mental condition is questionable (January 29th), that he is a proficient political liar (February 26th), that he is a puppet of Frankfurter and should commit suicide (March 30th), that he ought to be committed to an asylum (April 9th), that he is a profiteer himself (May 3rd)—the record over the air is indeed a biased one. No part of his opposition to Roosevelt would have sounded good in a treason trial, and perhaps this is the reason why the references to the President in the Cantos written while Pound was in St. Elizabeths are more guarded. Only one is explicit: "The total dirt that was Roosevelt,/and the farce that was Churchill" (87/30). Pound is more likely to let his rhetoric go when he refers to Churchill, occasionally achieving grotesque humor:

> . . . looking at the sputtering tank of nicotine and
> stale whiskey
> (on its way out) . . . . (84/118)

There is a clear case for deciding that Pound interpreted Roosevelt inexactly. His attacks on the American President also obscure the ideals he has been emphasizing in *The Cantos.* Canto 100 begins with a last typical shot at something which emphasizes Pound's lack of logic where Roosevelt was concerned:

> "Has packed the Supreme Court
> so they will declare anything he does constitutional."
> Senator Wheeler, 1939. (100/65)

This criticism is peculiar since the possible packing of the Supreme Court was suggested because all liberal legislation passed by the New Dealers was being outlawed. Pound is supposed to be on the side of the liberal legislation, even if he is fixedly opposed to any usurpation of constitutional powers.

Anyone who examines the historical record of economic reform must be amazed at the number of times liberal proposals have suffered from the fanaticism of their sponsors. When Social Credit had its great opportunity in Alberta, Canada, whatever advance might have been possible was hampered because only small parts of the promised program were attempted. In the United States many reform suggestions were tied to outrageous interpretations, each of them being introduced to aid special parts of the electorate and to appeal to sectional interests. Bryan had set the standard for alternately wide and narrow vision. Later Tugwell was supposed to be the most progressive brain behind the councils of the New Deal. Tugwell talked a remarkable game: "Profits would have to be limited and their uses regulated, prices controlled, gains eliminated . . . . When industry is government and government is industry, the dual conflict in our modern institutions will be abated."[21] This comes close to orthodox socialism, and however we interpret Tugwell's record, it is sure that he rarely persuaded Roosevelt to do much to implement his radical program for a planned economy. There have even been people like Howard Scott, the technocrat who urged the substitution for money of scrip based on ergs and joules or some other measurement of energy.

The great popular orator of the early Rooseveltian days was Father Coughlin, the priest who roused radio attention and rabid following by trying to mix Christianity with the reform of capitalism and the curbing of banking privilege. Coughlin's rhetorical addresses managed to include support for a vast number of economic cures, including what look like conflicting proposals. Senator Nye and Congressman Sweeney introduced a bill to implement some of Coughlin's suggestions, and it is hard from this distance to tell exactly how the bill would have worked if it had been passed. It has some of the Social Credit philosophy in it, and while its provisions distort the original recommendations, Pound is on record as praising Coughlin.[22] The crusading priest first supported Roosevelt and said that the "New Deal is Christ's Deal." Then by 1936 he charged the President with being allied to the United States Chamber of Commerce and the international bankers. The "New Deal" turned into what he called the "Jew Deal."

The beneficent Townsend proposed a bill to channel pensions to everyone over 60, $200 per month if everyone spent the money. Of course this was special privilege for the elderly, fantasy for liberal and conservative alike. Huey Long sounded like a Fascist Social Credit man part of the time, except that his sources were long on the Old Testament and short on mathematics. When he urged that wealth be shared, the figures he used indicated contempt for eighth grade arithmetic. His own ignorance, arrogance, and desire for personal power probably kept him from any workable proposals which might have helped the economy. Pound opposed Townsend, but was interested in Huey Long's intentions.

There were others, but they all give the appearance of impractical peculiarity. A man named Pelley launched the Silver Shirts on the day Hitler became Chancellor of Germany. Protestant, white, anti-Semitic, Pelley corresponded with Pound, although Ezra never seems to have fathomed his correspondent. Pelley was rabid about astrology, too. There were men like Gerald L. K. Smith and Gerald Winrod, who played on the anti-democratic tones of hate and white supremacy, calling on God in terms of their own image and rousing whatever rabble would follow them. Many reformers rallied round the third-party campaign of 1936, cheering Lemke and Frazier who proposed measures to refinance mortgages by issuing eight billion dollars' worth of greenbacks. Pound seems to have examined all these movements, since he was getting nowhere through ordinary channels. The total record of this kind of economic protest does not look very convincing in retrospect. Part of the conclusion is lack of any reasonable faith in the reformers themselves.

There may be an exception. This was Jerry Voorhis, the Congressman from California. Voorhis' speeches and proposed bills suggest a positive program for new government economic policies. Pound's silence about Voorhis arouses some wonder. I find few references to him, one in *What Is Money For?* where Voorhis is praised because he mentions Brooks Adams in a speech in the House.[25] Since Voorhis wrote a challenging book, *Out of Debt, Out of Danger,* explaining the history and background of the program which urges that Congress control the money of the country, one may note that the idealistic and positive parts of Pound's ideas (completely dissociated from his interpretations of Mussolini and Roosevelt, having nothing to do with Fascism or special sections of the economy) are best examined in the work which Pound either did not read or did not utilize to aid his own cause.

There is no easier way to understand Pound's economic thesis than to read Voorhis. The fact that the Congressman sounds reasonable, while Pound sometimes does not, is also a fact on the slopes of sympathy. Voorhis shows no signs of attempting to build personal power, nor did he associate with any fanatical groups campaigning for special segments of the electorate. In fact he resembles a typical descendant of the Jeffersonian tradition, particularly in his belief that an informed public is the only real force which can help permanent reform. Furthermore he knew the banking business.

Voorhis can be interpreted completely as an individual; but it is also fair to say that he served as the political counterpart of Irving Fisher, the economist who puts most cogently the case for reform in the way America handles its credit. Voorhis came into Congress late in the New Deal, at a time when no one was completely sure whether all the measures to restore prosperity were going to work. His speeches are models of sober analysis, a helpful element in *The Congressional Record*. Specifically he argued that the government should issue its own money by Congressional direction; credit should go to all business and all the people equally; the national debt should be gradually liquidated by replacing it with government money; inflation should be controlled by national regulation of the volume of credit made available to banks; and the government should either own or control its own banking system.[24]

Voorhis' friend, Congressman Wright Patman of Texas, introduced a bill in 1939 to implement the Voorhis proposals (H.H.4931). It is now curious to note that 150 congressmen were pledged to vote for it, but bills like this never seem to get out of committee. Voorhis says he talked to President Roosevelt and got his approval for the bill, then found that backing was withdrawn after the President consulted his advisers. Eccles was a liberal, but not that liberal, and there were few influential voices to join Voorhis in the inner circles of the New Deal. Perhaps Roosevelt suddenly saw that the new bill would change our financial system, and recalled that he had dedicated himself to some middle way of reform. Or perhaps he thought the bill was economic jargon.

The Patman-Voorhis Bill specifically proposed: (1) that the capital stock of the twelve Federal Reserve Banks be purchased by the government, thus making the central banks the property of the people; (2) that a new Federal Reserve Board be appointed, directly responsible to Congress; (3) that whatever amount of money was called for according to economic circumstances be paid into circulation through such programs as old-age pensions, wages on public works, loans to agriculture and industry (this would mean controlled issue of new debt-free money); (4) that money in circulation be kept at the level established in 1926 (this would stop Congress from wild expansion in printing money); (5) that banks be required to maintain dollar-for-dollar reserves behind demand deposits (this follows the direct proposals of Fisher); (6) that government controls over banking be simplified to guarantee compliance and safety of deposits.

It is easy to see, if one has been following the Pound story, how close this bill comes to many of the ideal recommendations he has been urging. Nothing so comprehensive was suggested in the Italy Pound praised, nor put in practice by decree of Mussolini. No one should have been surprised if Pound had added to his attack on President Roosevelt because he did not throw himself behind the Patman Bill.

Voorhis also made an effort to use modern credit devices to reduce the national debt. This came about after he had discussed exactly how it could be done with Irving Fisher. Voorhis' own explanation is interesting:

> The total amount of demand deposits held by all member banks of the Federal Reserve System as of March 20, 1945, was $61,175,000,000. The total amount of reserves carried by these banks against these demand deposits was $14,605,000,000 on the same date. But these same banks held $67,915,000,000 of United States securities. Thus the reserves held by such banks and the government bonds in their possession exceeded by $21,345,000,000 the total of their demand deposits . . . . As the bonds matured they would have been paid off by the government with new money created for that purpose. Every dollar of that new money would have gone into the Banks' reserves to replace the bonds. Thus $45,570,000,000 of the nation's debt to the banks would have been paid off in the same manner in

> which the banks bought the bonds originally—namely with newly created money. In this manner, without a cent of inflation or the necessity of levying a cent of taxes, the national debt would have been reduced by $45,570,000,000 as an incident in the establishment of a sound banking system.[25]

A few advanced liberal economists have at some time or other argued that our national debt will be retired as it was acquired, by the creation of credit translated into book figures, or new money substituted for that which "came out of nothing." The money actually subscribed for government bonds from salaries, savings, or cash would naturally be handled as any cash transaction or cash loan should be handled. Nobody loses, the government gains, the nation quits paying money on its national debt in interest from taxes. The matter seems simple, even if the manner escapes normal comprehension: "Ignorance of coin, credit, and circulation." Adams said it first, and the extraordinary thing is that it can rarely be debated in terms of negative capability. Special interests easily turn attempts at understanding into something dangerous to the national welfare.

Consider what happened to Jerry Voorhis. He supplied the first incident in the spectacular career of Richard Nixon, for Nixon was chosen as a good bet to defeat him. Rather dispassionately, Voorhis recounts the campaign which removed him from the national scene. He does not seem to blame Nixon particularly, but rather the forces which chose Nixon, financed him, and offered him expense accounts. Certainly the money put into a campaign to defeat a Congressman from California was all out of proportion to any importance a single seat would usually have had for the national party. Pound ought to have had a field day with the Nixon-Voorhis campaign. Voorhis was labelled the C.I.O. candidate; Communism was whispered; Banks seem to have shut off credit to merchants who supported Voorhis (he says he could never completely prove this); Community Chest solicitors carried Nixon advertising with them and left it at every house; the one editor who supported Voorhis was moved out of his home by his landlord; a member of a large New York financial house went to California to organize the campaign against Voorhis, describing him as "one of the most dangerous men in Washington."[26]

At least this is the way Voorhis describes his defeat. How easy it would be for Pound, with his talent for exaggeration, to read too much into the story or become partisan about the forces of Usury. Voorhis was removed from Congress, and other Congressmen have deduced that it is dangerous to become too interested in banking reform unless they are prepared to arouse powerful forces in opposition. Search of *The Congressional Record* shows, since the defeat of Voorhis, no very serious speeches by anybody but Patman about this kind of economic reform. The economy has been booming much of the time, the affluent society has been prosperous, and there is no crying need for reform apparent to the public, perhaps because of the business stimulus of the Cold War. Patman has not proposed any very embarrassing bills since 1939, but he raises his voice loudly whenever the Secretary of the Treasury or the Federal Reserve Board constricts credit.[27]

What Pound thought of America after the close of the second World War was mixed with his own predicament and his confinement in St. Elizabeths. He was avoided by many of his embarrassed old friends, but approached by extremists of all kinds plus some academic sightseers. We could hardly expect him to change much, but rather to be hardened in his views, whatever they were. Furthermore the character of some of the supporters who took up cudgels for him contributed to the picture of an irresponsible fanatical poet not to be trusted or supported. He refers to President Truman twice, the first time when Stalin is quoted as preferring to take Truman's word over Churchill's (84/118). This is a backward citation, used merely as another Pound volley at Churchill. In Canto 97 his reference to Truman is bitter: " 'And he, the president, is true to his caste'/'and that caste,' said old Lampman, 'the underworld' " (97/22). The journalist Lampman was attacking Truman's connections with the Pendergast machine in Kansas City, the organization which started him on his political career. "'Democracies electing their sewage," Pound says (91/75), but he adds no analysis of Truman's record as President in connection with his economic thesis. He might have pointed out that Truman removed Eccles from the chairmanship of the Federal Reserve Board, and that many appointments and connections with privileged business plagued Truman toward the end of his elected term.

No serious effort has been made to stimulate reform or change in the Federal Reserve System since the time of Voorhis, or even back to 1935. Yet gradually a kind of Keynsian cooperation between the Board and the President has developed, or between the Board and the Secretary of the Treasury. This situation began with the tenure of Eccles. Whenever inflation appears to be getting out of hand, meaning a general rise beyond a per cent or two per month, the Board tightens credit experimentally; whenever the tightening encourages a recession, the Board has loosened credit. Generally speaking this was the way the original drafters of the Act in 1913 envisaged its operation. There is an interesting example of what the Pound perspective would call the dangers of yesterday, and this incident stemmed from the office of the Secretary of the Treasury rather than from the Board itself. When Eisenhower was elected President a representative of big business, George M. Humphrey, was appointed Secretary. Humphrey's public statement of his economic philosophy went back to the days of McKinley and Coolidge, viewing with alarm social measures like government lending programs, housing, small business aids, and farm loans. He was also concerned about inflation. Social security and improved wages for labor apparently encouraged inflation. His remedy was to increase interest rates, tighten credit, raise the rediscount rate, and cut down on advances by the Federal Reserve Banks. Note that the Federal Reserve Board cooperated nicely with the government in all these moves.

This action was reminiscent of the Federal Reserve Board's tightening of credit under President Harding at the close of the first World War. Whether such procedure would have been extreme enough to create another depression is, of course, arguable. Humphrey changed his mind after awhile, and the Korean War stimulus to business was still working. Several times during the Eisenhower administration there appeared hints of recession, and each time the Treasury and the Federal

Reserve Board loosened credit strings to stimulate recovery. Perhaps we do learn by experience. Patman had a political fit when Humphrey began to tighten credit with his "Hard Money" policy. Pound does not seem to have noticed. He was lost in St. Elizabeths in study of Alexander del Mar, the records of Mons of Jute, Gansl, Antoninus, even Coke, who is now called the clearest mind in England (107/110). Most of us would occasionally like to retreat to the past or vanish into the future when the present puzzles us; Pound had more reason than most of us.

Pound did have a fleeting opinion of Eisenhower, although it does not come out with violence. Obviously Ike was not an economist, and his basic philosophy was comfortable middle-of-the-road conservatism. Pound says, with less venom than usual, that Ike finally got round to connecting issue with backing (97/24), a statement which cryptically and condescendingly assumes that the President had finally graduated from the first to the second grade in understanding economic theory. He also remarks that Field Marshals were once literate: "Art is local,/Ike driven to the edge, almost, of a thought" (97/30). After all it was Eisenhower who finally released him from confinement and let him go back to Italy.

The two divisions of *The Cantos* which follow the Pisan section, Rock Drill and Thrones, are filled with intensifications of the themes already presented. The original brilliance and vividness of *The Cantos* generally fades away. More bewildering historical data is set beside what we have read before. Most of the material concentrates on the past rather than the present. The economic thread Pound had woven through his analysis of the United States, Italy, and China is now extended to the significant facts he finds in ancient Constantinople, in early English history, in Egypt, Babylonia, and in other parts of the European story not previously explored. Pound's fire has not completely burned out, but the evidence is less spectacular and there are fewer examples of violent extremes. Perhaps the intensity of his feelings about Mussolini, Roosevelt, and the Rothschilds broke sharply against his emptiness in the hospital. The Thrones of Paradise are still in his dreams, but not in our world.

Yet despite the onus of being called insane, despite the bitterness of his ordeal in attempting to expiate the charge of treason, the old man fought on. His tragedy is a perfectly typical one, hallowed by the tradition of great literature. Like a tragic hero in Greek drama, he has not been overcome by fate. Rather he has suffered from a nemesis he began by his own decisions. Like Brutus in Shakespeare's *Julius Caesar,* he believed in an ideal which did not exactly fit his present situation. Brutus helped assassinate Caesar, believing himself to be aiding his country; the comparison to Pound is suggestive. The heroes of Shakespeare's plays are often accounted admirable in some sense for qualities of character which include nobility, but they reach catastrophe because they have tragic flaws. Pound is the hero of his own drama, and perhaps he also can be said to have a tragic flaw. But his ideals were always there too, even if we have difficulty in defining the quality of his nobility. After all, what other poet living or dead could have said, as he did:

> What thou lovest well remains,
>   the rest is dross
> What thou lov'st well shall not be reft from thee
> What thou lov'st well is thy true heritage
> Whose world, or mine or theirs
>   or is it of none?
> First came the seen, then thus the palpable
>   Elysium, though it were in the halls of hell,
> What thou lovest well is thy true heritage . . . .   (81/98-99)

It does not take many more lines like these to put a poet in the list of the few who are truly immortal. Even if his ideals are attainable only in infinity, his case in finite. Poets, like other men, suffer; they often believe intensely in what they write about; sometimes they give all for an unattainable goal. Sometimes their ideals are only indestructible in the mind.

There is a poetic footnote. The old ego, the old disdainful fire flashes in the last line of the Thrones Cantos, and lets Pound say with supreme arrogance: "You in the dinghey (piccioletta) astern there!" (109/126). We have certainly been pursuing him. His voyage, like that of Odysseus, has taken him over strange oceans to hell and back. Some of us have had to row madly to keep him in sight. Some of us wish he had occasionally gone in different directions or had listened to Tiresias. But there he is, the beard sticking out at an angle, the eyes flashing with the light of other worlds, the anchor of Social Credit pulled up safely inside the boat, his rudder set for Ithaca or what he imagines to be paradise. The vision is there somewhere before him. What a fantastic image he leaves behind him!

notes

All references to Pound's poems are from the American New Directions editions, unless otherwise indicated. Quotation from *The Cantos* is noted after the excerpt by the number of the Canto and the page in the New Directions edition on which this quotation occurs. For example, a quotation from Canto 2, page 8, is listed 2/8. All excerpts from Pound's broadcasts have been taken from the microfilm copy (December 7, 1941 to July 25, 1943) made by the Federal Communications Commission and issued in 1952 by the Library of Congress.

CHAPTER ONE

1. Ernest Hemingway, *A Moveable Feast,* 1964 p. 108.

2. Charles Norman, *Ezra Pound,* Macmillan, 1960, p. 412, quoting a letter from William Carlos Williams.

3. See Norman, *op. cit.,* p. 417, where this statement is recorded as Cerf's proposal to Julien Cornell, Pound's attorney, concerning Cerf's willingness to print Pound's poems.

4. Ray West, "Excerpts from a Journal," *Western Review,* Winter, 1950, reprinted from the O'Connor-Stone *A Casebook on Ezra Pound,* p. 68.

5. The Tate essay is available in several places, being often reprinted. See Peter Russell, *An Examination of Ezra Pound,* p. 67.

6. *Ibid.,* p. 72.

7. Hugh Kenner, *The Poetry of Ezra Pound,* see pp. 35, 67, 252, 291, etc.

8. *The Letters of Ezra Pound,* edited by D. D. Paige, 1950. Letter to Hubert Creekmore, February, 1939, No. 355.

9. Norman, *op. cit.,* p. 387.

10. Clark Emery, *Ideas into Action,* pp. 43, 46.

11. Eustace Mullins, *This Difficult Individual, Ezra Pound,* 1961, Chapter X, pp. 201 ff. Mullins presents a defense in detail against the charge of treason, printing safe and positive examples of the radio scripts.

12. See Pound's many contributions to *The New English Weekly,* covering the 1930's, where he consistently defends Mussolini and Fascism for economic reasons and where he seems unaware of the general horror felt by America and Britain caused by the excesses of Hitler and Mussolini.

13. FCC Microfilm, May 26, 1942.

14. Ezra Pound, *The ABC of Reading,* p. 68.

15. Yvor Winters, *The Pound Newsletter:* 10, April 1956, p. 17.

16. Norman, *op. cit.,* p. 315.

17. Reported by Wyndham Lewis, quoted in Norman, *op. cit.,* p. 322.

18. Malcolm Cowley, "Pound Reweighed," *The Reporter,* March 2, 1961, p. 38.

CHAPTER TWO

1. Many critics, like Eliot and Kenner, seem to say that this should not be done. Eliot once argued that the "meaning" of a poem is like the bone a burglar throws to the housedog to keep him occupied while the burglar

(the Poet) is going about his business of robbing the safe (writing the poem). This critical ideal is quite valid in its special sense, particularly if one is deprecating the Victorian tendency to write a poem and then explain its moral point to the presumably stupid or dense reader. It is also helpful as a teaching device in trying to persuade the beginning reader that he ought to do more than compose an interlinear prose translation for a poem in his own simple and uninspired language.

2. Clark Emery, *op. cit.,* describes this contrast of theme in a brilliant analysis on pp. 104-105.

3. Data about Sir Basil Zaharoff may be examined in Richard Lewinsohn's *The Career of Sir Basil Zaharoff,* Gollencz, 1929; Robert Neumann's *Zaharoff, the Armaments King,* Allen and Unwin, 1939; and Donald McCormick's *Peddler of Death,* Holt, Rinehart, Winston, 1965.

4. See Chapter Seven, pp. 161-162 of this book for further explication of this passage, taken from a Pound broadcast from Rome, June 19, 1942.

5. Technically these two quotations do not mean exactly the same thing. The latter statement assumes that the interests of the country and the business community are identical; the other says that self-interest rather than patriotism will rule the activities of the business class. Many people, however, read the "General Motors" quotation sarcastically as putting business interests above the good of the country as a whole.

6. Pound's *The ABC of Reading* states clearly his judgment of the traditional English poets and clarifies his evaluation of the standard creative representatives of literary history.

7. Ezra Pound, *Make It New,* p. 19.

8. *Guide to Kulchur,* p. 191.

9. *Make It New,* p. 19.

10. *The ABC of Reading,* p. 22.

11. *Gaudier-Brzeska,* p. 106.

12. Eliot has described the poetic process in the more familiar concept of the catalyst: words and ideas combine in the poem when the poet-catalyst is present, and after the combination is completed, the poet himself can be removed from the poem like the catalytic agent which has combined the elements without joining them.

13. *The Translations of Ezra Pound,* edited by Hugh Kenner, Faber, 1947, p. 214.

14. *Ibid.,* p. 237.

15. *Kulchur,* p. 51.

16. *The ABC of Economics,* p. 37.

17. *ABC of Reading,* p. 9.

18. Letter to Hubert Creekmore, see Chapter One, Note 8.

19. Kenner, *op. cit.,* p. 83.

20. Kenner, *The Invisible Poet: T. S. Eliot,* pp. 146-147.

CHAPTER THREE

1. See the authoritative analysis in John J. Espey's *Ezra Pound's Mauberley; a study in composition,* Faber, 1955.

2. From parts of *Hugh Selwyn Mauberley,* poems I, III, IV, and V.

3. Ezra Pound, "Obituary Letters to the Editor," *The New English Weekly,* November 13, 1934, p. 109.

4. A. R. Orage, *An Alphabet of Economics,* p. 53.

5. "I don't want to roast little babies. . . . I just happen to like the Fascist money system," he said to Virginia Rice. Cited by Norman, *op. cit.,* p. 371.

6. Pound makes very few references to Veblen, and there is no particular evidence that he read any of Veblen's books. It seems reasonable to assume that Veblen's theories were in the air about Pound and his associates,

whether or not there was direct influence.

7. Odon Por, *Italy's Policy of Social Economics,* translated by Ezra Pound, p. 37.

8. *The Annotated Index to the Cantos* indicates that Bukos is a pseudonym for Keynes.

9. The economist who reads the statement about stock-splitting usually is quick to point out that stock-splitting is not exactly the creation of new shares at the expense of the worker. That is, under this system, each holder of a share receives an additional share. This practice does not increase or decrease the proportion of the corporation owned by any stockholder. In practice this means that if you hold one share of stock valued at some simple numerical figure like $100, the stock could be split four ways and you would have four shares worth $25 each. The reason for doing this is that profits may be large and the dividends issued for the $100 share would look out of proportion, but the practice is also to encourage trading in the stock. It is this latter feature which offers the opportunity for the man on the inside to profit. His $100 share is no greater than four $25 shares, but these shares are likely to go higher immediately, and the insider who knows about the split can arrange to buy a great number of shares just before the split, and appropriately sell them just after, if they go up as expected. Further, there may be tax benefits. The man who owned ten shares of AT&T in 1930 is quite likely to have extraordinary capital if he has held his stock through all the years of subsequent splitting.

10. Anyone who has taken accounting realizes that the jargon of bank reporting seems to say the opposite of normal communication. That is, deposits are not called "resources," but "liabilities." Further, resources are reported as assets like cash holdings, securities, and borrowers' notes. The technical point is that banks *do* lend more than their liquid asset resources, and are able to do so because of the flow of money that depends upon deposits.

11. See Footnote 18, Chapter One.

12. See essay by T. S. Eliot, reprinted in Russell's *Examination,* pp. 33-34.

13. John Dos Passos, *U.S.A.,* "The Forty-Second Parallel," Modern Library Edition, p. 265.

14. *Ibid.,* "1919," pp. 339-340.

CHAPTER FOUR

1. *The ABC of Economics,* p. 128.

2. W. W. Rostow, *The Stages of Economic Growth, a Non-Communist Manifesto,* p. 158.

3. C. H. Douglas, *Credit Power and Democracy,* pp. 21-23.

4. Douglas, *The New and the Old Economics,* p. 19.

5. Arthur Kitson, *Scientific Solution of the Money Question,* 1894, p. 35.

6. See Malcolm Cowley, Chapter One, Footnote 18.

7. Christopher Hollis, *The Two Nations, a Financial Study of English History,* Routledge, 1937, pp. 19 ff.

8. Alexander Hamilton, report on "A National Bank," submitted to Congress, December 13, 1790.

9. The Constitution says specifically, "Congress shall coin money and regulate the value thereof."

CHAPTER FIVE

1. See Cowley, Chapter One, Footnote 18.

2. Pound uses as basic source of reference Joseph Anne Marie Moyriac

de Mailla's *Histoire Générale de la Chine, ou annales de cet Empire:* translation of the Tong-kien-kan-mou, 13 volumes published in Paris, 1777-85. An outline of the emperors and dynasties can be easily consulted in Edwards-Vasse *Annotated Index to the Cantos,* 295-303.

3. David Ricardo, *Works,* quoted from Montgomery Butchart's *Money,* pp. 244-245.

4. See Canto 74/22.

5. See Cantos 86/28, 98/37, and 102/80.

6. Silvio Gesell, *The Natural Economic Order,* translated by Philip Pye, 1934, p. 13.

CHAPTER SIX

1. It is convenient to use this summary of Brooks Adams' position, stated this way by Gorham Munson, *Aladdin's Lamp,* 1945, p. 50.

2. See Second Money Pamphlet, *Gold and Work,* p. 7.

3. *Jefferson and/or Mussolini,* p. 97.

4. In his contributions to *The New English Weekly,* all through the thirties, Pound goes through the motions of suspending judgment on Roosevelt and the New Deal. He grudgingly praises steps which lead to stirring up the American economy. In the July 12, 1934, issue he suggests that Roosevelt may be worse than the previous four unfortunate American presidents. On Jan. 3, 1935, he refers to F.D.R.'s "banking friends."

5. In the May 24, 1934, issue of *The New English Weekly* Pound calls Hitler an "almost pathetic hysteric." By April 2, 1936, he was beginning to praise him.

6. There is no desire to exaggerate this opinion. John Gunther, *Inside Europe,* 1933, devotes Chapter XIII to Mussolini and tells of his weaknesses along with his strength. The beginning of this chapter says, "His career is that of the most formidable combination of turncoat, ruffian, and man of genius in modern history" (1938 edition, p. 187). But Mussolini consistently fares better in this account than the other strong men of Europe.

7. Charles Beard, *The Rise of American Civilization,* I, 195.

8. *Ibid.,* I, 201.

9. *Ibid.,* I, 207, 211.

10. Summarized and quoted by Munson, *op. cit.,* pp. 52-53.

11. Kenner is the authority for saying that the missing lines had to do with the presence of the Rothschild yacht in Rapallo harbor.

12. The ammassi are mentioned: 53/8, 56/49, 61/81. The fontego is explained: 61/81.

13. *The Works of John Adams,* Charles Francis Adams, 1854, IX, 638.

CHAPTER SEVEN

1. See Footnote 12, Chapter Six.

2. *Sindacato e Corporazione,* October 1934, p. 469.

3. Pound, *Jefferson and/or Mussolini,* Liveright, 1935, p. viii.

4. *Ibid.,* p. ix.

5. *Ibid.,* pp. 33-34.

6. Pound, *What Is Money For?,* Russell, 1951, p. 6.

7. *Ibid.,* p. 7.

8. *Ibid.,* p. 11.

9. Pound, *Social Credit: An Impact,* Russell, 1951, p. 19.

10. *Ibid.*

11. Odon Por, *Italy's Policy of Social Economics,* translated by Ezra Pound, 1941, p. 37.

12. FCC Microfilm, April 27, 1942.

13. *Ibid.*, May 31, 1942.

14. William G. Welk, *Fascist Economic Policy,* Harvard, p. 34.

15. George Seldes, *Facts and Fascism,* p. 44.

16. Welk, *op. cit.*, pp. 241-242.

CHAPTER EIGHT

1. Several specific quotations from Pound's discussions in *The New English Weekly* may be appropriate here. In the November 14, 1935, issue (p. 85) he asks somebody to "ramble round to enquire whether anti-semitism, a red herring if ever was one, mayn't be a hidden war of the five Swiss protestant dynasties on the Rothschild. . . ." In the November 21, 1935, issue Pound is even more revealing. He says (p. 105): "Usurers have no race. How long the whole Jewish people is to be sacrificial goat for the usurer, I know not." Again: "Whenever a usurer is spotted he scuttles down under the ghetto and leaves the plain Jew to take the bullets and beatings."

2. Frederic Morton, *The Rothschilds,* p. 5.

3. Christopher Hollis, *The Two Nations,* bases his book on a quotation (used as the title) from Disraeli and discusses in detail Disraeli's early reform notions. These are all anti-Usury, most of them in harmony with Pound's general position.

4. Pound, *An Introduction to the Economic Nature of the United States,* Russell, 1950, p. 19.

5. See Chapter Six, Note 11, where authorities like Kenner say the lines have to do with the Rothschild yacht in Rapallo harbor.

6. Everyone seems to agree with this refutation except the anti-Semites. No study of Franklin's life and opinions substantiates it, so far as I have been able to find.

7. The question of Pound's opposition to Roosevelt is illuminated by his continued discussion of the President in *The New English Weekly,* from 1934 on. There are several examples of praise for the American President, as if Pound would be willing to support him whenever Roosevelt decided to institute debt-free financing of federal support for the economy. In the July 12, 1934, issue (p. 311) he says that "if Mr. Roosevelt takes home any tips from English systems of rotten finance . . . the loathing America feels for her last four presidential misfortunes will pale into malarial insignificance in ratio to the new hate." It should be noted that Pound was not sure F.D.R. was the lowest president following Grant until the war started. On November 19, 1936, he remarked that at least Roosevelt was better than Landon.

8. *Jefferson and/or Mussolini,* p. 108.

9. This quotation from a speech made by Woodrow Wilson when he was Governor of New Jersey, in 1911, is used by Supreme Court Justice Louis D. Brandeis as the headpiece for his book attacking the American money monopoly, *Other People's Money,* 1913.

10. The Federal Reserve Banks make no direct loans to business, but are "banker's banks." They make discounts (loans) to member banks and hold the reserves of these banks. The individual commercial banks which belong to the Federal Reserve System then use this credit to encourage whatever economic activity needs the money and can supply collateral to justify getting it. The point is, of course, that the public has no check on how much credit can be thrown into the economy, nor on how much interest can be charged.

11. Quoted by Jerry Voorhis, *Out of Debt, Out of Danger,* p. 122, where the effect of this action is analyzed in some detail.

12. In *The New English Weekly,*

October 8, 1936 (p. 425), he also says that he has reports that Eccles is trying to do good by increasing coverage. Earlier, April 4, 1935, he had praised the Roosevelt-Eccles Federal Reserve Reform Bill, except that it did not go far enough. Pound does not seem to connect any banking reform with Eccles himself.

13. Marriner Eccles, *Beckoning Frontiers, Public and Personal Recollections,* 1951, p. 166.

14. *Ibid.*

15. Arthur M. Schlesinger, Jr., *The Age of Roosevelt,* Vol. III, 1960, p. 406.

16. *Ibid.,* III, 650.

17. *The New English Weekly* comments on the New Deal are quite varied. His general attitude toward Coughlin is favorable. He laments the death of Huey Long, but still thinks these critics had important defects. In the February 13, 1936, number (p. 345) he says that Townsend "knows less economics than did Huey Long. He is apparently as stubborn as Upton Sinclair."

18. See Note 5, Chapter Six.

19. Pound, *A Visiting Card,* Russell, 1951, p. 15.

20. Pound does not seem to be acquainted with Soddy's works. His references to Fisher in *The New English Weekly* are quite profuse. He distrusts *100% Money* and generally shies away from Fisher's position because he finds it not down the Social Credit "line." See *NEW,* September 5, 1935. Pound also attacks Fisher in the January 5, 1939, issue of *NEW*. But one of Pound's last articles, April 11, 1940, praises the Voorhis bill based on Fisher's contentions.

21. See Schlesinger, *op. cit.,* I, 196, for discussion of Tugwell's proposals. The quotation here is from Rexford Guy Tugwell, *The Industrial Discipline.*

22. On April 11, 1935, Pound says in *NEW* (p. 530): "The Reverend Father with eight million enrolled in his league can very well stand on the defensive. He knows a great many of the facts, and no form of statement can be, in our time, stronger than a simple account of them." The conclusion may well be that he thought Coughlin's contribution was in bringing the money question to the attention of the American people, even if Coughlin did not have all the answers.

23. Pound, *What Is Money For?,* Russell, 1951, p. 15.

24. Jerry Voorhis, *Confessions of a Congressman,* 1947, pp. 165-167.

25. *Ibid.,* p. 181.

26. *Ibid.,* pp. 331-342 inclusive tell this story.

27. Patman has stayed in the Congress through the years and is now, in the Johnson administration, by seniority, chairman of the important lower house committee on banking and finances. His record is consistently on the side of loosening credit, and he has always been against the raising of interest rates or any other measures designed to tighten the economy. Note his published statements in 1966 against the Federal Reserve Board when it raised interest rates to combat inflation.

index

Adams, Brooks
viii, 76-78, 80, 81, 117-118, 136
Adams, John
10, 27, 32, 67, 69-70, 78, 87, 88, 96, 115, 121, 122-125, 131, 135, 136-144, 147, 148, 166, 181
Adams, John Quincy
125, 136
Alberta
100, 107, 192
ammassi
136
Aristotle
25, 40
autarchy
151, 163

Bach, Johann Sebastian
18
Beard, Charles
121
Benét, Stephen Vincent
130
Biddle, Nicholas
78, 90, 126-127, 173
Blast
52
Bollingen Prize
4
Browning, Robert
2, 35, 36, 67
Bryan, William Jennings
78, 92, 182
Butchart, Montgomery
viii, 78

Cabestan (Cabestanh)
38-39
Carnegie, Andrew
66
Catullus, Gaius Valerius
2
Cavalcanti, Guido
2, 27, 29, 33, 34, 126
Cerf, Bennett
4
Churchill, Winston
10, 35, 54, 130, 173, 192, 198
Cocteau, Jean
1
Cole, G.D.H.
49, 51
communism
32
Confucius (Kung Fu-Tse)
2, 10, 26, 31, 70, 80, 98, 117, 136-137, 144, 148
Coughlin, Father
108, 188, 193
Cowley, Malcolm
13, 64-65, 78, 79, 97
Cummings, E.E.
1, 44, 111
Cutting, Bronson
107, 189

Daniel, Arnaut
2, 29
Dante, Alighieri
2, 14, 19, 25, 26-27, 33, 34, 54, 133
del Mar, Alexander
viii, 76-78, 81, 136
de Vega, Lope
46
Dickens, Charles
173
Dickinson, Emily
46
Disraeli, Benjamin
134, 176-177
Doolittle, Hilda (H.D.)
48
Dos Passos, John
43-44, 65-67
Douglas, Major C.H.
viii, 23-24, 27, 31, 52, 60-61,

62, 73-78, 100-108, 112, 116, 128, 132, 136, 155-157

Eccles, Marriner
185-195, 199
Edwards, John
11
Einstein, Albert
25
Eisenhower, Dwight D.
199-200
Eliot, T.S.
1-2, 4, 40, 42, 48, 111, 118, 171
Emery, Clark
7
Engels, Friedrich
49
Erigena, Scotus
2, 27, 116

Federal Reserve System
62, 78, 83, 92, 113, 133, 165, 181-184, 196, 198-200
Fenellosa
34, 39
Ferdinand III (Tuscany)
117, 132, 134, 136
Fisher, Irving
viii, 190, 195
fontego
126, 136
Ford, Ford Madox
1, 48
Franklin, Benjamin
121, 138-139, 179
Frobenius, Leo
2, 23, 136
Frost, Robert
1, 48

Galbraith, John
viii, 31, 74
Gandhi, Mahatma
22
Gaudier-Brzeska, Henri
1, 52, 55
George, Henry
109
Gesell, Silvio
viii, 15, 31, 78, 100, 108-112, 116, 136, 149-150
Graves, Robert
44
greenbacks
129, 191
Griffith, Arthur
56
Guild-Socialism
50-51, 151

Hamilton, Alexander
78, 87-89, 92, 123, 133, 137-139, 142, 173
Handel, George Frederick
18
Hardy, Thomas
44
Heine, Heinrich
2
Hemingway, Ernest
1-2, 43, 44, 48
Hitler, Adolf
10, 80, 96, 109, 113, 119-120, 155-156, 161, 167, 169, 177, 188-189
Hobson, S.G.
49-50
Hollis, Christopher
vii, 78, 86
Homer
2, 14, 15, 26, 172
Hulme, T.E.
48, 55

ideogram
2, 18-19, 36-38, 171
intaglio
37-39
Ives, Charles
46

Jackson, Andrew
10, 78, 88-92, 105, 117-118, 123, 126-127, 128, 166, 181, 182-183
James, Henry
1, 46
Jefferson, Thomas
10, 27, 32, 67, 70, 87-89, 92, 105, 117-121, 122-125, 128, 130-131, 133, 137-138, 142, 144, 147, 148, 151-152, 166, 181, 182, 183
Johnson, Lyndon B.
99, 108
Joyce, James
9, 43

Kennedy, John F.
99, 108, 151
Kenner, Hugh
vi, 5, 6, 37, 41
Keynes, John Maynard
viii, 31, 60-61, 77, 113, 185, 187, 199
Kimball, Dexter
19, 21
Kitson, Arthur
viii, 75, 78

Landor, Walter Savage
36
Lee, Mary
44
Lenin, Nikolai
55
Leopold II (Pietro)
27, 70, 117, 132, 134, 136, 148
Lewis, Sinclair
46
Lewis, Wyndham
1, 48, 52, 111
Lincoln, Abraham
10, 78, 88-89, 92, 105, 117-118, 123, 128, 145, 166, 182
Li Po (Rihaku)
2
Long, Huey
108, 188, 193
Lowell, Amy
48

MacLeish, Archibald
107, 129-130
Madison, James
89, 142
Mairet, Philip
viii
Malatesta, Sigismondo
27, 29, 47-48, 67, 117, 148
Malthus, Thomas
viii, 75
Manes
147
Marconi, Marchese
19-21, 161
Marlowe, Christopher
173
Marx, Karl
viii, 30, 31, 49, 56, 70-76, 81, 100, 103, 124
Matteotti, Giacomo
168
Metevsky (*see* Zaharoff)
Mill, John Stuart
viii, 51, 75
More, Thomas
111, 118
Morgan, John Pierpont
59, 62-67, 78, 92, 118, 168, 173
Mullins, Eustace
7
Munson, Gorham
vii, 78, 107

Napoleon Bonaparte
124, 135, 149, 175-176
National Bank Act of 1863
178-179
New Age, The
49, 50
New English Weekly, The
107, 188
Nixon, Richard
197-198
Noh Plays
2, 39-40
Norman, Charles
7, 11

Odysseus
14-15, 19, 26, 28, 30, 34, 116, 134, 201
Orage, A.R.
viii, 49-51, 55, 106, 111, 151
Ouang-ngan-ché
27, 97-99
Ovid
2, 14, 26, 28, 34
Owen, Wilfrid
44

Paterson, William
85-86, 132-133, 173
Patman, Wright
195-197
Pearson, Drew
2
Penty, A.J.
49
Pinckney, Charles Cotesworth
180

Pisan Cantos
3-4, 27, 82, 113, 115, 145, 147-150, 169, 189, 200
Plato
111-112
Poetry Magazine
49
Por, Odon
viii, 51, 56, 78, 145, 151, 156-159, 163, 190
Propertius, Sextus
2, 34
Pujo Investigation
62, 64, 129

Remarque, Erich Maria
44
Ricardo, David
viii, 51, 75, 105
Richards, I.A.
39
Robber Barons
59, 118
Roosevelt, Franklin D.
7, 8, 10, 12, 60, 118-120, 133, 144, 169, 180-200
Rostow, W.W.
71
Rothschilds
62, 97, 120, 126, 128, 130, 133-134, 136, 149, 154, 162, 173-180, 200

Sandburg, Carl
130
Sassoon, Siegfried
44
Schlesinger, Arthur M., Jr.
126-127, 188
Shakespeare, William
29-30, 172, 201
Shaw, George Bernard
49, 50
Sheriff, Robert
44
Siena Bank
27, 84-85, 103
Smith, Adam
viii, 31, 75, 173
Soddy, Frederick
viii, 78, 190
Sordello
29, 67
Sorokin, Pitirim
30
Spengler, Oswald
30, 40, 98, 120, 131
Stalin, Joseph
115, 118, 120, 149, 198
Steffens, Lincoln
57, 64
Swift, Jonathan
11, 172
Syndicalism
49-51, 56

Tate, Allen
5, 39
Thyssen, Fritz
167, 189
Tiresias
28, 134, 202
Townsendism
108, 193
Toynbee, Arnold Joseph
30, 98, 115, 120
Truman, Harry
187, 198
Tugwell, Rexford Guy
190, 193
Twain, Mark
46

Van Buren, Martin
67, 78, 88, 90-91, 117, 123, 125-127, 128, 133, 136
Veblen, Thorstein
viii, 51-52
Vico, Giovanni Battista
30
Villon, François
2, 34
Voltaire (François Arouet)
172
Voorhis, Jerry
viii, 194-196
Vorticism
36-37

Webster, Daniel
90, 125

Wells, H.G.
50
Whitman, Walt
2, 41, 46, 130
Williams, William Carlos
1, 13, 107
Wilson, McNair
viii, 78
Wilson, Woodrow
22, 44, 66, 88, 113, 183
Winters, Yvor
17
Wörgl
100, 109, 131, 150

Yeats, William Butler
1, 44, 48, 111

Zaharoff, Sir Basil
19, 22, 25, 55, 128